# BRIGHT IDEAS
*for*
## Young Women
# LEADERS

# BRIGHT IDEAS

*for*

# Young Women

# LEADERS

By Trina Boice

spring creek
BOOK COMPANY
Provo, Utah

ISBN 13: 978-1-932898-59-0
ISBN 10: 1-932898-59-X

e. 1

Published by:
Spring Creek Book Company
P.O. Box 50355
Provo, Utah 84605-0355


www.springcreekbooks.com

Cover design © Spring Creek Book Company
Cover design by Nicole Cunningham

Printed in the United States of America
10 9 8 7 6 5 4 3 2 1
Printed on acid-free paper

Library of Congress Cataloging-in-Publication Data

Boice, Trina, 1963-

  Bright ideas for young women leaders / by Trina Boice.

    p. cm.

  ISBN-13: 978-1-932898-59-0 (pbk. : alk. paper)

  ISBN-10: 1-932898-59-X (pbk. : alk. paper)

  1. Young women--Religious life. 2. Mormon women--Religious life. 3. Church work with women. 4. Young Women (Church of Jesus Christ of Latter-Day Saints) I. Title.


BX8643.Y6B63 2006

267'.629332--dc22

                              2006012973

# Contents

# INTRODUCTION
## *Your Sacred Calling*

"You have been called to nourish spirits and feed souls of Heavenly Father's daughters. You will be able to fulfill your calling in full purpose with the help of God. Your family and the young women will see in you someone who loves the Lord and is strengthened by Him. You will be easy for them to follow because they will sense your great love for life and for them. They will see in you a woman of gentleness, goodness, refinement, and strength as you reach out to nourish their spirits and feed their souls, and they will want to be like you." (*Margaret D. Nadauld, October 2000*)

The First Presidency sent a letter in March 2006 to all stake presidents, urging them to double their efforts in meeting the needs of the youth. The leaders are concerned about the struggles of our youth now more than ever. Encourage your ward to support your Bishopric and free up their time so that they can attend every youth activity and spend that third hour in Church with the youth where they are supposed to be. Help your ward members rally together to form a loving wall of protection around your young women and young men against the powers of the Destroyer. We all need to work together to help these young people stand for truth and righteousness and be witnesses of God at all times and in all things, and in all places.

In 1979 President Ezra Taft Benson said, *"For nearly six thousand years, God has held you in reserve to make your appearance in the final days before the second coming of the Lord. Every previous gospel dispensation has drifted into apostasy, but ours will not. While our generation will be comparable in wickedness to the days of Noah, when the Lord cleansed the earth by flood, there is a major difference this time. It is that God has saved for the final inning some of his strongest children who will help bear off the kingdom triumphantly. And that is where you come in, for you are the generation that must be prepared to meet your God. All through the ages the prophets have looked down through the corridors of time to our day. Billions of the deceased and those yet to be born have their eyes on us. Make no mistake about it—you are a marked generation. There has never been more expected of the faithful in such a short period of time as there is of us. Never before on the face of this earth have the forces of evil and the forces of good been as well organized. Now is the great day of the devil's power, with the greatest mass murderers of all time living among us. But now is also the great day of the Lord's power, with the greatest number ever of priesthood holders on the earth. And the showdown is fast approaching." (BYU Press, 1980, p. 59.)*

Between the ages of 12 and 18 young women make choices that will affect their lives forever. The decisions they make as young women will determine the quality of the rest of their lives! Adolescence is the time when attitudes and values are significantly shaped. Their commitment to the gospel, to education, to service and to their roles as wife and mother are determined during these short years. They live in a treacherous world. As the world grows darker, our young women must shine brighter! You must be an illuminating light for them to follow. You must guide them to Him, who is the light of the world!

When you are set apart as a Young Woman leader you are given a mantel of authority and the right to receive personal revelation for those whom you serve. Pray to understand the needs of your young women. Every girl is unique and it will be your challenge to touch her life and her heart. To be an effective leader you will need to know her and understand her challenges.

Prepare yourself in every way as you invite His precious daughters to "come unto Christ." The most important thing you will do is to introduce them to Him and help them want to be more like Him, and be with Him. As you are prayerful and diligent, many ways to impact and touch their lives will be opened to you.

Let the girls know you love the Lord and find joy in living the gospel. Provide them with opportunities to practice living the gospel and see how to apply it to their lives as they go to school, work, spend time with friends, and live at home. Help them transfer their understanding of the gospel from their head to their heart. While preparing a lesson, prayerfully consider the girls' needs. You are not teaching lessons; you are teaching young women!

Statistics show that most parents average between five and seven minutes talking to their teenagers a day. Most of those conversations are spent dealing with homework, chores, and scheduling issues. Think about how much time you get to spend with those teenagers each week! Now you should realize what an important role you will have in their lives and the influence for good you can be. You can have a tremendous impact in the lives of young women. Make Young Women's fun! It should be a place of refuge, peace, safety, love and laughter!

When Brigham Young first organized the Young Women's auxiliary of the Church he said, "The time has come when the sisters must agree to set an example before the people of the world worthy of imitation. There is a need for the young daughters to get a living testimony of the truth. I wish our girls to obtain a knowledge of the Gospel for themselves. We are about to organize a Retrenchment Association, which I want you all to join, and I want you to vote to retrench in everything that is bad or worthless, and improve in everything that is good and beautiful. Not to make yourselves unhappy, but to live so that you may be truly happy in this life and the life to come."

Elder M. Russell Ballard said, "*Teachers would be well advised to study carefully the scriptures and their manuals before reaching out for supplemental materials.*" (*Ensign*, May 1983, p. 68.) Before reading this book you should first become very familiar with the material the Church has provided you, such as the manuals, handbooks and the website www.lds.org. You'll find that most every question you can think of has already been answered somewhere in the leadership guidebook or website. Once you familiar with the materials and the program, then you can infuse your own talents and personality into it and magnify your calling!

Have fun! Whether you serve in the Young Women's program for a few months or a few years, you will grow closer to the Savior as you develop pure love for His lambs.

*Young Women? Of course . . . I'll be happy to serve.*
*You say about one hour on Sunday, and one during the week?*
*That's the kind of a call every woman should seek!*
*I guess they forgot about camping and cooking,*
*And how hard it would be, to keep yourself looking*
*Well-groomed, and well-dressed, and just sort of warm*
*In an old "A frame" cabin in a mid-summer storm!*
*And nothing was said about youth conference and such,*
*And all of the meetings to just "keep you in touch,"*
*With schedules and parties, stake dances and sports,*
*And how to make sure the girls don't wear shorts*
*To the fireside next Sunday at 6:30 p.m.;*
*And if they have parents – be sure to bring them.*
*How could you know that tears would be shed,*
*As you prayed for your girls by the side of your bed;*
*Or your feelings when, with a nice lesson prepared,*
*You talked to the class, but it seemed no one cared?*
*But then sometime later; the joy which would come*
*When the spirit at last, touched the "questioning one."*
*And, she thanked you, through tears, for just being there,*
*And letting her know that you really do care.*
*The Lord makes us equal to what we must do*
*And He performs miracles especially in you.*
*For as you are humble and just do your part,*
*A treasure of love will be stored in your heart.*
*Not just for the girls, but for others as well,*
*Who have served at your side, and can certainly tell*
*Of how much you'll be missed; if by change or new call*
*Your paths may or may not, cross very much, if at all.*
*Our lives are much richer than at the beginning,*
*When we each said, "I'll be happy to serve in Young Women!*
(Author Unknown)

CHAPTER 1

# Getting to Know You & Ice Breakers

*"Friendship improves happiness, and abates misery, by
doubling our joys, and dividing our grief."*

JOSEPH ADDISON
*1672-1719, British Essayist, Poet, Statesman*

Julia Ward Howe was talking to a distinguished U.S. senator. She asked him to take interest in the case of a person who needed help. The senator answered, "Julia, I have become so busy I can no longer concern myself with individuals." She replied, "That's remarkable. Even God hasn't reached that stage yet."

Before we can serve the young women under our care we need to know them and understand their unique needs. Sometimes young women can be shy. Sometimes they need a little gentle prodding to open up. Sometimes wards get divided and you need to provide opportunities for the girls to feel more united. Sometimes girls just wanna have fun! For all those reasons and more, here are a few fun ideas to put some spark into your Mutual activities and Sunday lessons. Think of them as just a brainstorm to get your own creative juices flowing.

# ACTIVITIES

### "ABC'S OF FRIENDSHIP"

Invite the girls to create a list of friendship rules from A to Z. Create a contract they can sign that encourages them to be their best and create a loving class environment for others.

## "FLOWER OF FRIENDSHIP"

Each girl brings a flower that best represents her and explains why she chose that one. Create a bouquet and talk about what flowers need to grow, comparing your class to a blossoming flower. Have the girls make tissue paper flowers or learn how to arrange flowers as an activity.

## "BROWN BAG IT"

Give each girl a brown paper bag to take home and fill with things that describe her personality and life. Everyone returns the next Sunday or on Mutual with their brown bags and shares what is in them. Have a brown bag dinner. Give the girls a small item in another brown bag to take home that will remind them of what they have in common with all the other girls in the Young Women's program.

## "LIL SIS"

Have the Laurels each adopt a "Little Sister" from the Beehives and even the Mia Maids if you have enough girls to make it work out. The "Big Sister" can either be a secret and do nice things anonymously or else everyone can know everyone else's identity and they do things together during special combined activities, as well as sitting together on Sundays.

## "FRIENDSHIP BASKET"

There are several variations to this. One girl fills a basket with things that tell about herself. She talks about why she chose those items and then she picks a slip of paper out of a jar to read the name of the next girl who will get a turn to do the same thing next week. She can present her items as gifts to the next girl. To prevent competition and overspending, another variation is for her to simply do a "show and tell" and take the items back home.

## "PICTURE PERFECT"

Have each girl make a collage poster of things that describe her. The girls can try to guess who made each poster or they could simply take turns telling the others about why she created hers the way she did.

"THE BINDER THAT BINDS"

Each week a girl is chosen to take home a binder that has been filled with a questionnaire or simply blank pages. The girl answers the questions and/or decorates a blank page to tell about herself. She shares the information and then passes it on to the next girl to take home the subsequent week.

"FRIENDSHIP KNOTS"

Make pretzels or homemade bread knots and talk about the qualities of a true friend: Knot critical, Knot thoughtless, Knot judgmental or irresponsible. A true friend is Knot to be taken for granted, knot to be forgotten, knot just a blessing but a miracle. Let's Knot let it slip away!

"SWEET VICTORY"

Have a cake decorating contest between the Beehives, Mia Maids and Laurels. Give each group an unfrosted, single layered cake (or cupcake) and a bowl of frosting. Place small bowls filled with candies, fruits, candy sprinkles, chocolate chips, coconut, raisins, nuts, etc. in the center of the table. Set a time limit for decorating. Have pre-appointed judges award prizes when the decorating is done. Award prizes for the most original, most creative, etc., making sure each cake is awarded a prize. Gee, guess what's for dessert?

"TRUTH OR DARE"

Have girls pull (leader approved) questions out of a hat that they have to answer or else choose a "dare" card out of another hat. Make sure the questions and the dares will not offend or embarrass anyone but rather endear them to each other.

"AMISH FRIENDSHIP BREAD"

Begin "Amish Friendship Bread" by creating a starter dough that is then passed on to another and then another. By the time the dough has been shared by all of the girls have a bread-making activity.

FRIENDSHIP FUDGE

While singing the song in Opening Exercises pass around a bag of "Friendship Fudge". The girls mix the following ingredients together in a gallon ziplock baggie by gently squeezing the bag when it comes to them. Talk about how the rewards are sweet when we work together. (Be sure not to do this on Fast Sunday!)

4 cups powdered sugar
3 ounces softened cream cheese
½ cup softened margarine
½ cup cocoa
1 tsp. vanilla
½ chopped nuts

"HOUSE RULES"

Invite the girls to create a list of rules they all agree on for the group. They could even sign a contract, decorate it and display it as a reminder.

COMPREHENSIVE QUESTIONNAIRE

Vickie Hacking has created a wonderfully comprehensive questionnaire for leaders to have their young women fill out. It's a great starting place to learn more about each of the girls you have a stewardship over and is entitled "All About Me." It can be found at www.lds-yw.com/html/yw_files.html. (Look under the section "Leader Help.")

# GAMES

"PEOPLE BINGO"

Make a Bingo grid with a "FREE" space in the center. In all of the other spaces, write things such as "Has been to Utah", "Has completed a Personal Progress goal for faith", "Has seen the movie Napoleon Dynamite", "Born in another state", "Has pierced ears", etc. The young women have to walk around the room and get the signature of a person who meets the criteria for each section. Depending on how many people are playing the game, you might want to implement a rule that a person can only sign another player's paper in two spots. The first person with a completed card wins!

"BIRTHDAY LINE"

Take some tape and make two parallel lines on the floor about a foot wide. Everyone has to stand in a row inside the lines and make sure their feet aren't touching the tape lines. They can stand side by side in the line so that the task is not impossible. Now tell them that they have to arrange each other in birthday order without stepping out of or on the lines. As people step out of the line, they're eliminated and the amount of space you have to move around increases so it gets easier.

"SQUEEZE!"

This game encourages creative thinking. Get four long pieces of string to form a square on the floor. The object is to fit the entire group into increasingly small spaces. Once the group can fit into a square of one size, make the square smaller each time. Have a competition between the girls and the leaders to see who is more creative. Talk about how it's cool to be "square" by living the standards of the church. Have the girls decorate blocks of wood by adding faces and hair so they "wood" remember to live the Young Women values.

"WHAT'S IN A NAME?"

Participants stand in a circle, arms distance apart. Ask each person to think of a verb and action which starts with the same letter as the person's first name. (For example, "Jumping Janice" or "Kickboxing Kelly.") The person does the action and yells out their action-name, then points to someone else. Try to go faster and faster until everyone knows everyone's name or is laughing too hard to play any longer, whichever comes first.

"OVER THE WALL"

Divide the group into two teams. Two members of the team hold a rope about three to four feet above the ground. The object of the game is to get everyone over the rope. No one can go under the rope. Before you start transferring people over the 'wall', you meet as a team and decide how to get everyone over. Time the teams. If you don't have a large enough group, you can do this as one group.

## "THE THING ABOUT STRING"

Without telling anyone what the game is have each girl cut a piece of string or yarn from a roll. Tell them to make it as long or short as they wish. Now explain that the game is to have each girl take a turn and talk about themselves for as long as it takes them to wrap the string around their finger. Another variation is to assign each girl a cut piece of string that has a equal length that was given to someone else in the room. They have to find their match, sit together and then talk until they are finished wrapping the piece around one finger.

## "TIME FLIES!"

Have everyone write down a topic on a separate piece of paper and then put the slips of paper in a bowl or hat. Don't tell any other players what it is. Possible suggestions: famous Americans, TV shows, artists, music styles, cartoons, etc. Each person takes a turn picking a slip of paper out of the hat and talking for exactly one minute. Set a timer. If that person pauses, changes the subject or says "um" or "uh" then another person takes her place, yelling out "Time flies!" If the person can speak for the entire minute she earns two points. If someone else is speaking when the timer runs out she receives one point. The person with the most points when all the topics are gone wins!

## "TO TELL THE TRUTH"

Everyone thinks of 2 things about themselves that are true (I've skied on Lake Mead, I have eaten duck, etc.) and one thing that is not true but might sound reasonable (I won a burping contest, I won a baby beauty contest, etc). The group has to decide which of the three items are true and false.

## "TELLING A YARN"

Have everyone stand in a circle fairly close together and toss a ball of yarn to each other. When you catch the yarn you have to tell something about yourself, a hobby, or something that no one knows. You then hold on to a piece of the yarn and toss the ball to someone else. Keep tossing and talking until you form a giant spider web. Then get out a beach ball and put it on the web. Talk about how we need to be unified as a group to keep the ball on top of the string. Have someone use scissors to snip a few strings here and there, while giving examples of negative things we might say to one another. Eventually the ball will fall through the web. Emphasize how our actions and words affect the group as a whole.

### "M & M'S"

Get a bag of M & M's and some small cups (like Dixie cups). As each person comes into the room, give them a cup with a few candies and ask them not to eat any yet. After everyone has been seated in a circle, tell them you are going to go around the circle and for every color of candy they have, they have to tell the group as many things about themselves as the color represents. You can make up whatever categories you would like. For example, BLUE=Family, RED=Pets, BROWN = talents, GREEN = goals, etc.

### "THREE THINGS"

Each girl pairs up with another girl. They have to find three things they have in common and then present their findings to the rest of the group.

### "IT'S IN THE BAG"

Open a big, grocery-sized paper bag and place it in the middle of the floor. Each person takes turns picking it up, but you can only do it using one of these three methods:

—You must pick up the bag with your teeth

—You must stand on one leg only

—You must not touch your hands on the floor.

In the first round everyone gets a turn. If someone breaks one of the rules, she is out of the game. Before each round cut off one or two inches from the bag. The last one who is able to pick up the bag wins!

### "YOU'RE ALL A BUNCH OF ANIMALS!"

Give each young woman a slip of paper with the name of an animal on it. They must locate the other members of their animal group by imitating that animal's sound. No talking is allowed.

## "COOPERATIVE MUSICAL CHAIRS"

This activity is a twist on the familiar musical chairs game. Set up a circle of chairs with one less chair than the number of participants. Play music as everyone walks around the chairs. When the music stops, everyone must sit in a seat. Unlike the traditional game, the person without a seat is not out. Instead, someone must make room for that person. Then remove another seat and start the music again. The girls end up on one another's laps and sharing chairs! Afterward, emphasize the teamwork and cooperation the game took, and how the girls need to accept one another to be successful.

## "EVOLUTION"

Everyone begins as an "egg," so people have to pretend to be an egg. Find another egg and play "rock, paper, scissors" with the other egg. Whoever wins gets to "evolve" into a chicken, so now the chickens have to pretend to be chickens. Whoever loses remains an egg. Then the chickens must find other chickens in order to play rock, paper, scissors. The eggs must play with other eggs. Whoever wins evolves. Whoever loses "devolves." The loser between two chickens will become an egg again. The winner will become a dinosaur and pretend to be that. Loser eggs remain eggs. Again, like animals play rock, paper, scissors with like animals. Losers devolve into what they were previously. Winners between two dinosaurs evolve into the highest form of evolution: either ELVIS or the ENLIGHTENED ONE, in which case they would pretend to be ELVIS or sit down and say OM, depending on how you choose to play the game.

## "PEOPLE IN A POT"

Divide the group into two teams. Write down the names of famous people on slips of paper and include the names of everyone in the group. Another version of the game is to write the names of people in your ward. Each team gets 30 seconds to pull the slips of paper out of a bowl one at a time and give word clues until her teammates can guess the right name. When the group guesses the name, it gets to keep that slip of paper. The winning team is the group who has collected the most slips of paper.

## "MINE FIELD"

Create a "mine field" in a room by distributing balls, cans, foam noodles, and other objects on the floor. Divide the group into pairs. The challenge is for one of the girls in each pair to verbally guide her blindfolded partner through the minefield. Switch so that each girl can do both parts. See which pair can get through the maze the fastest.

## "TOWER OF BABEL"

Give each team the same materials: paper cups, empty cans, paper, balls—anything you can think of. Using all the materials (points deducted for each object not used) the object is for each team to build the tallest freestanding tower without talking!

## "BUILDING BRIDGES"

Using mini marshmallows and toothpicks, each team has to build a bridge. Set your criteria - longest bridge (that doesn't break in the middle); tallest bridge (inches from the ground); bridge that can support the most weight, most creative design, etc.

## "FRUIT BASKET"

Put out enough chairs for everyone minus one. Everyone playing needs to be given the name of a fruit (apple, orange, banana, etc.) The person without a chair yells out the name of one of the fruits. Each person who has been named that fruit then has to get up and move to another chair while the person in the middle tries to steal one of the seats. The person without a seat now becomes the caller. The caller can yell out two or more fruits at a time. If she yells "Fruit Basket" then everyone has to get up and move. The game continues until everyone has had a chance to be the caller. A way to learn more about the players is instead of calling out fruits, the person in the middle calls out something about herself or something she has done and they change places quickly, leaving another person in the middle. Make sure that they go beyond things like, "everyone who is wearing blue" or other simple things. It has to be something that is special about them—playing a particular instrument or knowing how to ride a horse, etc. Emphasize the fact that you want to get to know something about them you may not have known before.

"BALLOONS"

Choose three different colors of balloons to represent the Beehives, Mia Maids and Laurels. Blow them up and scatter them all over the room on the floor, including under chairs and tables. The girls are not allowed to touch the balloons with their hands, but by only using their feet they have to gather their colored balloons to a certain corner of the room without being stolen by the other groups. The winning team is the group who can gather all of their balloons first. Another element of the game is to put slips of paper inside the balloons and when the teams have gathered their balloons they can then pop the balloons to read assignments, solve a riddle or whatever task you want them to perform to determine the real winner.

"QUITE A PAIR"

Provide each young woman with two index cards. Ask each girl to write a brief description of her physical characteristics on one index card and her name on the other. Put all the physical characteristic index cards in a shoe box, mix them up, and distribute one card to each girl, making sure that no one gets her own card. Give the girls a few minutes to search for the person who fits the description on the card they hold. There is no talking during this activity, but they can walk around the room. At the end of the activity, tell the girls to write on the card the name of the young woman or leader who best matches the description. Then have everyone share their results. How many guessed correctly?

"HUMAN KNOTS"

Have everyone stand shoulder to shoulder in a circle. Explain that the group will be working through a challenge to untangle a human knot. Have each person stick their left hand into the circle without touching anyone. Then have them grasp the hand of a different person who is not standing next to them. This should tangle the group. Now have them work together to untangle the knot without letting their hands go. If you have an odd number of people in the group when you grab hands the first time you will have an extra hand. When everyone sticks their second hand into the circle you will find enough hands at that time.

## "SPONGE PLUNGE"

Divide into two teams. Place a bucket and a large sponge by the first person on each team. Place an empty bucket a certain distance away from each team. At the signal, the first person dips the sponge in the water, runs to the other end, and wrings the water into the empty bucket. When the first person runs back, the next person goes. The first team to finish, wins one prize, and the team that is able to squeeze the most water in the bucket, wins another. Talk about how we are each like sponges, soaking up the kind or hurtful words of one another.

## "TIC TOCK"

Everyone gets a slip of paper with a word on it such as "Disney" or "Root". They have to mingle with the others in the group until they find someone else whose word works with theirs such as "Disney-land" or "Root–beer."

## "LOVE ONE ANOTHER"

Have everyone sit in a big circle. One person is left in the middle and is "It." That person goes up to someone and says, "Do you love me?" The seated girl can answer "Yes" or "No." If she says "Yes" she then gives up her seat and becomes "It". If she says "No" she has to explain why such as "No, but I love everyone with blonde hair" or "everyone with red socks" at which time anyone who fits that description has to exchange places while the person in the middle tries to get one of their seats. The last person left is "It." Play until everyone has had a turn being "It."

## "SIAMESE TWINS"

Cut off one sleeve on an old T-shirt and sew it to another old T-shirt whose opposite sleeve has been cut off, making one giant T-shirt for two girls to share. Have them play games and sports together and then feed each other dessert.

## "SINK YOUR TEETH INTO THIS GAME"

Sit in a circle and have a contest to see who can do various tasks without showing their teeth, such as snorting, laughing, singing, etc. Whoever shows her teeth is out until the last player wins.

"STARING CONTEST"

You guessed it! See who can stare the longest without blinking or laughing.

"WHO'S WHO?"

Write the names of famous people on slips of paper and tape them to the girls' backs. They have to mingle and ask each other questions until they can guess their identity.

"HUG THE POT HOLDER"

Give everyone a pot holder they must hug without using their hands. Choose someone to be the "Judge" who will tell them if they're hugging the pot holder correctly or not. The Judge has a pot on her lap. See how long it takes for them to figure out they're supposed to hug the judge! (She is the potholder.)

"GIVE HER A HAND"

A fun game to play to get to know a new Young Women's presidency is for the new leaders to stand behind a table or blanket that is being held up by two of the girls. The leaders then put a hand out while the rest of their body is covered up. The rest of the girls have to ask yes or no questions to the hands, trying to guess who it is. To answer "yes" the leader gives a thumbs up and to answer "no" she gives a thumbs down or shakes her index finger.

"YES/NO"

Write the word "Yes" on one side of a paper and the word "No" on the other side. Simply ask the group questions they have to answer such as "Do you have a pet?", "Can you do a cartwheel?", "Do you like spinach?" etc. The girls will get a kick out of seeing how everyone answers the questions.

"PIG HEAVEN"

Tape everyone's noses up by putting a long piece of clear tape from the top of their lip to their forehead. That alone is cheap entertainment. Now have everyone take turns seeing who can do pig calls the best, snort like a pig, and sing a farm song.

## "STICKY FINGERS"

Tape everyone's thumb down to the palm of their hand and then have them do various tasks such as writing their name with a pencil, using chopsticks, clapping, snapping their fingers, putting a pillow in a pillow case, eating a snack, putting on a coat, etc.

## "DON'T EAT MOLLY!"

Make a board game with as many squares as there are girls. Draw a different face to represent each girl. Put a small piece of candy on each square. Have one of the girls leave the room while the other girls choose one of the faces on the board to be "It." When the girl comes back into the room she is invited to eat the small candies one at a time. When she chooses the candy that was on the "It" square all of the girls yell "Don't Eat Molly!" (or whatever the real girl's name is who is represented by that square.) The winner is the girl who can eat the most candy before choosing "It."

## "SOCK DARTS"

Every girl is given an old, but clean sock to decorate to look like her. Fill the toe area with beans and then tie it with elastic or yarn. Have the girls take turns tossing their sock towards a target such as a hula hoop or a circle drawn by tape on the floor. You could also write points on pieces of paper and the girls earn the amount they get their sock dart closest to.

## "TO TELL THE TRUTH"

Give everyone a paper to write down something amazing they have done. Choose one of the papers and have three of the girls stand in front of the group, being sure to include the one girl who really wrote the paper. Have the three girls try to convince the group that they were the one who actually did that particular thing. See if the group can guess who was telling the truth.

## "WATERMELON SEED SPITTING"

Who doesn't love a good old-fashioned watermelon seed-spitting contest? See who can spit their seed the farthest or to a certain target on the ground. Gee, guess what you're having for refreshments?

### "SHOE PILE"

Everyone takes off one of their shoes and throws it into a big pile. Then each person picks up a different shoe from the pile and finds the person it belongs to.

### "LIGHT SABERS"

Have the girls pick a partner and put their hands together, hooking them with an index finger sticking out like a light saber. The object of the game is to poke each other. Once you have been poked you sit down and the partner that's left finds a new partner until it comes down to the champion.

### "HULA HOOP CONTEST"

See who can hula hoop the longest or craziest. Have them make up tricks they can do with the hula hoop on their arms or one foot or with a partner.

### "SHOT PUT THROW"

Blow up a bunch of balloons. Each person gets three chances to throw the inflated balloon as far as possible. Another variation is to play on teams and play shuffleboard with balloons.

### "COOKIE DASH"

Divide into two teams. Place a plate with a large cookie on it and a glass of milk a certain distance from each team. Instruct teams to form a line. At the signal, the first person from each team runs to the cookie and eats it. She must not only eat the cookie but must drink the milk before running back. (Be sure to check for food allergies first.) The next person runs down quickly, eats a cookie, and drinks a glass of milk. Each person must take a turn. Have a person at each end pouring glasses of milk and replacing cookies. The first team to finish wins.

### "ZIP/ZAP/ZOP"

Everyone sits in a circle and someone begins by pointing to another person in the circle and saying "ZIP!" That person then points to yet another person and says "ZAP!" That person points to another person and says "ZOP!" This continues, but the words must be said in order: ZIP, ZAP, ZOP. If someone makes a mistake and says a word out of order, that person is out of the game. Eventually, the circle dwindles to just a few people, then to only 2 people, who are staring at each other, yelling ZIP!, ZAP!, ZOP! Continue until one of them makes a mistake.

### "HAVE YOU EVER?"

All of the young women stand in a circle. Each takes a turn asking a question, "Have you ever_____" (filling in the blank). Those who have, answer yes by walking to the center of the circle and slapping a "high five" with whoever else has done the action.

### "WATER BALLOON TOSS"

This one is always a hit. Another variation is to use raw or hard-boiled eggs. Choose partners and stand facing each other. Toss a water-filled balloon to the other person. After each toss, the partners must take a step backward. The last set of partners to have an unpopped balloon wins.

### "PILE UP"

Have the girls sit in a circle in chairs with a little bit of space between chairs. Have a leader in the center of the circle give directions such as "Everyone wearing jeans move three spaces to the right" and the moves are made. Continue calling out different commands for things about who is wearing earrings, what type of shoes people have on, the color of shirts, make-up, etc. Most likely the girls will end up sitting on top of each other, sometimes 4-5 deep. Teach the girls to celebrate the differences and enjoy one another.

### "UTENSILS"

Everyone sits in a circle. One person gives a fork to the girl sitting next to her and says "This is a fork." The receiver says "A what?" and the giver repeats "A fork!" The receiver then says "Oh! A fork!" and then repeats the conversation with the girl sitting next to her. Somewhere else in the circle another girl has started a similar conversation with a spoon going in the opposite direction. Include a knife, a spatula, and whatever other utensils you want to use. The game is pretty much over when everyone is laughing.

"SOFT SCULPTURES"

Have a bubble blowing contest first. Then, once the gum is sufficiently soft, have each girl create a sculpture of a Young Woman or any other item. Put each sculpture on a 3 x 5 card and have an unbiased judge select the winner.

"JELLY BEANS"

Have girls guess the flavor of various jelly beans. JellyBelly has great ones. Next have them design a jelly bean that reflects their personality without the other girls seeing them work. They need to color a jelly bean design on paper and then select a name and display real jelly beans that illustrate their concoction. Finally, display the jelly bean creations and see if the girls can guess who made them. Have each girl explain why she designed her jelly bean the way she did.

# WEBSITES

Here are some great websites with ideas for more fun "get to know you" games!

- www.ce.byu.edu/yp/ythconf/games/initiative.htm
- www.funattic.com
- www.funandgames.org
- www.adulted.about.com/od/icebreakers/
- www.eslflow.com/ICEBREAKERSreal.html
- www.poped.org/icebreakers.html
- www.teach-nology.com/ideas/ice_breakers/
- www.geocities.com/EnchantedForest/Glade/6694/icebreak. html

CHAPTER 2

## Personal Progress

*"Let's tell young people the best books are yet to be written; the best painting, the best government the best of everything is yet to be done by them."*

JOHN ERSKINE
*1878-1951, American Poet, Essayist, Novelist, Musician*

The Personal Progress program is the meat of the Young Women's program. It helps each girl to learn gospel principles and then apply them to her own life in practical ways. The booklet she is given will help her crystallize what it is she really wants to do and be in life. By setting personal goals she will learn how to stand in and create holy places wherever she is.

Help the girls understand that the suggested tasks in their book are not "busy work" but actually introduce the girls to things they will be doing the rest of their lives: studying the scriptures, setting goals, learning, growing, serving.

Sunday lessons and Mutual activities could offer ways for her to accomplish her goals. Every girl is unique and progressing at a different rate, so it's important for her to understand that the goals she selects are for her to improve herself and not to compete with others. Help parents to understand the program and offer suggestions for them to support their daughter. Help the girls and their parents look at the activities they are already involved in and see how they could apply towards meeting some of the goals.

Ultimately, the young women will hopefully learn not to compartmentalize their activities into "Personal Progress" and "My activities", but see that they can be the same. Remember, Personal Progress is just that—it's personal! Every girl should choose what she wants to do, not feel compelled to do something because that's what everyone else is doing. Group activities are fine every now and then, but each girl's progress should be an individual experience. Be sure to have the girls report on their progress to you frequently, whether it be in a formal interview setting, weekly chart-marking, or in some other way so that they are accountable for their choices. (They should be very familiar with the idea of accountability!)

# MOTIVATION AND RECOGNITION

Be sure to check out all of the helpful ideas at www.lds.org. Click on "Serving in the Church" and then "Young Women." There are talks, video clips, links, inspiring quotes and so much more! There is even an entire section on "Encouraging Young Women to do Personal Progress." There are some helpful training lessons that can be shared with the leaders, parents and even the girls. Here is some food for thought:

- Have a monthly or quarterly P.I.E. night. This is "Personal Interview Evening" where each girl sits down with a leader and goes over her goals. While the other girls are waiting for their turn they can bake pies, eat or even work on a group project like making a quilt for a graduating Laurel.

- Help the girl to focus on one value each month. Remind the young women to ask themselves "What do I want to become?" not "What do I want to do?"

- Create a Values Binder where she can collect handouts from lessons and organize them according to the values. When she gets ready to choose a Value Project she can refer to the handouts.

- Create a Personal Progress Binder for each girl to either keep at Church or take home. Things you could include are a copy of the Personal Progress book, the Young Women theme, a copy of The Articles of Faith, a copy of *The Family: A Proclamation to the World*, a class list with phone numbers for the girls and the leaders, a monthly calendar, and notepaper.

- Include a Personal Progress article in a monthly newsletter to spotlight some of the girls' accomplishments.

- Whenever there is a special program or ceremony to present the Young Womanhood Recognition award, invite the girls who have already received theirs to sit in a special section of the room, kind of like the Boy Scouts' "Eagles' Nest." You could call it the "Recognition Circle" or "Medallion Club" or something that makes them feel extra special.

- The Young Women general presidency sends out letters of recognition upon request for young women and leaders who have earned their Young Womanhood Recognition award. To request such letters, send an e-mail, fax, or letter to:

    Office of the Young Women General Presidency
    76 North Main Street
    Salt Lake City, Utah 84150-6030

    Fax: (801) 240-5458
    E-mail: youngwomen@ldschurch.org

- Have a "You CAN do it!" can where the girls can select treats each week when they pass off activities.

- Each girl can make a doll (wood, porcelain, fabric) and receive other elements for it each time she completes a personal progress project. Items could be hair, jewelry, miniature cell phone, etc.

- Each girl makes a "Noah's Ark" craft and receives an animal each time she completes a personal progress project.

- Give each girl a charm bracelet or a necklace chain when she becomes a Beehive or moves in. Each time she completes a project she earns a charm to add to her jewelry. You could also award charms for other special efforts such as attending girl's camp, Young Women in Excellence or on birthdays. Check out www.charmedmoments.com.

- "Personal Progress isn't just for Sundays." Hold an evening where the girls can work on their Personal Progress. Each time they pass off an item they earn a ticket to redeem for a topping on an ice cream sundae that night.

- Each time a girl completes a task toward her Personal Progress she earns a square of fabric that can be used to make her very own quilt or pillow. Have a big quilt-making party at the end of the year.

- Buy an oil lamp and have the girls drop some "oil" into the lamp each week if they have completed a project or even worked on one. The girls could each have their own lamp or you could have one large one for all of the young women combined. The "drops" of oil could be colored marbles, gumballs or candies to reflect the Value colors. Once the lamp is full you could choose to have a party or some other special reward.

- Have a Personal Progress Spotlight on Sundays or during Mutual when the girls can report on what they've done during the week and get a little treat out of a basket.

- Create a poster with the girls' names posted, placing a sticker next to every girl who passes off a task each week. Once she has earned 5 stickers she gets a special treat. Use stickers that coordinate with your monthly or annual theme.

- Present each girl with one piece of a 7 piece Nativity set when they have finished all of the goals for a particular value. This is something that will be cherished in her home now and when she has her own family.

- With the Bishop's approval, present a special award to each girl in Sacrament Meeting when she has completed a Value Project. Your ward will learn more about the program and be happy to support all of the Young Women.

- Present a quilt square in the value color that has just been finished. When the young woman completes all seven she can make a special pillow. Have a pillow-making party for all of the girls who are ready to sew their "reward."

- Plan a big awards night like the Oscars where you can present the awards. It could be a great annual tradition for your ward or stake.

- Be sure your Bishop understands the Personal Progress program and ask him to include questions about it during his interviews with the young women.

- Present the girl with a picture of her shaking hands with the Stake President, Bishop, or Young Women President (or all of the above!) when she has completed a project or earned the Young Womanhood Recognition.

- Add a pearl or charm to a bracelet that is being created for every accomplishment the girl passes off. Have a jewelry-making activity for all of the girls to get excited about it.

- Keep the girls' Personal Progress books at church and provide copies of pages they are working on to take home. That might help prevent their books from disappearing into the black hole that is their bedroom.

- Make a Personal Progress Family Home Evening lesson packet to help family members understand the program and how they can support the Young Woman in their family. Choose goals they can work on together.

- PPP = "Personal Progress Pal"  Pair girls up randomly or according to needs. Invite the "Pal" to give reminders, bring special treats, and celebrate when her pal finishes a goal.

- Invite a guest to speak to your Young Women once a month on one of the Personal Progress goals or areas you are working on.

- Have an evening all about "purses" . . . our Purse-onal journey here on earth, scriptures up close and purse-onal, how we progress in life purse-onally, etc. Show different kinds of purses that represent stages in our lives: little girl dress-up purse, backpack, make-up bag, prom purse, temple bag, travel bag, missionary bag, book bag, grocery bag, Church calling bag, etc. Decorate a bag with the Young Women values on it.

- Play "Personal Progress Feud" like the TV game show. Ask the girls to answer various questions ahead of time so you can create a poll such as "What is your favorite value?" "What is the hardest value to work on?" "Name one value experience for Good Works" "Name a person in the scriptures who represents Integrity", etc.

- Make a plaque like the missionary or Eagle Scout plaques that hang on the walls at church. Engrave the names of the girls who earn the Young Womanhood Recognition Award.

- Have the girls make magnet reminders to put on their mirrors or refrigerators at home to remind them to work on their projects.

- "Triple P" (Personal Progress Party) The girls can wear and bring anything that starts with "P" such as their Personal Progress book, Pretzels, popcorn, pillows, etc. Then watch a "P" Movie (*Princess Bride, Pete's Dragon*, etc.)

- During Mutual, invite each girl to a short visit where she will bring her Personal Progress book and you will chat about her goals.

- Designate one week every month when you will all work on goals and give rewards for accomplishments.

- Provide a "You Nailed It" basket the girls can pick from when they finish a goal. The basket will include a variety of nail polish, glitter, stick-ons, Emory boards and other nail care items.

- Give the girls some cute little reminder to work on their goals such as a piece of gum with a note that says "Stick To Your Goals."

- Have the girls earn value-colored beads to go on a necklace. The girls could bring their necklaces once a month on "Be and Bead Night" to add more when they pass off their goals.

- Give each girl a votive candle holder and talk about the symbolism of light. Each time they complete a value project they can earn a value-colored candle to put in their holder.

- Have a weekly Spotlight moment each week where you could shine a flashlight on each girl while she talks about her accomplishments.

- Have a "Value Sunday" where everyone wears clothes in the color of the value they've been working on.

- Put value-colored stones into a lamp (like the parable of the 10 virgins) or some other receptacle when the girls complete a project. When it becomes full you can have a special activity or party to celebrate their accomplishments.

- For Personal Progress ideas check out:

  www.lightplanet.com/mormons/ywc/pp/morelaurel.htm

- Find a nice receptacle to put value-colored candy or gumballs in as the girls complete their assignments. When the jar is full, present it to the Bishop to put on his desk in his office for him to share with future visitors.

- Personal Progress is CHARMING. Have a special lesson and present the girls with bracelets they can add charms to every time they complete a Personal Progress achievement.

- Stations Night. Set up seven value-colored tables that the girls can rotate through. Post a list of requirements at each table. Provide things they will need in order to pass off a couple of items for each value such as scriptures, hymnals, paper, pens, pedigree charts, family group sheets, etc. Invite a leader or parent to sit at each table and sign off the girls who complete tasks. Award girls with a value-colored treat at each table.

- "Jump Start" Show the girls that it's easy to get started on their goals by doing one all together the first week of the month. Play jump rope, learn about jumping beans, and have the girls do a few jumping jacks before they get refreshments.

- Kneel with the girls in prayer as you begin your interviews with them. Let them hear you pray for their success.

- Create "Pingo" cards by making a Bingo grid and writing different key words from the Young Women values and Personal Progress book. Make sure each board game has the words scrambled in different order. While each girl is going over her Personal Progress book privately, the other girls are playing "Pingo." The winner of each round will get a prize that starts with "P".

- Encourage the leaders to work towards earning their Young Womanhood in Recognition award and let the girls know it. They will be impressed and motivated by their leaders' examples. Have a healthy competition between the girls and the leaders to see who can pass off the most goals within a certain time period. Whichever group "wins" is treated to a special event.

- Have each girl or class take turns decorating a Young Women bulletin board with Personal Progress information.

- Encourage the Bishopric to ask the girls during interviews how they are doing on their Personal Progress goals.

- "Pie Plunge" For every goal passed off within a certain time frame the girl gets to throw a pie at the Bishopric or Young Women leaders on "Pie Plunge Night." Cut holes in big sheets of plastic for the leaders to put their heads through. Thrown pies could just be whipped cream on pie plates. Save the real pie for dessert!

- Create a craft item that will need seven gem stones such as a frame, mirror, bracelet, necklace, etc. Reward a value-colored gem when all of the tasks have been completed in that particular area: Diamonds for Faith, Sapphires for Divine Nature, Rubies or Garnets for Individual Worth, Emeralds for Knowledge, Topaz for Choice & Accountability or Good Works (as they can be yellow to orange), and Amethyst for Integrity. Gold could also be used for Good Works. See www.aboutgems.org for more information on gems and their meanings.

- Write Personal Progress goals on slips of paper and have the girls draw one out of a hat to decide what they're going to do that night.

- When the girls finish a Personal Progress activity they get to put their name in a jar. Once a month draw a few names of winners to receive a special treat.

- If you want to create a progress chart to display on the wall for everyone to see, then have each girl make up an alias name so that the girls won't be embarrassed.

- When only one girl shows up for Mutual save that great activity you had planned for a larger group and use the opportunity to go over her Personal Progress goals.

- Have the girls bring blankets, pillows, and their Personal Progress books. Make popcorn and have the girls watch the video "Wives and Daughters of the First Presidency" while the leaders pull one girl out at a time to update her Personal Progress book and go over her goals.

- A great Value Project might be for a young woman to make a year's worth of Personal Progress reminders that could be passed out each week.

CHAPTER 3

*Parental Support*

*"We never know the love of the parent till we become parents ourselves."*

HENRY WARD BEECHER
*1813-1887, American Preacher, Orator, Writer*

Getting support from the parents of a young women is extremely important for the progress and success of your program. When the parents see that their daughter is being blessed by her attendance they will be more eager to make sure she goes to Church.

Parents will become very supportive when they see your activities and efforts are helping their daughter to strengthen their home and family! Teenage girls have very busy lives and, most likely, their parents are trying to coordinate the activities of several children.

When you communicate with the parents and let them know ahead of time what you've planned for their daughter, they will be able to support your calendar with enthusiasm.

Here are a few ideas to help get more support from the parents:

- Send them weekly e-mails with an updated calendar.
- E-mail them pictures that were taken from last week's activity night.
- Send them a monthly newsletter.
- Find out what their talents are and recruit them to teach classes or activities where they can share their skills.

- Make sure they have copies of their daughter's Personal Progress goals.
- Do in-home visits with their daughter and include them.
- Invite them to hold a special activity in their home for the Young Women.
- Invite them to attend a special day and time when parents of all the Young Women will be in the temple, praying for their daughters.
- Honor them at a special Parents Night.
- Encourage their daughters to write them thank you letters.
- Provide opportunities when the girls can make special crafts and gifts for their parents.
- Always speak positively about the parents in front of the girls so they will see that you respect them.
- Invite the parents to take turns bringing refreshments for special occasions and to be involved in the events.
- Write them a thank you letter, expressing how much you appreciate all of the good things that they have taught her.
- Call them up and ask them what they think you could do to better touch their daughter's heart and help her want to live the gospel.
- Invite them to be guest speakers in a panel addressing a particular topic during your Sunday lesson.
- Take lots of pictures of each girl. Parents love getting copies.
- Write complimentary articles about each Young Woman that could be submitted to your ward newsletter.
- Let parents know which Young Women's value you're emphasizing each month and include a list of things they could talk about and do with their daughter at home to reinforce what the Young Women's program is teaching that month.
- Have a look-alike contest, showcasing photos of the girls and their parents when they were babies.
- Involve the parents in a big craft project or something they can work on with their daughter.

- Have a 50s, 60s, 70s or 80s night and invite the parents to come and share their experiences of being teenagers. Help the girls to appreciate their parents.
- Have a family tree climbing activity where the girls can bring photos, pedigree charts, and other memorabilia to share what they know about their ancestors. If you invite the parents they will be grateful for the opportunity to talk about the legacy their parents have left so that it won't be forgotten.
- Have a Father/Daughter or Mother/Daughter cooking contest.
- Ask the parents how you can help them to get their daughter to church and activities on time.
- Ask parents to keep you informed of their daughter's special events such as piano recitals, sports events, competitions, performances and other occasions you could attend to show you care.
- Visit her home and see her bedroom. Let her tell you about her favorite things in her room. Let her parents hear you expressing interest in what she does.
- Pray for the parents and let them know you are praying for their success in raising such a wonderful young woman.
- Encourage the parents to write a "love letter" to their daughter for a special occasion.
- Send your daughter home with ideas for Family Home Evening lessons, refreshments, games and other activities for her family.
- Create a special scrapbook for each girl. Add photos of her and other momentos during her time in Young Women. She can even work on it with you. Present it to the parents when she graduates or at the end of each year.
- Help each girl recognize the unique challenges her family faces and talk about how she can be a blessing to her parents and family.
- Have the girls decorate a mat that will go around a framed copy of *The Proclamation on the Family*.
- Encourage the Young Women to seek a father's blessing.

- Have all of the Young Women adopt one of the girl's families each month. The girls could write letters of appreciation, do a "heart attack", bring them goodies, give them an award, help baby-sit, help them with yard work, or invite them to be the guests of honor at a special evening.

- Have a cooking contest and then create a special Young Women's cookbook with all of the entries. Each girl can choose her mom or dad to help so it's a team effort and contest. You can even throw in a family history twist to it by requiring that all recipes be either a family favorite or one that has been passed down in their family.

- "Family Fun Jar." Here's a new twist on that "Journal Jar" idea. Put ideas for creative, fun activities on colored slips of paper and then into a decorated mason jar or even one of those round, cardboard oatmeal boxes. Have every girl create one for her own family to use and talk about how the family who plays together stays together! Talk about other fun family traditions and ways to strengthen the family closeness and create special memories.

- Encourage your Bishopric to hold a special Parents Meeting on the 5th Sunday of each month, perhaps during the Sunday School hour or during a combined Relief Society/Priesthood lesson that focuses on the youth and how parents can support them. Familiarize parents with the goal programs so parents can ask their children informed questions at home and celebrate their progress.

# FATHERS

As the young women develop close relationships with their fathers they will be able to better understand how much their Heavenly Father must love them. Be sensitive to the girls who don't have a father available to attend special events by inviting their Home Teacher, Bishop or even an older brother.

### "DADDY'S LITTLE GIRL"

Invite the dads to bring baby pictures of their daughters and tell all about their daughter's life growing up.

## DADDY/DAUGHTER DATE NIGHT

This could be a formal dinner and dance or a more casual western hoe down with Sloppy Joes. Create a fun evening where the girls can play with their dads and create special memories. Be sure to take one of those "prom-type" pictures of each girl with their father in front of a specially-decorated background.

## HEAVENLY FATHER

Spend some time talking about Heavenly Father and his divine attributes. Point out that a loving Heavenly Father gave us earthly fathers so we could learn more about what our father in heaven is like. Have the girls' fathers walk into the room carrying flowers for each girl. Invite each father to share what he has learned about Father in Heaven by becoming a father.

## DADDY/DAUGHTER NERDS NIGHT

Dress up like real goobers and play nerdy games. Make the invitations look like pocket protectors. Play games using calculators, math, trivia, duct tape, and broken glasses.

## "DONUTS & DADS NIGHT"

You guessed it . . . play games with donuts such as trying to eat a donut hanging from a string, Tic Tac Dough, donut hole rolling contest, Guess the Flavor contest, see how many donut holes the dads can get in their mouth at once, etc.

## "DADS & DAUGHTERS IN DUNGAREES"

Have them perform a dirty service project such as pruning a widow's trees, painting a house, cleaning up a yard, etc.

## "DANCING WITH THE DADS"

Teach the dads and their daughters how to ballroom dance. Include a sentimental dance when the girls can stand on their dad's shoes and waltz around like when they were little.

## "DAD'S DUDS"

Help the girls learn about boys' and men's fashion by doing a makeover on their dad.

## "SUGAR DADDY"

Have each father/daughter pair enter a dessert-making contest or see what they can construct using sugar cubes.

## GYM NIGHT OR "PLAYGROUND PALS"

Play broom hockey, slide across the floor in socks, jump rope, and do some of the other games suggested in the chapter on Combined Young Men/Young Women activities.

## "DAD'S CAR"

Give each father/daughter a large appliance cardboard box that they transform into a car. Watch a movie together at the "drive in."

## "FOOTBALL"

Play flag football outside on the grass! Have each father and daughter make up a cheer.

## SONGS WITH A TWIST

Teach each group to sing the following songs to each other:
(The fathers sing this to the tune of the Primary song "Popcorn Popping.")

*I looked out the window and what did I see?*
*My little girl changing right in front of me.*
*Life has brought me such a big surprise.*
*She is growing up right before my eyes.*
*Wish I could take her and hold her tight.*
*Keep her forever in my sight.*
*But it can't be so. . . it's just not the plan.*
*Someday she'll find her a special man.*

(The YW sing this to the tune "I'm So Glad When Daddy Comes Home.")

*I'm so glad when Daddy comes home.*
*I'm waiting for the keys.*
*I clap my hands, and shout for joy,*
*The car is mine. . . I'm free!!!!*
*I need some cash, I need it quick.*
*I can't go out like this.*
*Don't worry though. I'll be back home*
*For what? Your goodnight kiss!*

VIDEO MESSAGE

Video tape sweet messages from the girls' parents and play it for the girls. It might surprise you how it touches the hearts of both the parents and the girls.

WORKING UP A SWEAT

A father/daughter service project that involves something more physical like painting a widow's house or pruning a widow's trees can really bring the spirit of service to your girls.

PICNIC AND HOE DOWN

Begin with a simple picnic at an outdoor pavilion, then move the tables to have a hoe down! It has probably been awhile—if ever—since the fathers have participated in a square dance. See if any of the older couples in the ward would be willing to come teach the group some basic steps. Provide some music, and let the fun begin!

"TURNING HEARTS TO FATHERS"

Have the fathers join their daughters in the Family History Center to see what information they can find together. Serve heart-shaped cookies for dessert.

DON'T FORGET MOM

The fathers and daughters could do the unexpected by making a special gift for their wife and mother.

AUTO REPAIR 101

Learn how to fix cars and do simple maintenance together. Hopefully an automotive-minded father would be willing to share his expertise with the group.

"DADDY/DAUGHTER DINNER DANCE"

Dress up very formally for a fancy dinner, dancing and etiquette night.

"LUAU"

Teach fathers to do the hula and one of those stick dances, and then eat a traditional Hawaiian meal.

## "WHEELBARROW BASEBALL"

The girls hit the ball with a bat and then hop into a wheelbarrow to be pushed around the bases by their dads.

## MISSION IMPOSSIBLE

Dress up like spies and solve mysteries together (like how to understand girls).

## MEXICAN MADNESS

Make piñatas together, eat Mexican food, learn a Mexican dance.

## MISSIONARY MOMENTS

Invite the dads to share experiences, photos, and food from their missions. Have each father/daughter pair do creative door approaches like they're missionaries.

## FUN CONTESTS AND RACES TO PLAY WITH DADS:

- The dad has to braid his daughter's hair.
- The daughter has to shave her dad's face blindfolded. Use tongue depressors as the razor.
- The father and daughter have to run a distance with the daughter standing on his shoes.
- The father and daughter work together to solve a brain teaser.
- The dads stand behind a sheet with little holes cut out, sticking their noses through the holes. The girls have to "pick" which one belongs to their dad.
- The girls stand barefoot behind a divider (rolling chalkboard) and the dads have to find their daughter's feet.
- The girls have to tie a tie on their dad.
- Tape-record each father's voice and see if the girls can guess who they are.
- Answer questions about each other.
- See who can eat a plate of Jello the fastest.

## "GUESS WHO?"

Ask the dads ahead of time to tell you one crazy thing they had done when they were younger. Write them on slips of paper and read them one by one, having the girls vote on who they think it was.

## "WHOOPS!"

The fathers lay on their backs with an ice cream cone in their mouth (opening facing up). The girls stand on a chair over their respective father with a bowl of tapioca pudding or ice cream and a spoon. The race is to see who can fill the cone first. Then they switch (father on chair, daughter on floor). Hey, fair is fair!

## "SHAVE A BALLOON"

Put shaving cream on a blown up balloon. Race to shave it first.

## "FOOD RELAY"

Have identical items in two different paper bags. Put one bag on a chair at the opposite side of the room. Form two teams. One person at a time races to the bag, pulls something out, eats it completely (opens their mouth to prove it), then runs back so the next person can go. Suggestions: a big dill pickle, a juice box, 4 saltine crackers, a banana, a piece of bubble gum (chew and blow a bubble), a fruit roll-up, etc.

# FATHER'S DAY GIFT IDEAS

The Young Women are often given the task of creating a special Father's Day gift for all of the men in the ward to be passed out after Sacrament meeting on Father's Day. Here are a few ideas:

- Big Hunk ties—Using gray cardstock, cut a rounded triangle that looks like the knot of a tie when folded in half. Glue ribbon in the fold and a Big Hunk candy bar between the open bottom halves. Tie them on to the fathers like a real tie.
- Wrap several Treasures candies in colored cellophane with a ribbon and attach a note that says, "A good father is a TREASURE beyond measure."
- Cinnamon rolls with a note saying, "You are so sweet, Dad!"

- Sugar Daddy boutonnieres—Using floral tape, wrap the ends of a Sugar Daddy candy and attach either paper leaves or real ones so that it can be pinned on the dads like a boutonniere.
- Small package of Nutter Butter cookies with a note that says "There's Nutter Butter Dad than you!"
- "Cookies and a Kiss." Attach the following poem to one giant cookie:

*Daddy's come in lots of shapes*
*But whether fat or slender*
*There's something that they can't resist*
*It's common to their gender*
*For when they come from work at night*
*One thing they love is this*
*A cookie and a glass of milk*
*A big hug and a kiss.*
*So on this special Father's Day*
*We want to share this treat*
*A cookie and a kiss for you*
*We think you're super neat.*

- Take pictures of the Primary children and youth that could be placed into those inexpensive mouse pads for their dads.
- Make a coupon book designed to look like a man's tie. Use several different colors of paper and cut each piece of the tie a little bit shorter than the last one, so that it will look like a striped tie once stapled together. On each tie piece write a different quote about fathers.
- Photo Tie. Take pictures of the daughters and cut out in a circle to make the knot part of the tie. Cut out the rest of the tie on colored cardstock.
- Go to www.lds.org and check out the song "I'm Glad That God Chose Me to Be Your Son" that appeared in the *New Era*. Change the word "son" to "child" and sing it in Sacrament Meeting.
- Father's Day graphics and ideas at www.maryslittlelamb.com.
- Attach a note to a can of "Dad's Rootbeer" saying "We CAN hardly wait to wish you a Happy Father's Day!"

- Make "Almond Joy" bow ties by drawing a cute oversized bow tie on cardstock and writing "All Men Are That They Might Have Joy" on it.

- Give each father a mini loaf of bread with a note attached that says something like " No matter how you SLICE it, you're a great dad!", "Thanks for always RISING" to the occasion", "Thanks for always being there when you are KNEADED", "Thanks for never 'loafing' on the job".

- Serve goodies to the men at the end of Priesthood meeting. They'll proably appreciate this gift more than a tie!.

- Make giant Hershey's kisses by using Rice Krispie Treats or chocolate and then shaping it in a funnel. Once they are cooled you just pop them out of the "mold" and wrap with aluminum foil, leaving part of a tag sticking out that says "Kisses to you on Father's Day!"

- Another cookie and poem idea:
  *Cookies and Dads are both so much alike . . .*
  *After the first taste you can't stop at one bite.*
  *They're both irresistible and a treat that's second-to-none,*
  *When the jar is full and Dad's at home, it's time for family fun.*
  *Cookies are rough around the edges, with a middle so tender—*
  *Dad's are like that, too—well-rounded, in all their splendor.*
  *Cookies are always better when they're lovingly homemade,*
  *Just as Dads create home-made memories that will never fade.*
  *Cookies warm a stomach, while Dads warm a troubled heart,*
  *So, thank goodness for them both and the meaning they impart!*
  HAPPY FATHER'S DAY!

- Tie a note to an apple that says "Thanks for being the core of your family!"

- Fold paper into the shape of a shirt. Staple it close to the neck and insert a candy bar like Big Hunk or Sugar Daddy.

- Serve pie, donuts, or some kind of treat during Priesthood meeting.

- Tie a ribbon and a note to a package of Pop Rocks that says, "My Pop Rocks!"

- Put a ribbon and a note around some chocolate chip cookies that says "Happy Father's Day from a chip off the ole block."
- Attach this poem to a "100 Grand" candy bar, a "Pay Day" candy bar or to a little bag of chocolate coins:

MY MILLION DOLLAR DADDY
*My dad is really special. He's the best Dad there ever was.*
*Let me tell you about him and some of the things he does.*
*He's the best example of fatherhood.*
*He's smart and handsome and smells real good.*
*He helps me with things that are hard.*
*He helps me when I work in the yard.*
*He leads us in family prayer at night.*
*He makes me feel better when I've had a fight.*
*This Dad of mine shows me the way*
*To laugh and joke when we play.*
*If I had a dollar for every time he makes me glad,*
*I'd have a lot of money, because he's my million-dollar dad!*

- Using old ties that have been donated for the cause, decorate the bottom 12 inches with wiggly eyes, buttons, pom poms, sequins, etc., and attach this poem:
*Happy Father's Day! We love you so;*
*We wanted everyone to know*
*So we designed this nifty tie,*
*'Cause you're really a special guy.*

*Wear it with pride. Don't be afraid.*
*(Wait until you see what the other kids made.)*
*And anyone who stops to stare*
*Will only see how much we care!*

- Fill a small jar with Hershey's kisses and hugs and attach this poem on the label:

*Dad,*
*Take this jar to work with you*
*And put it in your drawer,*
*it has a special purpose—*
*Let me tell you what it's for.*

*On days when you are tired or stressed,*
*When your work is long and hard*
*That's the day to open your desk*
*And remember about this jar.*

*You'll notice it's filled with chocolates—*
*Some "KISSES" and some "HUGS"*
*And though they are just candy*
*Let them remind you of our love.*

*We appreciate your work for us,*
*Our family is truly blessed*
*To have a dad who cares for us,*
*We think you are the best!*

# MOTHERS

As a Young Women leader you want to be a positive role model for the girls, but you should be careful not to allow the girls to place you above their own mother in esteem, attention or time. Help forge the bond between mother and daughter. Create opportunities to support their relationship and create lasting memories for them together. Work with the Relief Society to meet the needs of the mother and daughters in the home, especially as the young woman begins to make the transition from one auxiliary to the other. The experiences you create for her in Young Women's will lay the foundation for her in Relief Society and help her to appreciate the special bonds of sisterhood that are available to her in the Church.

- Work with your Relief Society leaders to plan special events for mothers and their daughters at an Enrichment Night or other event.

- Mother/Daughter Service project. Sew baby blankets for hospital, crochet newborn hats, bake cookies for widows, make curtains for the church building, etc.

- Play a Mother/Daughter Newlywed game to see how well they know each other.

- Fashion Follies. Fun fashion show of either real fashion tips or goofy ones. This could also be a great time to review "For the Strength of Youth" standards.

- "Proper Manners Party." Decorate tables with rose petals and fine china. Serve crumpets, and learn about etiquette.
- "Mums The Word." Learn how to arrange flowers together.
- "Garden Party." Decorate with outdoor theme or actually hold a party outside! Play croquet, wear fancy hats, and speak with British accents.
- "Spa Night." Learn how to make bath salts, do facials, pedicures, manicures, etc.
- "Wedding Day." Invite mothers to share photos and memories from their wedding day. Embroider handkerchiefs and serve wedding cake.
- "A Mother's Touch." Learn how to give massages to each other.
- "Sugar and Spice and Everything Nice. Learn how to make fancy desserts such as swan cream puffs, éclairs, flambé, etc.
- "Joy Luck Club." Serve Asian food, talk about the importance of girlfriends and celebrate sisterhood!
- "A Woman of Virtue Is More Priceless Than Rubies." Learn how to make different kinds of jewelry. Read stories out of *The Book of Virtues* by William J. Bennett.
- "Annie Get Your Gun." Western theme party. Learn how to cook various food items on a BBQ, have a squirt gun contest (aim at plastic items outside) and talk about strong women in history.
- "Beach Party." Have a fashion show with modest bathing suits, talk about skincare, sit on beach chairs and learn how to make tropical drinks.
- "Scrapbook Queens." Learn new techniques for creating photo albums and beautiful scrapbooks.
- "The Mall." Create "stores" in the cultural hall to look like a mall and "go shopping" together. Mother/daughter pairs earn play money to spend by filling out a questionnaire of things they have accomplished that week (study the scriptures, Family Home Evening, laundry, dishes, homework, help someone, etc). Learn exercise tips at the sporting goods store, buy a manicure at the spa, attend a fashion show at the clothing boutique, and "buy" refreshments at the food court.

- "Glamour Shots." Dress up the mothers and the girls with fun accessories and take pictures of them separately and together. Show make-up and hair tips.

- "Wax Strong." Women love candles. Teach them how to make different kinds, scent them and decorate with them.

- "Dating Panel." Invite mothers to share their dating experiences and answer questions.

- "Extreme Makeover." Invite the mothers to learn makeover tips with their daughters or have them dress and style each other.

- "Generations." Invite grandmothers, mothers, and daughters to share a special evening together, talking about the legacy women have in families.

- Invite the mothers to share their humorous and poignant motherhood experiences with the girls to help them know how to prepare for their own future families. You could even invite the Mother of the Year from your state to speak to everyone. Contact www.americanmothers.org.

- Make or collect items for a Women's Shelter together. Talk about domestic violence and learn how to protect against it.

- Talk about all of the mothers in the scriptures and how we can be more like them.

# GIFTS FOR MOTHER'S DAY

There are so many craft websites with ideas for creative gifts the Young Women could make to pass to all of the women in the ward on Mother's Day Sunday!

- Teach the Young Women how to make bath salts, bath balls, or bubble bath. (See instructions in Chapter 6.)

- Hershey's kisses rose buds www.lds-yw.com/hgml/yw_files.html.

- Wrap floral tape around a pen or pencil and add a flower at the top.

- Wrap some gummy bears with a ribbon and attach a note saying, "We could BEARly make it without a wonderful mom like you!"

- Wrap a soup mix with dried beans, veggies and spices in cellophane with a note attached that says, "We think you're a SOUPer mom!"
- Attach a note to a small bag of Whopper candies that says, "We think you're a WHOPPER of a mom!"
- Decorate small frames.
- Buy small containers of potted flowers to give to each mother such as African violets or pansies. Have the girls stick little hearts taped to sticks into the dirt with a loving message or quote from the scriptures or Prophet about the importance of mothers. Wrap in polythene and tie it closed with a ribbon.
- Teach the girls how to make chocolates or lollipops with candy molds.
- Make giant chocolate-covered Rice Krispie kisses.
- Make tissue flower bouquets.
- Make a pop-up flower garden card.
- Decorate votive candle holders.
- Make decorative soaps.
- Attach a note to a bag of M&M's that says, "Me & Mom time is sweet!" or "You are a Marvelous & Magnificent Mom!"
- Make potpourri or sachets.
- Dip plastic spoons in chocolate, wrap in cellophane with ribbon and attach a note that says, "A spoonful of love for you on Mother's Day!"
- Make flower corsages out of ribbon. For instructions, go to www.daniellesplace.com/html/mothersday.html.
- Recipe card holders.
- Cute pin cushions made out of baby food jars and a padded lid with ribbon.
- A pretty bookmark with lace, ribbon or pressed flowers for her scriptures.
- Heart-shaped brooches out of Plaster of Paris.
- Puzzle pin. Spray paint puzzle pieces red or pink and glue together in the shape of a heart. Glue a pin on the back.

- Necklace hanger. Cut out a piece of cardboard into the shape of a heart and cover with batting and pretty fabric. Screw small hooks into the front.
- Pretty paperweight.
- Make one of those photo holders out of twisted wire and secure onto a decorative weight made out of clay.
- Flower coaster, coffee table decoration or paperweight. Arrange flowers in between two small pieces of glass. Wrap metallic tape (slide masking tape) around the edges.
- You can purchase those small booklets at LDS bookstores or else you could create your own! Have the girls do artwork and include quotes from Church leaders about motherhood.
- Decorate small jars with a sign that says, "Girls Night Out" or "Mom's New Dress" so the family could put their loose change in it so Mom can buy something she wants with it.
- You can buy $20 gift certificates for See's Candy at Costco where you'll pay less than $20 for them. Then with those certificates go to See's and buy their little one piece boxes to give to each mother.
- Individually wrapped chocolate-covered strawberries that the young women can make.
- Teach the girls how to make cute refrigerator magnets with inspiring quotes and their own artwork. Wrap them up with some candy in a clear bag, some of that decorative shredded crinkle paper and a ribbon.
- Decorate "Do Dads" by gluing a magnet on the back of a clothespin and write "Do Dad" on the front of it. This will let Mom hang a list of jobs on the refrigerator for Dad to do around the house. Dads just love that, don't they?

Enter "Mother's Day Poem" on any search engine and you'll find a million to choose from to attach to the gift. Here are some websites for a few more craft gift ideas.

www.enchantedlearning.com/crafts/mothersday/
www.dltk-kids.com/crafts/mom
www.theholidayspot.com/mothersday

www.daniellesplace.com/html/mothersday.html
www.kidsdomain.com/craft/_gifts.html
www.familycrafts.about.com/od/mothersday/
www.123child.com/easter/mother.html
www.theideadoor.com/MotherDay.html
www.garvick.com/annual/mothers_day/crafts.html
www.homeandfamilynetwork.com/holidays/mothers.html

CHAPTER 4

## Leadership

*"When you educate a man you educate an individual;
when you educate a woman you educate a whole family."*

ROBERT M. MACIVER

Leadership is more than just being in charge. It involves service, teaching, training, patience and vision. The church is about people, not programs. The programs exist to help the people learn about the gospel and to practice living it. Those of us who have had a challenging calling know that we were not given our assignment because we were perfectly competent or the one who could do the best job; we are given callings because the Lord knows that's how we will learn and grow and become more like Him.

When you are baffled with a leadership problem, always remember to look to the Savior's example. He taught and led people according to their capacity and potential, requiring enough of them to stretch their souls but not so much that they would fail and succumb to despair. He ministered personally to the individual. He taught them correct principles and then let them choose. He knew when to delegate and when to personally attend to matters. He prayed and fasted and served. He withheld judgment. He knew His sheep. He loved them.

President Gordon B. Hinckley counseled, "With all of our doing, with all of our leading, with all of our teaching, the most important thing we can do for those whom we lead is to cultivate in their hearts a living, vital, vibrant testimony and knowledge of the Son of God, Jesus Christ, the Redeemer of the world, the Author of our salvation, He who atoned for the sins of the world and opened the way of salvation and eternal life. I would hope that in all we do we would somehow constantly nourish the testimony of our people concerning the Savior." (*Ensign*, Aug. 1997, p. 3.)

We should spend more time on our knees and with the girls than attending meetings. After speaking with many Young Women leaders and their priesthood advisors the following list of tips was created to help you magnify your calling, enjoy your experience, and grow closer to the Savior as you serve His precious daughters:

## LEADERSHIP TIPS FOR ADULTS

- Take care of yourself and your families.
- Take time to study the scriptures every day.
- Pray, pray, pray. Then listen.
- When planning with both adults and young women have them ask:
    1. What do we want to have happen? Not, What do we want to do?
    2. What experiences could help us reach our goal?
    3. What do we need to do to carry out the plan?
    4. After the activity or lesson ask, "How well did we achieve our goal?"
- Fill your spiritual cup. Sign up for daily inspirational messages from LDS leaders at www.egroups.com/group/DailyWOW
- We have the tendency to think that if all of our activities aren't perfect then we have failed as leaders. Just remember, if you have prepared your best and given it your all then your offering will be acceptable to the Lord.
- Carry a notebook with you in your purse, car, in the kitchen, or by your bed stand. When you pray for inspiration to lead these young women you will receive help, so be ready to receive it whenever and wherever it comes!
- In your personal prayers mention your young women by name and express your concerns for them.
- Give teachers and leaders a little thank you gift monthly or quarterly.

- We all know the adversary is working very hard on the youth. Have you ever considered that the adversary may be working even harder on the leaders to discourage them in their individual callings and to even cause contention between them? If Satan can cause the leaders to stumble, imagine how much easier it would be for him to work on the youth of the Church!

- Rotate the Young Women leaders in all of the classes on Sundays so they can get to know all of the girls better. Be sure to include the Personal Progress leader (if you have one), Camp Advisor, Presidency, Secretary, Music Leader, and other leaders you might have working on your Board.

- Present a "Teacher Appreciation Coupon" or a "Guilt-free Pass" that your teachers can cash in on a day when they can attend Relief Society instead of staying with the Young Women.

- Remember that you don't have to do everything. All of your young women should constantly be looking for Value Projects and could help you with certain tasks!

- Make a calendar for all of the Young Women leaders that includes birthdays, meetings, interview dates, activities, Sunday Evening Discussions, Youth Conference dates, who is conducting BYC each week, etc., so that no one will get any last minute surprises.

- Pray for vision. Take the time as a presidency to get a vision for what you want to have happen in your young women program. Then set small goals to achieve this vision. Once you have your goals, share your vision with the class presidencies to get them excited and involved in making it happen.

- Invite a Stake leader to come teach a leadership lesson to your adult leaders and/or class presidencies. That's what they're there for!

- When passing out a written agenda for a meeting, be sure to include a space called "Action Items" so each participant can go home with a very specific list of things they need to do.

- Don't do everything for the girls to make it "nice" for them. Help them learn how to do it themselves and become leaders rather than followers.

- Make a "Young Women Leader Survival Kit" for each of your Board members that could include such items as:
  —Box of Band-Aids to mend hurt feelings
  —Pair of ear plugs for noisy activities
  —Phone card to call for help when needed
  —Cute stickers (since the leaders need to stick together)
  —Hershey's kisses (everyone needs a kiss now and then)
  —A disposable camera for keeping the memories alive
  —A pocket calculator so they can add up all the fun memories
  —A packet of tissues for wiping away Young Women's tears
  —Breath mints (so they're always open to FRESH new ideas)
- Make a "Get Connected Starter Kit" for each leader that could include:
  —A card to send to a young woman
  —A phone list so she can call a young woman
  —A bookmark or little gift she could take to one of the girls
  —A list of goals the Young Women leaders have set for their ward
- As a leader attending Sunday class, take your turn praying in class. Identify girls by name and let them know you talk to the Lord specifically about each one of them.
- Don't try to be the girls' best friend. Be their leader, teacher, and example. Be a role model. A leader is simply someone who sets a good example with a title: Miss Example.
- Don't compete with their parents. Strengthen their relationship with their parents.
- Divide the names of the girls amongst all of the leaders so that each girl is assigned to a loving leader who will periodically send surprise notes, give extra hugs, call, offer rides, etc.
- Create a phone tree in case of emergency or last minute change of plans.
- Write a leadership letter each month to all of the adult leaders and a different one for the class presidencies. Include tips, quotes, updates and express gratitude.

- Create a program for the leaders to develop a greater love for those whom they serve such as:

    Week 1: "The Hand of Love" – Write a letter to a young woman, expressing your appreciation of her. Identify her gifts and talents.

    Week 2: "The Voice of Love" – Telephone a young woman just to chat or say thank you.

    Week 3: "The Deed of Love" – Take something you have made or bought to a young woman to express your love.

    Week 4: "The Heart of Love" – Pray for each girl by name.

    Week 5: "The Touch of Love" – Make sure you give all of the young women a hug or pat on the back for something great they have accomplished.

- Kneel with the girls in prayer.

- Go to the temple often as a Young Women's presidency or Board.

- If you have specific concerns about one of the girls put her name on the prayer roll in the temple.

- Bear your testimony often.

- Read the *New Era* magazine and share what you learn from it with the girls.

- If you haven't already received the Young Womanhood recognition award, work towards earning it yourself.

- Help the girls connect every activity and lesson with the gospel.

- Visit with the girls' parents and see if there is a need you can help with.

- Be worthy to receive inspiration for your calling.

- Do all you can to come unto Christ.

- Don't be afraid to delegate. You don't have to do everything yourself or you will get burned out. God's authority is given to man by priesthood power. If God can share His power than so must we. Delegate power and responsibilities to provide others with learning opportunities.

- Do more listening than talking.
- Love each girl for what she is.
- Have a sense of humor. Lighten up when everything doesn't go as perfectly as you had hoped!
- Plan 3 months ahead but be flexible if a change has to be made.
- Work together as a TEAM. It's amazing how much gets done when it doesn't matter who gets the credit.
- Read the manual! Most questions you'll think of will already have written answers!
- Watch the Leadership Training Video.
- Be familiar with all of the Young Women materials.
- Attend all of the Young Women broadcasts and choose one specific thing you will work on to improve yourself and the way you approach your calling.
- Visit the Church's website often at www.lds.org to be up to date on what is going on.
- Evaluate your efforts. The Gadarene Swine Law says that just because a group is in formation does not mean that it is going in the right direction!
- Listen to the other leaders. Neal A. Maxwell said "You and I are usually pretty good at paying attention upward, but we are not nearly as good at heeding that which comes from other directions."
- Attend all of your meetings.
- Start everything on time, even if there is only one girl there.

## LEADERSHIP TIPS FOR THE YOUNG WOMEN

You can put girls together, but that doesn't mean they will be a group. One of your tasks as a Young Women leader is to provide opportunities and guidance for the girls to become leaders.

They are young and will need practice developing leadership skills. Help them to understand what their responsibilities are and what is expected of each of them. Teach them how to act when they have a commitment. Teach them to love one another. How do you do all that? Following are a few helpful suggestions:

- Be in touch with the class presidencies weekly.

- Encourage the Bishopric to provide a short leadership training during Bishop's Youth Council.

- Teach the girls how to fellowship one another.

- Help the girls learn how to conduct a meeting properly and speak in front of a group.

- Teach the girls how to conduct music properly.

- Constantly remind the girls that the main goal of the Young Women's program is to help the girls "Come Unto Christ." Have them evaluate all of their efforts according to that singular goal.

- Teach the girls how to make a reminder phone call to the others.

- Help the girls understand what it means to follow up on an assignment.

- Critique the girls gently but praise them generously. Remind them that we all make mistakes.

- Teach the class presidencies to be gracious and send thank you notes when someone has helped them with an activity.

- Help the girls identify Christ-like qualities so they can practice developing them.

- After planning an activity with the class presidencies, have them evaluate past events and talk about what they learned and how they could improve on it for next time.

- Help them see the big picture and the role that each girl plays in it.

- Offer leadership training lessons frequently.

- Identify simple, specific things the class presidency can do.

- E-mail the class leaders weekly to remind them of tasks they committed to do.

- Provide each girl in a class presidency with a leadership binder that contains:
    - A calendar
    - A list of all the girls and their phone numbers
    - A description of her specific duties and responsibilities
    - A copy of the Young Women's theme and manual
    - A copy of *For The Strength of Youth*
    - Paper where she can keep notes and write down questions she might have
    - Blank agendas for Sunday Opening Exercises
    - Mutual Opening Exercises agenda
    - Guidelines/worksheet for planning activities
    - Sample agenda or worksheet for running a class presidency meeting
    - A copy of the Proclamation To The World
    - A copy of "The Living Christ"
- A sample template for Sunday's Opening Exercises could include some of the following:
    - YW Conducting
    - Welcome
    - Visitors
    - Opening Song
    - Opening Prayer
    - Spiritual Thought
    - Theme
    - Announcements
    - Birthday spotlight
    - Missionary Moment
    - Friendship Basket
    - Turn the time over to _____ for our lesson
    - Thank teacher for the lesson and make one comment about what you learned
    - Thank everyone for coming and contributing
    - Closing Prayer
- Have the Bishopric cook breakfast on a Saturday morning, and offer different leadership classes the youth can rotate through.

- Begin the tradition of a "SOUPer Saturday." This is where the class presidencies and YW Presidency meet in a home for presidency meetings and eat soup! You could do planning, leadership training, discuss goals, etc.

- Have a nautical or cruise theme training based on teaching about "StewardSHIP" where the girls visit various ports of call (workshops) such as: President's Point, Calendaring Cove, Bishop's Bay, Secretary's Summit, Leadership Lagoon, etc. Teach them how to chart their course and what the Officers' duties are. Be sure to serve submarine sandwiches on the Leader Deck along with Caribbean Chips, South Seas Soda, and St. Croix Cookies.

- Be sure to give each girl in a class presidency something to do so she will feel needed. Perhaps you could assign someone to set up the room for Opening Exercises, keep track of who gives Sacrament talks, or be a door greeter.

- Have a luncheon with sandwiches and talk about how we often "sandwich" our calling between all of our other demands. You could make clever analogies such as:

  **Bread** = *foundation of a sandwich, Jesus is the "bread of life"*

  **Butter** = *love is the smooth coating that rounds off any uneven textures of our calling*

  **Miracle Whip** = *You will see many miracles unfold as you faithfully follow the Savior*

  **Mustard** = *Variety adds the spice to our Young Women activities and lessons*

  **Meat** = *We need to "meet" regularly as leaders to plan and evaluate our goals*

  **Cheese** = *Don't act like the "Big Cheese" but as one of the Lord's servants*

  **Tomato** = *Some say "tah-MAY-tah" and others say "toe-MAH-toe". Learn to appreciate the differences in all the girls as well as their leadership styles.*

  **Pickle** = *Don't get caught in a pickle by procrastinating your assignments*

  **Lettuce** = *LETTUCE work together and LETTUCE be prepared*

**Chips** = *Everyone needs to 'chip' in to make a successful activity*

**Lemonade** = *We all need to make lemonade out of lemons and have a good attitude*

**Ants** = *The adult leaders don't want to have to "bug" you to be a good leader*

**Utensils:**

**Knife** = *A sharp class presidency & teacher plan 3 months in advance*

**Fork** = *Dig into every assignment*

**Spoon** = *A spoonful of love should be used to make each young women feel needed and important*

**Glass** = *Quench the spiritual thirst of those whom you have stewardship over*

**Plate** = *Dish out the gospel by providing lessons and activities with substance. People come to church to be spiritually fed*

**Napkin** = *Get absorbed in your calling*

- Break the girls into four groups and tell them they're going to make music. One group claps, one group whistles, one group taps on their seats, one group makes shushing sounds with their mouths (like cymbals). Each group plays their sound when you point to them. The object is for each group to get itself coordinated into something that sounds good without talking to the other member(s) of the group. In order to accomplish this they have to listen to what each other is doing and adjust accordingly. Point to the groups one at a time, letting each group get their act together. Then, start adding the groups together allowing time for them to adjust what they're doing until they start to sound good. Eventually, you'll have all the groups going at once in a well coordinated ensemble. When the concert is over, ask the girls what made this activity fun and why it required cooperation to make it work. What would have made it work better? If it didn't work, why not?

- Pass out a bunch of old pens that don't work anymore and ask the girls to write down a scripture. Talk about how important it is to be dePENdable.

- "Putting Your Best Foot Forward"
  1. Chicken Feet : Leaders who lack confidence, are shy, don't feel they can make a difference. To overcome chicken feet you need to do more than scratch the surface of your calling by digging deeper. Be familiar with the manuals and the girls.
  2. Calloused Feet: Leaders who become hard and insensitive. Soak in service.
  3. Cold Feet: Leaders who procrastinate and don't warm up to the girls. Set a faster pace and hot foot it over to your knees to pray.
  4. Bored Feet: They've been around and think they know everything. Try on some new shoes and ideas.
  5. Ingrown Toenails: Leaders who are wrapped up in themselves. The prescription is service.
  6. Tired Feet: Don't lose your tread by running in too many different directions. Learn to delegate.
  7. Stinky Feet: Don't be a stinker and drop the ball. Do your part.
  8. Ugly Feet: How beautiful are the feet of those who proclaim the gospel. Bear your testimony often!
- Blow up 10 balloons and tell one girl to keep them all up in the air at the same time. Most likely she won't be able to. Add other girls, one at a time, to help her until they are able to perform the task. Talk about how important it is to have everyone help accomplish a goal.
- "Three Heads Are Better Than One." Tell all of the girls to write down five things they can think of about a penny. Compare what each girl has written. Most will be quite different. Now have them work together in small groups and come up with five more.
- Have the girls sit on top of a blanket. Now, without touching their feet on the floor, have them turn the blanket over. Afterwards, talk about how they had to work and think together in order to accomplish the task. Point out how communication was extremely important.

- Teach the girls how to brainstorm. Get a chalkboard or lots of paper and have them spit out ideas. Fast and furious. No judgments, no shooting down bad ideas. Point out that even a bad idea might trigger a good one. After all the ideas have been written down, then start to consider which ones will actually work. The brainstorm session should get everyone excited and talking about new possibilities they may not have previously considered.

- Using a flower theme, talk about how our leadership skills can blossom when given the room and right conditions. Talk about what those would be in a Young Women's class presidency situation.

- Have the girls play JENGA with a twist. Mark an X on one of the pieces to represent the Young Women's President or a class president. As the girls move their pieces on to the top have them recite an excuse for not attending a meeting or activity, why they couldn't help with an assignment or a reason for not sustaining a church leader. As the blocks stack up they will become less stable and eventually fall. Reinforce the idea that when we aren't dependable we make others' burdens heavier.

- Place a dozen raw eggs on a table and stack some heavy books on top. The eggs won't crack if they're together. Take away all of the eggs but one or two and they will crack. Reinforce the idea that "many hands make light work."

- Show a SOS pad and talk about the strength of steel. Have the girls create a new acronym for SOS such as "Seek Out Service," "Serve Our Savior," "Save Our Souls," etc.

- Real estate offices and Hallmark have free calendars you can give to all the class presidencies to help them plan on a calendar.

# CHAPTER 5

# Activity Ideas for Mutual or Value Projects

*"The youth-of the Church are hungry for things of the Spirit; they are eager to learn the gospel, and they want it straight, undiluted. If you teach youth, you may sometimes think that they do not want to talk about doctrines and principles of the gospel. You may be tempted to simply be friendly to them, keeping them entertained and talking with them about their social activities and their experiences at school. This would be a serious mistake."*

J. REUBEN CLARK
*Quorum of the Twelve Apostles, US Ambassador to Mexico, Under Secretary of State*

Which kind of activities should be provided for the young women: spiritual or fun? How about both?! If the gospel of Jesus Christ is called the "Plan of Happiness" then we should be the happiest people around! Our Young Women's program should be fun and joyful! Teach the girls how studying the scriptures and living the principles of the gospel can be exciting and wonderful!

Even after playing a game or working on a craft project, a short spiritual lesson could be given to point out the gospel application in our lives. The youth want to have fun, but they're also too busy in their lives to just pass time with no purpose during Mutual. Make sure your activities meet their needs, whether they be spiritual, physical, emotional, intellectual or social.

Provide activities that offer opportunities to develop talents, support and strengthen families, nurture the girl's testimony and self-esteem. When she and her parents see that you are planning valuable activities that enrich her life you will have their support. As you plan activities remember to ask, "Will this activity make us more Christ-like?" "Will it strengthen our testimony of the Savior and His Church?"

When you include the class presidencies in your planning you'll be able to come up with some great events. Talk to your Relief Society Enrichment Leader for some creative ideas as well and check out the book *Easy Enrichment Ideas: Thinking Outside The Green Gelatin Box* (written by yours truly) for even more fun suggestions. Sometimes all you need is a good brainstorming session to get your own creative juices flowing again. Here is one to get you started!

# PLANNING

The Church has provided a helpful activity planning sheet at www.lds.org/pa/images/ym/activityplan.pdf

Before looking at an empty calendar and feeling overwhelmed, try organizing the month into a routine format such as:

Week 1: Value-oriented activity to introduce theme
Week 2: Combined Young Men/Young Women activity
Week 3: Work on Personal Progress goals
Week 4: Combine all of the Young Women together
Week 5: Leaders' Choice, Girls' Choice, or Surprise Night

*or*

Week 1: Personal Progress Goals
Week 2: Combined Young Women
Week 3: Combined Young Men/Young Women
Week 4: Parent activity
Week 5: Cooking

*or*

Week 1: Strengthen home and family activities
Week 2: Stand as a witness (missionary activities)
Week 3: Make & keep sacred covenants activities
Week 4: Blessings of the gospel and exaltation
Week 5: Yearly Mutual Theme

A fun way to plan activities with the young women is to write the values on seven pieces of paper and have them write their suggested activities on the value page that best corresponds. Another format would be to analyze the Young Women's theme and place main ideas on separate pieces of paper, writing down the activities on those pages that best relate.

Help the girls to see that while they are having fun they can be accomplishing Personal Progress goals and meeting the needs of the girls at the same time. Teach them how to plan with purpose and be sure to let them feel a sense of ownership over the activities so that they will follow-through with assignments.

Another way to organize Mutual Night is by reading through the Personal Progress book and combining activities that work well with the calendar, holidays, annual theme and Young Men goals. Be sure to check the chapters on "Get-to-Know-You Games", "Personal Progress" and "Values" for more fun Mutual activities!

Also be sure to check out the New Era for ideas! The November issue each year has lesson helps and activity ideas that correlate with Personal Progress goals. Search the archives and you'll be amazed. As you go through the Young Women manuals you may also see some ideas that, with a bit of updating, could make for great activities!

A wonderful website that lists activities to coordinate with the lessons in the manuals is www.jennysmith.net. Thanks, Jenny!

When only one girl shows up for Mutual, save that great activity you had planned for a larger group for another day, and use the new opportunity to go over her Personal Progress goals with her. Many of the following ideas could also be used as Value Projects by the girls.

# FAITH

- Have a "PJ's" night: Prayer, Journals, Scriptures. Wear (modest) pajamas and throw a mini slumber party where the girls can make pretty journals, mark their scriptures, make prayer rocks, decorate bookmarks, etc.
- Design "Pass Along Cards" they could hand out to non-member friends or give to the missionaries to use.

- If you can still find them, watch some of the Church's old filmstrips and see if the girls can narrate them without listening to the corresponding cassette tape.

- Challenge all of the girls to read the *New Era* magazine for one month. Be mindful of the girls who can't afford a subscription and encourage all of the girls to share their copy when they're done reading it. On the night of the activity, split the girls into two teams. Ask questions about the contents of articles, comics, news, etc. The team that rings a bell or buzzer first gets to answer the question first and score a point.

- Learn about other religions and how to show respect for other faiths.

- Watch some of the Church's old, classic movies such as *"Johnny Lingo"*, *"The Mailbox"* and *"The Bridge."*

- Make temple clothing hangers, clothing packets, etc. There are some very cool sewing machine software programs that embroider temples on whatever fabric you choose.

- Stencil dish towels that could be donated to the ward kitchen or bath towels that could be given as gifts at baptisms. Tie them up with a ribbon and attach a note that says:
    *"May this ABSORB your troubles, BLOT out problems,*
    *SOAK up sorrows, and WIPE Away difficulties!"*

- If you're lucky enough to visit a Mormon handicraft store you can find molds of temples and other LDS things for making candy or even decorative items such as those shredded paper shapes that can be mounted on frames.

- Invite returned missionaries to speak about their preparation and experiences. Try to find sisters in your ward who have served missions who could speak. Talk about how we could all be better member missionaries as well.

- Plan a special activity with Primary children to help them pass off their "Faith in God" goals.

- Make Family Home Evening packets that include stories, visual aids, refrigerator magnets that emphasize certain scriptures that relate to the lesson, and recipes for refreshments.

- Play "General Conference Bingo" in October or April. Watch a session together.

- Learn about the 12 Apostles before General Conference so the girls will appreciate the Church leaders better and be more interested to listen when they hear them speak.

- Make packets for the Primary to give to children who are getting baptized and then a craft/gift that could be given to them on their special day.

- Make packets for new converts in your ward. Include copies of the Church magazines, pictures of Christ, a ward directory, tithing envelope, calendar of upcoming events, and a special note from the Young Women congratulating them on their decision to be baptized and welcoming them into the ward family.

- Make ornaments for small holiday trees for Christmas, Easter, Valentine's Day, etc. Talk about how our faith can be strengthened by holiday traditions that focus on the Savior.

- Talk about the importance of praying when we wake up and go to bed at night-time. Make seasonal pillowcases for the girls' bedrooms, using fabric for Halloween, Christmas, Easter, Valentine's Day, etc.

- Teach the girls how to make quilts. Check out this website for an inspiring temple design: www.quiltatemple.com/freeprojects.htm

- Make costumes for your next Pioneer Trek.

- Play "Scriptionary." It's the same concept as Pictionary (Drawing Charades) but use Seminary Scripture Mastery verses or ones that go with the Young Women Values. Talk about the importance of memorizing scriptures and how that can help us. Invite a Seminary teacher to share tips on how to memorize.

- Meet the Mormon Musicians. Introduce the girls to new LDS musicians by playing their music. Write letters or e-mails to the artists to thank them for sharing their talents and musical testimonies.

- Make statues of Christ, Young Women, people praying, etc.

Check out www.myweb.cableone.net/loupeck

- Decorate "Sunday Boxes" and fill with activities that are appropriate for the Sabbath Day.

- Make "Quiet Books" to help keep little ones in their family quiet and busy during the Sacrament. Design pages that reinforce scripture stories and build faith.

- Using glow-in-the-dark paint have the girls paint the words "Did You Pray?" on a wall hanging the girls will be able to see when they're laying in bed and have turned off their light.

- Dress the girls in white and take their pictures in front of the temple. Decorate pretty frames to display the photos in.

- Invite members who have recently attended the temple for the first time to share their thoughts about preparing for their temple experience.

- Feel like having a dinner with the girls? Turn it into a real spiritual evening and call it "Feast Upon The Words of Christ." Create a special menu where the items to be ordered are actually scripture verses. They can be scriptures that talk about certain foods or verses that reinforce what was taught the past Sunday. Someone could teach a mini-lesson between courses.

- If you're lucky enough to have them near you, visit some Church sites, Visitors Centers, landmarks, and museums. Talk about the great heritage we share as members of this faith.

- Learn how to make a glass etching of a temple.

- Host a contest for the Primary to build temples out of Legos, sugar cubes, modeling clay, PlayDough, etc. Have the girls create certificates and prizes to award to the children.

- "Scripture Scrabble" Play the game like regular Scrabble, but if the players can find a scripture that uses the word they want they get double points.

- Plan a babysitting evening so couples could drop off their children and attend the temple. Talk about what your girls could do to improve temple attendance in your ward.

- Make Nativity costumes for the ward to use during Christmas parties and performances.

- After a Fast Sunday have the girls write letters to the members who bore their testimonies and thank them for sharing their hearts and experiences with the ward.

- Write letters to the Bishopric and Stake Presidency, expressing gratitude for all they do. Make and bring treats to them.

- Write letters to people who have influenced and strengthened your testimony.

# DIVINE NATURE

- Go on a hike and talk about all the beautiful things the Lord has created.

- Talk about the importance of families and share ideas for fun traditions.

- Have a progressive dinner where the girls start in one home eating appetizers, then go to another house for salad, then another house for the entrée and a final house for dessert. At each home have a short lesson on various aspects of divine nature and compare the progressive dinner to our progression back to our heavenly home.

- Meet the Mormon Musicians. Introduce the girls to new LDS musicians by playing their music. Write letters or e-mails to the artists to thank them for sharing their talents and musical testimonies.

- Talk about their "sweet" spirits and teach them how to make their own perfume, mixing different oils and fragrances. Have them design a name and logo for their creation.

- Decorate purses and backpacks to help the girls remember who they are and whose they are.

- Learn how to make different kinds of candles and talk about what it means to "wax strong" like in the scriptures.

- Make Young Women value flags for your ward to display at special occasions. Hang one each month in your classroom as you focus on a particular value. Talk about how wonderful the Young Women program is and how it helps us discover our divine nature.

- Teach the girls various kinds of "handiwork" such as crocheting, cross-stitch, knitting, and tatting. Talk about nature and the Lord's handiwork.

- Decorate T-shirts, bags, canvas shoes, backpacks, jeans and other items with fabric paint. Have samples of the Young Woman torch logo, temples and other inspiring models.

- "De-stressor Night." Help girls remember to keep an eternal perspective when they're feeling stressed out. Teach them relaxation techniques and show them how to make "Potpourri Gel Smells":

   Boil 1 cup of liquid potpourri on the stove. Stir in 4 Knox gelatin packets until dissolved. Let the mixture cool and add a dash of salt (to prevent molding) and 1 more cup of liquid potpourri. Pour it into jars, cute bowls or decorative dishes. Cover with plastic wrap and cool it in the refrigerator. When it has thickened up a bit add plastic flowers and toys for variety to both the mixture and the outside of the containers.

- Talk about how the Church magazines help us remember who we are.

- Look at some of the comics in the "Extra Smile" section of the *New Era*. Now have the girls design their own. They could even submit some to the magazine!

- Have the girls bring blankets, pillows, and their Personal Progress books. Make pop corn and have the girls watch the video "Wives and Daughters of the First Presidency" while the leaders pull one girl out at a time to update her Personal Progress book and go over her goals.

- Teach the girls how to let their divine nature shine through by offering a skin care class! I know that's a bit of a stretch, but when your spirit shines your skin glows too! Talk about specific products for acne, cleansers, foundation, sunscreen, and makeup.

- Go to a local planetarium and learn about this incredible universe Heavenly Father has created for us! Many local colleges have free shows and observatories you could visit.

- Invite your Stake Patriarch to speak to the young women about preparing to receive their patriarchal blessings. Have him explain the interview process, the Tribes of Israel, what the promises made to Abraham mean, and how they apply to us.
- Hold a "Tacky Night" where everyone comes dressed in tacky clothes, eats tacky food (Spam, beans out of a can, etc). Talk about how to dress and behave in a "classy" manner that is becoming of someone who truly has divinity within them.
- Part of our divine nature includes getting married. Offer a Round-Robin setting where girls can visit several stations about planning a wedding such as cake decorating, fun traditions, choosing an appropriate wedding gown, food selection, etc.
- Make cute photo albums using different kinds of styles and talk about the importance of our families in this life and throughout eternity. Show some scrap booking techniques as well.
- Decorate journals and talk about how writing can be therapeutic, enabling us to see our divine nature and potential.
- Talk about what a blessing our families are. Share ideas on their favorite Family Home Evening lessons. Prepare a lesson the girls could use next week at home with their families, including visual aids, refrigerator magnet and recipe for refreshments.

# INDIVIDUAL WORTH

- Create a simple hope chest by covering the base of a box inside and out with wallpaper. Cover the inside of the lid with wallpaper but on the outside use quilt batting and fabric. Decorate with ribbons, silk flowers, buttons, etc.
- Before the activity find out details about each girl. At the activity provide each girl with a list of questions she has to answer about the other girls. For every question answered correctly she earns an item for her ice cream sundae (bowl, spoon, ice cream, whip cream, bananas, etc.) Talk about the importance of each girl and how each one has many yummy layers to discover. Encourage the girls to get to know one another better. Remind them that they don't have to be best friends, but simply learn to appreciate the wonderful variety.

- Attend a concert, sporting event or some other performance of one of the girls in your Young Women's group. Talk about the importance of supporting one another in developing our talents.

- Teach the girls how to cut hair, do fun updos for prom and other formal occasions, and take care of their hair.

- Talk about eating disorders such as anorexia, bulimia, and diet fads. Discuss the Word of Wisdom and how the Lord has prepared a way for us to take care of our bodies. Share the reasons why women, especially, need to care for their bodies and offer suggestions for ways the girls could talk to their friends who might be having problems.

- "Spa Night" Teach the girls how to do facials, manicures, pedicures, and hot oil treatments. Have them practice on each other so they can then go home and treat their mothers to a spa night.

- Teach the girls how to do Yoga or Pilates and care for their bodies.

- Attend a water aerobics class together or create your own in a member's pool.

- Make cute hair décor items such as scrunchies, bows, headbands, etc. Have them make white ones they could take to the temple to wear when they are doing baptisms.

- Help the girls design their own stationery that they can then use to write letters to missionaries, servicemen, other young women who have gone away to college, etc.

- Make a photo calendar the girls could give their families or they could use themselves.

- Every birthday should be celebrated! Share creative ideas for fun birthday parties and how to make someone feel loved on their special day.

- Work with your Family History Consultant to teach the girls how to do genealogy, find names on the computer, do extraction work, etc. Talk about how they play an important role in their family's legacy.

- Teach the girls how to take, display, and hang great pictures. Talk about how keeping family photos is a part of doing our genealogy and showing how everyone is an important part of their family tree.
- Teach the girls to care for the one and only body they have. Discuss and sample ideas for quick, easy, and healthy snacks.
- After the high school proms teach the girls how to dry flowers and make various decorations using dried flowers such as flower arrangements, bookmarks, hanging double glass décor, etc.
- A really fun activity that young women love because it makes them feel really special and pampered is to make bath salts, bubble bath and other luxurious bath products. Here are a few simple recipes that can be made during a Mutual activity as gifts or to take home and use:

BUBBLE BATH
     1 cup Epson Salts
     1 ½ cup liquid soap (like Ivory or baby)
     1 cup Rock Salts (for water softener . . . optional)
     Food coloring (1 drop at a time for desired shade)
     4-5 Drops of Glycerin (drug stores)
     Essential Oil (desired scent) *(optional)*
     Mix well to assure even distribution of color and fragrance.
     Portion serving: ¼ cup per bath or enough for desired amount of bubbles.

MILK BATH
     1 cup powdered milk
     1 cup baking soda
     2 Tbsp cornstarch
     1 Tbsp cream of tartar
     15-20 drops of essential oil
     Mix all ingredients in a glass bowl and store in an airtight container. Mix in ½ cup just before climbing in. For added effect, add 2 Tbsp of dried lavender flowers, rosebuds or other dry herbs.

BATH SALTS

  1 cup Epsom salts

  10-15 drops of essential oil

  1-4 drops food coloring

  Mix all ingredients in a glass bowl and pour into a bottle or specially decorated container. Let the salts sit for 2 weeks to infuse and to reach the maximum scent. Place 1-2 Tbsp into your bath just before entering.

FOAMING VANILLA HONEY BATH

  1 cup oil

  ½ cup honey

  ½ cup liquid soap

  1 tablespoon vanilla extract ( pure is better )

  Mix together all the ingredients and pour into a clean bottle with a tight fitting stopper or lid. Shake before using. Pour ¼ cup into the bath under running water. Yield: 16 ounces, enough for 8 baths.

- Create puzzles and games, using the girls names. Go to www.acrynym.com to create new words out of the girls' names. Show the scrambled-up words and have them guess whose name it is! Also, check out www.puzzlemaker.com You supply the words and create word games for the girls to solve. Plug in their names, the Young Women values, or even concepts from last Sunday's lesson!

- Have the girls create a Time Capsule either as a class or for their own family. Give them a list of items to gather representing their school, church, family, talents, friends, etc. Include a newspaper, her testimony, pictures, and her written "wish for the future." Put the contents in a #10 can and seal (most Stakes have a sealer for food storage that could be used for this). The cans don't have to be buried, but simply stored in a basement or closet until a designated time. Talk about their future and how they are planning for it now.

- Sometimes girls just need to hold hands and skate around a rink together. Most ice skating and roller skating rinks offer group discounts.

- Have a "Stand Up Comedienne Night" where the girls can tell jokes and develop their talent of performing in front of an audience. Also talk about standing for truth and righteousness in the things we choose to laugh at.
- Instead of making friendship bracelets that only two girls can share, create some that the girls can wear to identify that they are united as a class.
- Teach the girls self-defense techniques. Talk about how listening to the Holy Ghost can be our best tool in protecting ourselves from danger. Some karate schools have "performing" groups who would love an opportunity to do an exhibition for your group if you just ask!
- Teach the girls the value of a life by getting them certified in CPR. Check your local hospital, fire station, or community health center to get a speaker or certified teacher.
- Learn what firemen do to save lives by visiting a fire station and going through one of their "Smoke Houses". Bring the firemen goodies and thank them for their service.
- Find out some interesting facts about the ancestors of each girl. Share the stories and information to see if the girls can guess whose ancestors they are. Focus on the great heritage each of the girls have and the legacy they can continue.
- Create a Family History Fair for your ward and/or community.

# KNOWLEDGE

- "Homemaking Olympics" Have fun and silly competitions that test such skills as sewing a button, reading a story, making a sandwich, ironing a shirt, balancing a checkbook page, and braiding hair. Include an Opening Ceremony with flags the girls design, entertainment, and the Olympic theme song.
- Do a "Video Scavenger Hunt."
- "Melodrama Night" Perform live or record on video. The cornier the better! You may need to teach the young women what a melodrama actually is. Use your Mutual theme, a Young Women value, or make-up a line or props they have to include in their play.

- Teach the girls how to make different kinds of pizza: deep dish, vegetarian, fruit, dessert, thin crust, meat lovers, etc. Learn how to make different kinds of crust too: Boboli, hand-made, Bisquick, cookie, etc.

- Sit on pillows, munching snacks while listening to a podcast of BYU devotionals, General Conference, or LDS music at www. apple.com/itunes.com.

- Enter a local flower show, craft fair or 4-H event.

- Have a "Handywoman" class where you teach the girls how to fix a squeaky door and repair other household items.

- Start a book club or show the girls how to start one in their community, by choosing good books and creating a list of discussion items that could be included in a group setting.

- Take the girls to their local library and help them open an account and get a card if they don't have one already. Talk about the importance of reading good books throughout our lives.

- Invite speakers from the local hospital to teach babysitter-certification classes to your girls.

- Teach the girls how to make cinnamon rolls from scratch using different kinds of wheat (hard red, soft winter, etc.) Have them take home a batch for their families or their Seminary class.

- "Powder Puff Mechanics." Learn how to purchase a vehicle and do basic car maintenance.

- "College Night." Talk about how to choose the right college or trade school and discuss the importance of furthering one's education after high school. Show the DVD that explains what programs are available through the Church Education System.

- Learn how to make jewelry and/or care for jewelry properly.

- Learn how to make piñatas or other paper maché items. Talk about what we can learn from other cultures and their traditions.

- Put together a "Final Exam Survival Kit" for the girls including items such as chocolate, gum, pencils, and a reminder to read the scriptures and pray.

- Practice cooking simple recipes that can be used in college.

- My niece loves "Cooking Night" in her ward. Once a month a different Young Woman leader teaches the girls how to cook something and then gives them a recipe they can add to their growing collection. One night could be spent decorating a cute recipe book or folder and creating dividers based on categories the girls want to learn about such as: breads, things to do with pumpkins (after the fall holidays), desserts, chicken dishes, appetizers, fun drinks, etc.

- Invite your Ward Emergency Preparedness Specialist to teach a lesson on how to be better prepared for emergencies. Have the girls put together an emergency car kit, first aid kit or something they could add to their family's 72-hour home kit.

- Invite speakers from your local "ToastMasters Club" or college Speech and Debate team to teach the girls how to prepare an effective Sacrament Meeting talk.

- Talk to your ward and stake Seminary teachers to get ideas that would support the course of study the girls are working on that year. You could even have a special "Thank you" event where the girls could do a special dinner, program or party to thank their Seminary and Sunday School teachers for giving them so much good knowledge.

- Play "Stump The Bishop" (or whomever you want to stump) Have the girls bring miscellaneous items from home that are placed in a special box or bag. The "Stumpee" has to pull each item out and then explain how they relate to gospel principles. The girls could also do this with each other. You'll be impressed how creative they can be!

- Learn how to do outdoor cooking in preparation for Girls Camp such as Dutch Oven cooking. Have a contest with the Scouts to see who can cook the best main course or dessert.

- Invite your stake webmaster to talk about the resources available on the Church's website and how to use them. Find out if your ward has its own website and see what's on it.

- Invite a representative from LDS Social Services to speak on family relations, adoption, child abuse, mental health, and the services that the Church offers.

- Teach the girls how to sew. Have them make bean bags for games in the Primary or, if their skills are more advanced, teach them to sew modest clothing.

- Learn how to bake bread. Reserve two or three loaves for next Sunday's Sacrament service. There are some recipes on-line for bread that can be prepared and baked in the short amount of time during Mutual.

- "Ask the Bishop Night" This could also be done with your Stake Young Women's President, Seminary teacher, or another leader. Girls write questions on slips of paper that are put into a box and presented to the speaker who then selects them one at a time and answers the questions. The girls will be more willing to ask real questions if they know that their identity will remain anonymous.

- Learn about reflexology and how to do pedicures. Use value colors to polish the girls' nails. Talk about standing in holy places, "how beautiful are the feet of those who spread the gospel" and discuss what we can learn from when the Savior washed the disciples' feet.

- Have goofy Olympic contests to get the girls excited about the upcoming Olympics. Learn about the host country. Ideas can be found at www.ywconnection.com.

- Teach the girls how to cut different kinds of fruit. Make a fruit salad, ambrosia, or have a taster's table. Discuss all of the scriptures that talk about different kinds of fruit. Discuss the idea "By their fruits ye shall know them."

- Learn about the different kinds of foods that were available in Bible Times.

- Teach the girls magic tricks they can use at home to wow their families during Family Home Evening.

- Teach the girls to be "street smart" and protect themselves. Introduce them to some of the following websites:
    —www.vcpionline.org/mousetrap/index.html
    —www.netsmartz.org
    —www.missingkids.com
    —www.familywatchdog.us

- Before General Conference help the girls learn more about the First Presidency and the Twelve Apostles. You can make game cards with their photos and biographies and play "Go FISHers Of Men"! For game cards go to www.lds.about.com/library/bl/games/apostlecards2.pdf

- Learn about other countries. Invite returned missionaries to give mini-lessons on the country where they served. Create a travel box where the girls can store special vacation photos and souvenirs by decoupaging maps, postcards and other travel memorabilia.

- Learn how to take good pictures. If you live near a temple you could use that for a background and teach them about composition, light, etc.

- Invite the Mayor or City Council member to teach the girls how your local government works. Attend a City Council meeting or visit City Hall and meet the people who work there.

- Invite someone from a local bicycle store to teach the girls how to choose the right bike and take care of it. Go on a bike ride together. Find out if there is an amateur racing team in your town who could also come talk to the girls about what they do.

- "Scripture Clue Night At The Mall" Help the girls think harder about the scriptures in a fun way. Divide the girls into small teams and provide each group a set of scriptures and scripture reference clues that will direct them to various stores in the mall. Meet at the food court for refreshments.

- Teach the girls how to snorkel by practicing in someone's pool. Place items at the bottom that they have to dive and retrieve. Include lifesaving skills and water safety instruction.

- Arrange to go on a tour of a local university or trade school. Find out what services the girls could be using now to further their education.

- Teach the girls different styles of dance: western line-dance, hip hop, ballroom, salsa, etc. Choreograph a fun routine that could be performed at Girls Camp or in a Road Show. Make a cute music video to a song by a LDS artist.

- Homework/Pizza Night. Divide the girls into "Study Buddies", linking up girls who are strong in a particular subject with those that might need help in that area. Have them test one another on vocabulary words, do flashcards, and work for 15 minutes before each pizza break.

- Teach the girls some sign language and check out the Church's website about American Sign Language at www.asl.lds.org.

- Learn what it takes to put a play or concert together by attending a dress rehearsal of a local show. You'll be able to get in for free or else at a greatly reduced price and probably be able to meet the performers afterward.

## CHOICE & ACCOUNTABILITY

- Teach the girls how to be smart with their money, avoid scams, and make wise financial choices. Invite your local financial planner to teach them how to save and budget.

- "Hollywood Here We Come!" Everyone has to write down a famous line from a movie, such as "Go ahead, make my day!" or "I'll Be Back". Divide into groups that will rotate through rooms. In the first room, the first group picks two of the slips of paper with famous movie lines on them. One will be the opening line of their skit and one is the closing line. They have ten minutes to create a short play and five minutes to film it onto a camcorder. The group then moves to the next room. The second group enters the room and only draws one line—that's the closing line. Their opening line is the same as the closing line of the last group. For example, if the team ahead of you had the closing line, "Napoleon, don't be jealous that I've been chatting online to babes all day." (from the movie *Napoleon Dynamite*), that would be the first line of the next skit. Each group could be given props. When all of the skits are filmed you play the movie, eat popcorn and laugh until your sides hurt. Talk about how the actions of others can affect what you do.

- Choose some hymns or other songs by LDS artists and make music videos to them. Compare the differences in what effects the world's music and the Church's music have on us.

- Talk about the dangers on the Internet and how to keep safe. Share websites that promote the Young Women values and are better choices for "surfing" the net. Compare web filters.

- Have a fashion show that helps the girls choose clothing that is more modest, as well as stylish.

- Career Night. Have a round-robin style evening where the girls can attend each class and learn about several different careers to choose from. Invite speakers to explain their profession and what education or training was required.

- Have sister missionaries speak about their choice to serve a full-time mission. Discuss how they prepared and the blessings that followed. Prepare some care packages that could be sent to the missionaries serving from your ward or branch.

- Offer creative dating ideas and talk about proper dating etiquette. Share ideas for fun ways to ask a boy out to a "Sadie Hawkins" dance.

- Make packets for new converts in your ward. Include copies of the Church magazines, pictures of Christ, a ward directory, tithing envelope, calendar of upcoming events, and a special note from the Young Women congratulating them on their decision to be baptized and welcoming them into the ward family.

- Teach the girls about making good financial choices and being accountable for their money by organizing a Mall Scavenger Hunt. Divide the girls into teams and give each team a certain amount of money that they have to use to gather various items in the allotted time. Put items on the list the girls can get at the mall for free such as perfume samples, shopping bags, and wrapping paper. The team that can find the most items on the list without spending all of the money wins.

- Have your ward librarian give you a tour of your building's library and introduce you to all of the wonderful resources that are available for Family Home Evening lessons, talks, Sunday lessons, and Mutual activities. There is so much to choose from!

- There's a cute "So You Want To Marry A Moroni" activity found at www.lightplanet.com/mormons/ywc/activities/moroni.htm Talk about the choices the girls will make while dating and how to prepare to make the right ones.

- Show how to make lots of different kinds of popcorn for the girls to choose from (buttered, caramel, Cracker Jacks, cheese, herb, candy, chocolate covered, etc) and provide recipes for the girls to take home. Read the "Parable of the Popcorn" and talk about the choices we have when we go through trials.

### "THE PARABLE OF THE POPCORN"

*Behold, at the time of harvest the ears of corn did bring forth kernels which were dried and prepared for the popper's hand.*

*And then it was that the popper did take the kernels, all of which appeared alike unto him, and did apply the oil and heat. And it came to pass that when the heat was on, some did explode with promise and did magnify themselves an hundred fold, and some did burst forth with whiteness which did both gladden the eye and satisfy the taste of the popper. And likewise, some others did pop, but not too much.*

*But lo, there were some that did just lie there and even though the popper's heat was alike unto all, they did bask in the warmth of the oil and kept everything for themselves.*

*And so it came to pass that those which had given themselves did bring joy and delight to many munchers, but those which kept the warmth and did not burst forth were fit only to be cast out into the pail and were thought of with hardness and disgust.*

*And thus we see that in the beginning all appear alike, but when the heat is on, some come forth and give their all, while others fail to pop and become as chaff to be discarded and forgotten.*

- "Mormon Movie Madness." Introduce the girls to movies they can choose that have been created by LDS members. Show movie clips and talk about how the girls can use their talents to build the kingdom of God.

- Find a corn maze the girls can go through and then afterward talk about how life is like a maze.

- Invite wives of the Bishopric to speak to the young women about dating, supporting the priesthood, or serving in the Church. Another fun night would include a panel of the wives and their husbands where the girls could ask them questions on a given topic.
- Have the girls make up their own board game to play on large poster paper. Have them choose what game pieces to make and what rules to follow.
- Talk about all of the wonderful places in the world. Invite foreign-exchange students to talk about their country.
- Arrange to have a tour of a local TV or radio station. Talk to their Directors about what the girls can do to encourage more positive programming.
- You can get free calendars at many real estate offices, online or even at Hallmark to give to the girls at the beginning of the year. Illustrate that life is full of choices by asking them how they will fill the pages of their calendars. Bring stickers they can place on Mutual nights to remind them to attend.

## GOOD WORKS

- Some terrific resources where you can learn about service organizations and projects the girls could get involved with are: www.volunteermatch.org , www.serviceleader.org , www.volunteers.com and www.servenet.org
- Learn to crochet squares for the Red Cross "Warm Up America" Program. They collect squares from volunteers and then create blankets out of them for the needy. For information call (704) 824-7838 or go to www.warmupamerica.org
- Hold a car wash but don't charge anyone money for the service. Give patrons a Pass Along card and let them know you were there to serve the community.
- Organize a book drive for your local Boys and Girls Club, hospitals, or shelters.
- Volunteer at the Salvation Army, Deseret Industries, or a local food bank.

- Girls love making crafts and they can do good works at the same time. Check out www.bevscountrycottage.com and www.allcrafts4charity.org to learn about projects they can do for other people or organizations.

- For outdoor service projects sponsored by the Keep America Beautiful Foundation go to www.kab.org

- Teach the girls how to knit projects like clothes for stuffed bears that are given to children in crisis by Precious Pals or Project Linus (www.projectlinus.org).

- Get the girls involved in collecting food that can be distributed locally through Second Harvest (www.secondharvest.org).

- Collect toys for needy children before the holidays that can then be distributed through the Toys For Tots organization (www.toysfortots.org ).

- Write letters or birthday cards to the prophet or apostles. Their birthdays are listed in *The LDS Church Almanac*. The letters can be sent to: The Church of Jesus Christ of Latter-day Saints

  Church Office Building

  50 E. North Temple

  Salt Lake City, Utah 84150

- Find out how the young women in your ward and/or Stake can participate in National Youth Service Day or *USA Weekend*'s Make A Difference Day.

- Go to the temple parking lot and leave little notes on the windshield that thank the patrons for their service.

- Make visual aids that could be given to the Primary teachers such as flannel board stories, music aids, object lessons, etc. Laminate the pictures so they will last a long time.

- Hold an "Unsung Hero" service project. Find out who in the ward has "quiet" callings such as a librarian, Church Magazine Rep, choristers, pianists, bulletin board person, Sunday program printer, etc. Invite them to a special dinner where you honor their efforts and let them know they are appreciated.

- Sign up to be clowns in a local parade and pass out candy to the children.

- Organize a blood drive by calling 1-800-GIVE-LIFE.
- Show support by attending community events. Involve your girls in volunteering and participating in them by making a float for a local parade, passing out snacks at a craft fair, etc.
- Adopt a specific military Troop to pray for by signing up at www.presidentialprayerteam.net/manageadoptionslogin.php
- Pack up all of your stamping supplies and visit the children's trauma unit in your local hospital. Help the children decorate cards to give to their families, friends or even the hospital staff.
- Take any old cards you have received or made and cut the fronts off and send them to Sherrill Graff. She will add cardstock to them to make them a full card and add an envelope for each one. She and her young women will deliver them to her local Ronald McDonald house. They use them to thank their volunteers and cheer up sick children. The children's families can also use them to thank people for their support and help in their time of need.

Sherrill Graff<br>
605 Kendrick Place<br>
Boulder City, NV 89005

- Prepare a special activity and invite the Activity Days primary girls.
- Do something for the Cub Scouts or Boy Scouts to let them know you support the good works they are doing. See if you can help a Cub Scout with his goal to "do a good turn daily."
- Teach the girls how to make cinnamon rolls from scratch using different kinds of wheat (hard red, soft winter, etc.) Have them take home a batch for their families or make some for a Seminary class.
- "Secret Grandmas" Get a list of all the older sisters in the ward and assign a few young women to each senior sister. Deliver secret gifts to them for a month. Bring them flowers, cards, goodies, and crafts. At the end of the month invite the senior sisters to a special presentation and reveal who their secret "grand-daughters" were.

- "Spa Night" Teach the girls how to do facials, manicures, pedicures, and hot oil treatments. Have them practice on each other so they can then go home and treat their mothers to a spa night.
- "Feed A Soul" or "We CAN Do It" Divide the girls into teams who will call ward members to let them know that next week the Young Women will be stopping by to pick up donated canned food items. Have a contest to see who can collect the most.
- BINGO! Many retirement homes have big BINGO nights that the youth could help with.
- Stuff envelopes for a school, PTA, a charity, or some other non-profit organization.
- Have sister missionaries speak about their choice to serve a full-time mission. Discuss how they prepared and the blessings that followed. Prepare some care packages that could be sent to the missionaries serving from your ward or branch.
- Have everyone bring non-perishable items to include in care packages for missionaries and military who are serving from your ward. Include uplifting letters.
- "Santa's Helpers" Offer to baby-sit children so busy parents can go Christmas shopping. Keep the children happy by doing crafts, playing games, reading stories, decorating cookies, etc. This service could also be offered around Mother's Day to give exhausted moms a break.
- Make curtains for the ward's kitchen, nursery, the Young Women's room, Relief Society room, Bishop's office, or other classrooms.
- Make "Welcome To The Area!" packets for new move-ins. Include maps of the area, phone numbers, a ward directory, school and utility information, Parks & Recreation catalogs, etc.
- Make gifts the girls could give to military servicemen and women on Veteran's Day or Memorial Day such as a patriotic craft, plaque, cookies, an award, etc. Invite a war veteran to speak to the girls about his/her experience serving this country.

- Stencil dish towels that could be donated to the ward kitchen or bath towels that could be given as gifts at baptism. Tie them up with a ribbon and attach a note that says:

  *"May this ABSORB your troubles, BLOT out problems, SOAK up sorrows, and WIPE Away difficulties!"*

- Using clean, dry soup cans or those big food storage cans, paint designs on the outside and fill with treats that can be given to others as gifts.

- "Hands On" Teach the girls how to give themselves manicures. Talk about all of the good service we can do with our hands and how we can place our lives in God's hands.

- Arrange to visit an animal shelter to play with the animals and help clean up the stalls.

- Read children's stories into a tape recorder and package the books and tapes together as a set so they be given to a hospital, Boys & Girls Club, library, preschool, school for the blind, or daycare center.

- Find out how your girls can participate in a Women's Walk for Breast Cancer, the March of Dimes, or some other local event to help fight terrible diseases.

- Talk to the Facilities and Public Works Department of your city to see what service projects your girls could do. They can usually think of ideas that would readily work, such as painting over graffiti or cleaning up parks.

- Talk to your Bishop to see if your Young Women or ward could get involved in the Adopt-a-Highway or Adopt-a-Waterway programs.

- Using the girls' handprints paint T-shirts, pots, aprons, binders, Plaster of Paris handprints, or other items. Talk about how we use our hands to bless others and how we can place our lives into the Lord's hands with our faith.

- Paint and wallpaper a shelter. Make curtains and other decorative items to make it feel like a home.

- Find out if there are some projects with Habitat for Humanity that your girls could help out with.

- Write to your local Congressman about issues that affect your community. Invite a local civic leader to speak about how they can contribute in a positive way. Write letters of appreciation to Congresswomen for setting such a great example of leadership.
- Learn about well-known members of the Church at www. famousmormons.net and help the girls think about positive ways they can contribute to the world.
- Teach the girls some sign language and check out the Church's website about American Sign Language at www.asl.lds.org. See if there is a school for deaf children where the girls could practice their new skills and help out.
- Surprise everyone in your building by cleaning it! Tackle the kitchen and make labels for the cabinets, organizing their contents and cleaning the shelves. Reserve a cabinet or box for Lost and Found items.
- Have a progressive dinner, performing various acts of service in between courses.
- Teach the girls how to make a quilt that could be given to a shelter, a young woman leaving for college, new babies in the ward, or someone in need.
- Go to the Bishop's Storehouse and can food for families in the ward who are unable to do the manual labor themselves.
- Invite a representative from the Red Cross to teach the girls about disaster relief, preparedness, and how the girls can help in their community.
- If you're lucky enough to have sister missionaries in your area, do investigator visits with them.
- Do something nice for the Bishopric and/or presidencies of each auxiliary in your ward to let them know their hard work is appreciated.
- After learning how to do manicures, go to a retirement center and offer to give the ladies manicures and hand massages.
- Hold a special dinner or game night for the foreign exchange students who attend the girls' school. Learn about their countries and make them feel welcome here.

- Help your ward's Activity Director prepare for the next party or event by making decorations, centerpieces, posters, etc.
- Create a "Taste the Sweetness of Service" jar by filling a specially decorated jar for the Bishop and putting a piece of candy in it for every act of service each young woman gives.
- Make meals for a widow or sister on bedrest she could freeze.
- Sing the Seven Dwarfs song "Hi Ho" but have it stand for something new—Happiness Is Helping Others.
- "Land of Oz." Wizard of Oz themed evening to talk about getting a heart, head and courage to do service.
- Sign up ward members who are widows, elderly or home-bound to join the "Letter A Month Club." Prepare nice cards and letters that could then be mailed every week to uplift and inspire them.
- Put together "Finals Survival Kits" to send to college students from your ward. Include a bag of "brain candy" to help them get through those long study hours.
- Plan a special dance for the married couples in the ward in the style of a prom, complete with photos, dinner, and crowning of a King and Queen.
- Learn about literacy and the Church's emphasis on helping others to read. Offer to help students in a Boys & Girls Club, after-school facility or members of your own ward.
- Crochet leper bandages, baby caps, infant layettes, as well as other products used by the Church's Humanitarian Department. For more information contact the department on weekdays from 8 a.m. to 4 p.m. (Mountain Time) at (801) 240-6060. Or write to the following address.

Latter-day Saint Humanitarian Center<br>
1665 Bennett Road<br>
Salt Lake City, UT 84104

- Call your local LDS Social Services office. They usually have all kinds of projects they need help with.
- Make gift baskets to give to military wives for Mother's Day, Easter and/or Christmas.

- Make newborn hats that can be donated to hospitals. You can even buy one of those round looms which makes the project go very quickly and easily!
- Learn about Locks of Love if you have girls with very long hair who are considering cutting and donating it.
- Invite the girls to take their pets to a retirement home to visit with the residents.
- If you have artistic Young Women take them to a retirement home or children's hospital and have them draw portraits of the residents. If they aren't very good at drawing you could take Polaroid pictures or even digital pictures that could be printed out and brought back on another day.
- Take cookies to widows on Valentine's Day or other holidays.
- Create a Family Service Coupon book that the girls can give as gifts to their families.
- Have a "Random Acts of Kindness" contest and see which team can complete the most in an hour.
- Plan a dinner for all of the Seminary teachers and their spouses so they can eat together before the annual CES "Meet A General Authority" broadcast in the winter.
- Decorate lunch bags for missionaries and fill them with yummy food and snacks during their zone conferences.
- Help an older person write his/her autobiography, record a video of them being interviewed, organize their photos, etc.
- Make hospital gift tray items such as nice poems rolled up with a ribbon and piece of candy.
- Find out how your girls and ward can help with Special Olympics.
- Paint and wallpaper a shelter or Boys/Girls Club.
- Build a Pinewood Derby track for your Cub Scouts if your ward or stake doesn't have one.
- Build toy boxes or shelves for your building's nursery.
- Build cabinets or shelves for Seminary students to hold their materials.

# INTEGRITY

- Take the girls rock climbing and discuss their experience afterward, comparing it to life.

- Watch movie clips that demonstrate integrity. There are some great Church videos that teach powerful lessons in good character.

- Share websites where integrity and other good character traits are promoted.

- Have a progressive dinner where the girls start in one home eating appetizers, then go to another house for salad, then another house for the entrée and a final house for dessert. At each home have a short lesson about people throughout history who have been tremendous examples of integrity and honor.

- Teach the girls how to make their own jewelry. Talk about how a righteous woman is more valuable than rubies.

- Teach the girls how to make soap. Cleanliness is next to godliness.

- Make fun Shrinky Dinks that remind the girls to stand for truth and righteousness.

- Teach the girls how to do cross stitch and make lovely wall-hangings for their home that remind them to do what is right. Check out this website for inspiring designs: www.angelfire.com/biz/CottageSewing/free.html

- Decorate inexpensive flip flops with value-colored fabric, balloons, beads, shells, ribbons, charms, buttons, etc. Talk about how not to flip flop in the gospel.

- Paint terra cotta pots to use as candle holders. Talk about how our example can be a light to others.

- Decorate door hangers, light switch plates, mirrors and other décor for the girls' bedrooms, using Mutual themes, the Young Women's motto or other catch phrases that inspire the young women to remember their standards and the Savior.

- Paint sisal door mats with the Young Women logo or other inspiring designs that will remain the girls of their standards every time they enter their home.

- Talk about how what you say can reveal your true character. To emphasize the importance of speaking sweet words, teach them how to make lip gloss! Grate paraffin wax or Beeswax onto wax paper. Measure ¼ tsp. into a plastic bag and add 1 tsp. coconut oil, 1 tsp. petroleum jelly, 1 candy melt, and ⅛ tsp. of the flavoring of your choice. Seal the bag and put it in a bowl of hot tap water to melt the ingredients (3-5 minutes). Change the water if it cools. (Use only hot tap water. Never use a microwave or stove to heat.) Remove the bag from the hot water and squish the ingredients around in the bag to mix. Clip off a tiny corner of the bag and squeeze the gloss into small containers such as film canisters, pharmacy bottles or even plastic Easter eggs. Let it set for about an hour or put it in the refrigerator for about 15 minutes.

- Invite the girls to bring Church magazines or other publications that can be cut up to create a collage that represents a person with integrity or things that are of true value in their lives.

- Introduce the girls to such websites as www.onemillionyouth. com where they can learn more about how to make a difference in the world by standing for truth and righteousness with other good people. Spend time on the Internet looking for other organizations like www.presidentialprayerteam.com.

- Teach the girls how to tie dye T-shirts and have them write "Integrity" on the sleeves with fabric paint pens.

- Teach the girls how to make different kinds of jam. Afterwards, talk about how sometimes we get in a jam at school, work, and at home and can be tempted to lower our standards. Equip the girls with tools they can use to stay strong and maintain their standards even in difficult situations. Do role plays with various scenarios.

- Write "Letters to the Editor" of various girl magazines, thanking them for printing good articles and encouraging them to focus on more uplifting material.

- Make patriotic decorations for their home or to display during a ward party on the 4th of July or Memorial Day. Discuss the integrity of those who fight to protect freedom.

CHAPTER 6

*Transitions*

*"Youth is not a time of life; it is a state of mind; it is not
a matter of rosy cheeks, red lips and supple knees; it is a
matter of the will, quality of the imagination, a vigor of
the emotions; it is the freshness of the deep springs of life."*

SAMUEL ULLMAN
*1840-1924, German-born American Educator, Writer, Poet*

## WELCOMING NEW BEEHIVES

The beehive symbol was picked because of its worker bee significance. Industry is a part of our heritage of Latter-day Saints. Twelve and thirteen year old girls are excited to help, work and be productive. Church leaders in 1913 had the right idea when they decided to make the beehive the symbol of the lively and busy girls!

The Beehive Girls program was first organized as the sister organization to the Boy Scouts for girls ages 14-17 and offered summer activities such as hiking, parties, and studying literature. Later Church leaders focused on studying the bee and its example of service, creating three ranks for the girls to achieve: Builders of the Hive, Gatherers of the Honey, and Keepers of the Bees. The names have since been changed several times, but the beehive symbol remains as a constant theme for our newest young women.

Most girls are thrilled to be graduating from Primary and yet a bit apprehensive about joining the older teenage girls. There is a big difference between the needs, interests, and maturity level of a 12-year-old girl and a young woman of 17!

Help her to feel welcome, wanted, and needed. Let her see that she is an important part of your group and that she can contribute much to the learning and success of the program in your unit.

- Organize a special Beehive/Deacon conference.
- Plan a "Bee All That You Can Bee" evening for the new Beehives to show them how much they can learn and grow during their next few years.
- Teach her some camp songs before camp so she'll feel comfortable joining in on the fun once she gets there.
- Help her memorize the Young Women theme so she doesn't feel awkward on Sunday when all of the other girls are saying it aloud together during Opening Exercises.
- Plan a special Bee event and discuss President Hinckley's "Be's".
- Give her a "Young Woman Survival Kit." Cute suggestions can be found at www.christysclipart.com/survival.html
- Have a Beehive Orientation breakfast where they learn about the program and are welcomed by all of the young women.
- Invite the Beehive's parents to introduce their daughter to the rest of the Young Women on her first day. They can bring baby pictures, tell funny stories about her growing up, talk about her talents, and slobber all over her in front of the other girls for a few minutes.
- Create a "Welcome" packet that includes all of the Young Women materials and welcome letters from all of the other girls.
- Assign a "Big Sister" from one of the girls in the Laurel group to make sure she has someone to sit next to during Opening Exercises, knows about the activities, gets some fun treats or surprises in her mailbox, teachers her about the programs, and introduces her to the other girls.
- Spotlight new Beehives on a bulletin board or in a newsletter.
- Find out what her talents are and have her teach a class to the other Young Women at Mutual.

- Sit down with the parents of the new Beehive and explain all the ins and outs of Young Women's. For a first-time Beehive parent it can be overwhelming!
- Have all of the young women and their leaders go into the Primary room with balloons or flowers to escort the new Beehive to the Young Women's room on her first day.
- Begin a tradition of kidnapping each new Beehive and taking her out to breakfast.
- Give her a set of scriptures with her name engraved on them.
- Have a "Get To Know" you game night so everyone can get to know her better and she can learn everyone's names and feel a part of the group.

# TRANSITIONING LAURELS

What a difference only a few years make! Somewhere between the time when a giggling girl eagerly graduates from Primary and becomes a second-year Laurel she is transformed magically into a young woman with the future at her doorstep. She is excited to leave the nest, but still wants to feel a comforting wing around her for just a moment longer. She may be uncertain about the world, but confident that she can conquer it. Her schedule is filled with school, work, Seminary, sports, performances, dances and maybe even a boyfriend. Her presence at Young Women's may be sporadic, but when she comes she lights up the room. The Laurel symbol comes from the Greek or Romans' use of laurels which was a symbol for excellence.

Often times the Laurel girl feels she has outgrown the Young Women program, but she can't imagine herself in the same organization as her old mother! Studies have shown that it is exactly at this transition that so many young adults lose activity in the Church.

There are many things we can do to help ease her from the comfortable and familiar surrounding of Young Women's into the loving hands of her older sisters. Whether she is going away to college or staying home, here are a few suggestions to help her get excited about the next step:

- Encourage the Laurel's mother to work with you in easing the transition, especially by talking about how Relief Society has blessed her life.

- Work with the Relief Society presidency to get to know your graduating Laurel and welcome her with open arms. Have them explain what options are available in terms of singles wards and her home ward. If she is staying at home but interested in a singles ward, have your Relief Society presidency get in contact with the leaders in the singles ward to extend an invitation.

- Have Mutual activities that involve the Young Women and some of the older Relief Society sisters. For example, create a "Then And Now" evening where older and younger sisters team up to answer trivia questions from their era. Have them teach each other popular dances from their time. Your Young Women could also "Adopt A Grandmother."

- Invite the Relief Society presidency to a special Mutual dinner about how their organization works. You could have a panel atmosphere so that the girls could ask them questions about the similarities and differences of the two organizations.

- Invite the Relief Society to a special Mutual dinner.

- Work with the Relief Society Enrichment Leader and Counselor to plan special Mother/Daughter events.

- Find out if there are some mid-week Enrichment activities that would appeal to your Laurels and attend some of them together.

- Have the Relief Society President come into Young Women's with balloons or flowers for the graduating Laurel and then escort her to the Relief Society room on her first day.

- Have an "Enrichment Night in Training" evening, modeled after the Relief Society evenings. Offer several classes the girls can choose from to attend. Have a spiritual thought before the girls divide and offer refreshments at the end with time for the girls to socialize.

- Encourage the visiting teachers of the girl's mother to talk to her about visiting teaching and how she will some day be one, too.

- Present each graduating Laurel with a Relief Society gift basket with such items as the Relief Society theme on a bookmark, "Charity Never Faileth" stickers, a copy of the Enrichment Night calendar, visiting teaching cards, lesson manual, etc.

- Talk to the girls about how much you love Relief Society and share what you learn at Enrichment Nights so they will get excited to join you some day.

- Invite the Relief Society to compete against the Young Women in various contests such as daily scripture reading, memorizing scriptures, church attendance or whatever.

- Take the Laurels on a "field trip" to attend a Relief Society class one Sunday. The next week talk about the similarities and differences. Ask the girls what they think they could contribute to the Relief Society as well as what they think they could learn.

- Invite the Relief Society sisters to a playful "Game Night" so the young girls can see how young at heart the older women are.

- "Meet and Greet" Attend Opening Exercises in Relief Society once a month. Have the young women stand and recite their theme and then have the Relief Society sisters stand and recite theirs.

- If the girl's mother receives Visiting Teachers, talk with them privately about visiting her and explaining how the program works.

- Find an older sister in the Relief Society who could be a mentor to each transitioning Laurel. Try to match up similar interests and hobbies.

- "Sister To Sister." Have both the Relief Society and the Young Women draw names of someone in the other organization to bring surprises and treats to her secret sister for a month. Hold a special event where they can reveal their identities and enjoy their new friendships. Have the young women give the older sisters a flower with a handwritten note attached that says, "Sister to Sister – Heart to Heart. You were my friend right from the start."

- Invite the graduating Laurels to attend the March Relief Society Commemoration Enrichment Night (usually an extra nice event) so they can become more familiar with the history and culture of the Relief Society, as well as get to know some of the sisters.

- Point out to the graduating Laurel what talents and gifts she could offer to the Relief Society so she feels valued and needed.

- Organize a fun activity with the Laurels and their mothers where they rotate through stations and learn about basic homemaking skills such as: how to get stains out of clothing, how to not burn rice, planning nutritious meals, sewing on buttons, repairing zippers, cleaning tips, etc.

- You'll find that often times the Laurels will claim they are too busy to attend a particular Mutual activity, but if you invite the Priests to join you, all of a sudden, their interest is piqued.

# GRADUATING GIRLS

As Laurels graduate high school and move on, there are some special things you can do for them to let them know they will be missed and forever loved:

- Present her with a pearl bracelet or necklace and tell her that she is a Pearl of Great Price!

- Present her with an oil lamp or pretty light to let her know that you appreciate how she has been a shining example for all the other young women.

- Have a "Graduating Seniors Honor Night" where you spotlight each girl and her accomplishments.

- Create a "This Is Your Life" event for all of the graduating girls. Invite their parents and make it a really special honor.

- Invite all of the young women to write a letter of appreciation for the graduating Laurel and put them in a specially decorated binder with photos of everyone so she can take it with her to college.

- Present her with some stamped envelopes and pretty stationery so she can write to your ward while she is gone off to college.

- Hang pictures of all graduating seniors on a bulletin board with information about their accomplishments and what their future plans are.

- Give her a picture of your nearest temple and a basket with some things she'll need when she goes to do proxy work, such as a white hair scrunchie, comb, picture of Christ, journal, white knee highs, a book about the temple, etc.

- Get a pizza place to donate one of their boxes and create a "college survival kit" with silly items she might need while living in the dorms.

- Make a "spiritual survival kit" that she can use while she's out there on her own such as a bookmark, the temple schedule, a journal, a list of favorite scriptures that all of the Young Women have written down, an uplifting book about prayer, etc.

- Give her a list of emergency numbers she might need and include some scripture references for emergencies.

- As a Young Women's presidency, take the graduating Laurels out to lunch or dinner (or cook them a dinner in your home).

- Have all of the young women make her a quilt for her dorm room if she's going away to college.

- Create a "Living On Your Own" budget contest among all of the Laurels. Give them some pretend dollars to spend on college, housing, food, etc and see who can spend the least amount for certain tasks. Teach them how to keep a checkbook, rent an apartment, etc.

- "Stocks R Us" Give each Laurel some pretend money that she can use to invest in whatever stocks she would like. Watch the stocks for several weeks and have a contest to see which girl can make the most money.

- Present her with a photo album of all the pictures you've taken of her at Mutual and other events throughout her time in Young Women's.

- Teach the girls how to write checks and balance a checkbook. Help them open an account at a bank (with their parents' permission, of course) and learn how to keep a budget.

- Make patriarchal blessing envelopes. The instructions are found at www.groups.yahoo.com/group/lds-youngwomenfiles2/files/patriarchal%20blessing%20envelopes/
- Present her with an "Easy College Recipes" cookbook that includes favorite recipes from all of the other young women, as well as recipes for yummy refreshments that have been served at special Young Women events.
- "Real World" Competition. Set up stations where the girls will compete in timed events such as ironing, sewing on a button, looking up the phone number for the DMV in a phone book, balancing a checkbook, checking the oil level in a car, making a peanut butter and jelly sandwich, etc.
- Have plaques made that can be hung on the wall by the Bishop's office for all of the girls who have received their Young Womanhood Recognition award.
- Host an evening with the graduating Young Men and Young Women where you slobber praises all over them and let them know they'll be missed.
- Make and decorate a drawstring laundry bag that the girls can take to college. Include the scripture "And let all things be done in cleanliness before me" (D&C 42:41) or the quote "Cleanliness is next to Godliness."

CHAPTER 7

*Birthday Celebrations*

*"Sisters, you were not born at this time and place by chance. You are here because this is where the Lord wants you to be.... As the Church grows, there will be a need for more women who are leaders, for more women everywhere who have the courage to proclaim their testimony of Jesus Christ, women who will pray and study to find out what the Lord requires of them and who will then make right choices and put themselves in the hands of the Lord."*

ZINA ELIZABETH BROWN

## YOUNG WOMEN BIRTHDAY COMMEMORATION

While the name and activities of the young women's auxiliary have evolved over the years, the goal has remained the same: to help young women "Come Unto Christ."

Below are a few ideas for a special activity night in November when you can commemorate the organization of the Young Women's program and celebrate your part in it.

This is a great time to involve all of the Young Women so they can bask in the blessings of the Young Women program together, honor the rich heritage they share as members of the Church, enjoy their unique sisterhood, and have a renewed desire to live the gospel.

## HISTORY OF THE YOUNG WOMEN'S PROGRAM

Have someone give a special presentation about the history of the Young Women's program in the Church and/or in your specific city, state or country. For an informative time-line check out www.lds.org/pa/library/0,17905,5072-1,00.html.

Memorabilia and old photos could be displayed. Did you know that all Young Women were called Beehives for years? Did you know they wore special uniforms and earned patches that were sewn onto the sleeve?

There is a great article in the November 2003 issue of the *New Era* that shares the origins of the program and even shows how the reward jewelry has evolved over the years. Have the girls pull hand-made taffy for dessert. Have someone read a list of some of the requirements the Young Women had to do in 1916 to earn their award:

1. Care successfully for a hive of bees for one season and know their habits.
2. Give the six distinguishing characteristics of six varieties of hen and cattle and tell good and weak points of each.
3. Exterminate the mosquitoes over an area of ½ mile square by pouring a little kerosene on the surface of all standing pools of water twice each month during April, May or June.
4. Make 2 articles of underwear by hand.
5. Cover 25 miles on snowshoes in any six days.
6. Learn to float in the Great Salt Lake and propel yourself 50 feet.
7. During three consecutive months abstain from candy, ice cream, commercially manufactured beverages, and chewing gum.
8. For one month masticate (chew) your food so thoroughly that it slips down without any visible effort of swallowing it.
9. Successfully put a new washer on a faucet.
10. Care for at least 2 kerosene lamps daily.
11. For three months take care of the milk and cream from at least one cow and see that the pails, pans, strainer, and separator are thoroughly cleansed.

12. During two weeks keep the house free from flies or destroy at least 25 flies daily.

13. Have your toilet moved to an isolated place in the garden. Have a frame of chicken wire built about three feet away and plant quick growing vines such as cucumber or morning glories to screen it from observation.

14. Whitewash your toilet inside and out.

15. Know and describe three cries of a baby.

16. Without help or advice care for and harness a team at least 5 times; drive 50 miles during one season.

17. During 2 summer months clean ice chest thoroughly twice a week.

18. Discover 10 reasons why the Columbine should be made the national flower.

19. Clear sagebrush off of one half acre of land.

20. Know 6 blazes used by Indians.

## YOUNG WOMEN YEARBOOK

Begin a Young Women's scrapbook for your ward. Begin taking pictures at each week's Mutual events to reflect what activities and lessons were presented. Take pictures of each of the girls in your ward and have them write their experiences and feelings about the Young Women's program to include in the scrapbook. At the "birthday" party there could be a scrapbook table set out so the girls could create pages from the past year's photos, handouts, and momentos. This could also be a fun tradition that is ongoing every month or quarter.

## YOUNG WOMEN PRESIDENTS

Learn about all of the former General Young Women Presidents. Have your ward's Young Women presidency share a little about themselves to get to know them better. You could also share the history of Young Women leaders in your ward over the years. This would also be an excellent time to spotlight your class presidencies!

## FANCY SCHMANSY DINNER

Have the young men dress up as waitress, complete with folded towel over their arms, and serve the girls a special dinner. Find talented people in your ward to provide entertainment while the girls eat. If you have some really talented musicians in your ward it would be fun to have a strolling violinist or Barbershop Quartet perform from table to table. Include an inspiring speaker and a pretty backdrop where the girls could have their picture taken. Help the girls to feel special and that it is a unique blessing to be a part of the Young Women's program.

## CELEBRATE SISTERHOOD

Play a lot of icebreaker games where the girls can really get to know each other. A fun game to play involves girl writing on a slip of paper something she has done in her life that is unique. All of the papers are gathered and then read aloud while the group tries to guess who did that thing. The same type of information could be gathered ahead of time and written down on one sheet of paper that each girl is given. She has to write down the name of the person she thinks did that thing and the young woman who gets the most correct answers wins a little prize. See the chapter on get-to-know-you games for more ice-breaker activities. Show the girls that they share a special sisterhood with all of the other girls in your ward. Teach them that they don't have to be best friends with one another, but by being members of the Lord's Church they have a unique bond and will be blessed by their association with each other.

## GET TO KNOW YOU

Have the young women bring three items that describe themselves, their talents, or hobbies. Be sure to include the leaders in the fun! Items could be set out on a table and the girls would have to guess who brought them. Each young woman would then take a couple of minutes to identify her objects and talk a little bit about herself. Reinforce the idea that every girl is unique and that's what makes your ward's Young Woman program so wonderful. Help them to celebrate the differences!

YOUNG WOMEN BLESSINGS

Invite a panel of speakers to share how their lives have been blessed by the Young Women's program in the Church. Panel members could include girls who have recently graduated, older sisters in the ward, and parents. Show the girls how their lives will be blessed by participating in the Young Women's program.

THE BEAN GAME

You could also play "The Bean Game":

Everyone sits in a circle and is given a certain number of beans (or whatever item you want to use). Each girl takes a turn telling the group something she has never done in her life that she thinks everyone else in the group has done. Examples could include: I have never said a bad word, I have never watched the movie *E.T.*, I have never been to Salt Lake City, etc. The girls who HAVE done that thing then have to throw one of their beans into the center pot. If they have NOT done it then they get to keep their beans. The winner is the girl who has the most beans at the end of the game.

QUIZ SHOW

Turn any popular TV game show into a Young Women version. Use questions and answers about Church history, former General and local Young Women Presidents, ward trivia, characters from the scriptures, and interesting tidbits about your girls. Tape record the music from TV to play so everyone really gets into the spirit of the game. Fun TV game shows that work really well are *Jeopardy, Hollywood Squares, Wheel of Fortune, Who Wants to Be A Millionaire,* and *$10,000 Pyramid.* Help the girls to see the rich history they are a part of by belonging to the Church.

JELLY BEANS

Each girl picks a jellybean when she enters the room. The color of her jellybean determines which table she will sit at. Tables should be decorated with color-coordinated tablecloths or centerpieces. Have speakers talk about the "sweet" blessings of participating in the Young Women's program.

"MORMON BAR"

Here is a bar the young women can actually go in to . . .

For refreshments set out a long table with all kinds of toppings for a Taco Bar, Potato Bar, Salad bar, or Ice Cream Sundae Bar. Another version of this is to play a game where the girls have to answer questions about the gospel, the Young Women values, or anything else you are studying together. If they answer the question correctly they get to roll some dice. The questions could ask how much they know about one another. The numbers on the dice correspond to various items: napkin, fork, cup, plate, and the various food ingredients. As they answer questions correctly they begin to accumulate the items from the bar and can eat once they have all been gathered. Talk about how great it is to be members of the Young Women's program and be able to go to the kind of "bar" where Church standards are upheld.

PAJAMA PARTY

Have the girls wear modest pajamas and lounge-wear to enjoy a fun evening of girl talk, make-up tips, doing each other's hair, bedroom decorating tips, junk food munchies, and even a few innocent games where you wrap each other in toilet paper like mummies or freeze a token bra for old times' sake. Talk about "PJs"— prayer, journal, scriptures—the three important things we should all do before going to sleep at night. Help the girls to appreciate the sisterhood they share in the Young Women's program.

"A LAMP UNTO YOUR FEET"

Do a special presentation about the parable of the Ten Virgins. Decorate with small clay lamps. Talk about what sisters need to be and do to join the five wise virgins in being prepared for the Bridegroom's second coming.

"LEADING FAMILIES TO CHRIST"

Center your theme around Sheri L. Dew's statement, "We no longer have the luxury of spending our energy on anything that does not lead us and our families to Christ." Discuss ways sisters can focus more on Christ in their homes with their families.

### "YOUNG WOMEN ARE PRICELESS"

This is a fun activity to do if you're having a special dinner event. Each table in the room has a decorated jar full of pennies as the centerpiece. The girls take turns picking a penny out of the jar and then they have to tell something about themselves that happened during that year. If the date is before she was born she has to pick another penny. Include a guest speaker who talks about how valuable the young women are and how Heavenly Father knows their true worth.

### CARNIVAL

Have booths where sisters have to complete tasks or games to earn prizes. Fun and simple tasks might include answering a Young Women's history quiz, remembering past Mutual activities, "Name that Face" game using pictures of sisters in your ward, matching temples with locations, or you could even have the sisters come up with clever missionary door approaches to earn prizes. Use gospel twists to traditional carnival games like Ring Toss, Bowling, Bean Bag toss, fishing for a prize. Sisters are given tickets to spend at booths and "buy" refreshments. Reinforce the idea that the Young Women's program is fun and full of wonderful surprises!

### VALIANT SISTERS

Share stories and examples of good LDS women in history as well as in the scriptures. Help the girls see that they are a part of a powerful Church history.

### "GOD'S ARMY"

Using a military theme, help the girls to understand that we are in a battle for souls and that they are part of the Lord's army, fighting for truth and righteousness. You could talk about the armor of God and the girls could even create their own armor out of cardboard.

### YOUNG WOMEN UNITE!"

Invite all of the Young Women in your stake for a big birthday bash. Celebrate the unity of the girls in your stake and the wonderful sisterhood you share in the Church in your area.

DAY OF LEADERSHIP

Get back to the basics when the Young Women's organization was first organized by the Prophet Brigham Young and the daughters of Zion were called to set the standard for the world. Have speakers talk about the role of leadership the young women can play in their homes, schools and communities. Celebrate the achievements the girls have already accomplished and spotlight other LDS young women in the world who have set the standard.

# SHINING A SPOTLIGHT ON THE BIRTHDAY GIRL

There are so many ways to celebrate a young woman's birthday. The most important thing is to make her feel special and loved. Here are just a few ways to shine the spotlight on her, as well as some small gift ideas to let her know you care:

- Take a picture of each girl on a special "Glamour Shots" night or whenever you can get a good shot of each girl. Put a big mat on it and have each of the Young Women write a loving message to the birthday girl on the mat. Frame it, wrap it, and present it with hugs from everyone!

- Make "Birthday Cakes In A Bottle" by using ½ pint wide mouth jars. Spray the jars with oil and fill ⅔ full with brownie batter. Bake until done. Heat up the lids in hot water while the brownies bake and then quickly place the hot lids and rings on the jar to seal. Put a small wooden spoon on top and wrap with cellophane paper when cooled, tying it with cute ribbon or raffia.

- Create a framed copy of the picture on the front of the Personal Progress book (Christ with the temple overlay) to present to the birthday girl.

- Present a white rose and a white hankie that has her name written on it that she could take to the temple when she "makes and keeps sacred covenants."

- Fill a basket with inexpensive gifts from the $1 store so that the girls can choose any item they would like on their special day. Every girl is different and this way you can appeal to a lot of different tastes and styles.

- Make a bookmark or frame with the Young Women Values written nicely, adding pressed flowers of value colors.
- Present the birthday girl with a small Christus statue. They can be made fairly inexpensively at a local pottery store.
- Kidnap the birthday girl early in the morning and take her out to breakfast in her pajamas.
- Give her a bag of Hershey's candy with a note attached that says "HearShe's having a birthday."
- Make the birthday girl wear a tiara and one of those "Miss America" banners, but instead have it say "Birthday Girl" or "Young Woman Just Got Older."
- Decorate a brown paper bag, fill it with treats, and tie it with raffia for a country look.
- Present the birthday girl with a bunch of "Good For One" home-made coupons. You could even have the other Young Women make a bunch of coupons in advance and they each have to offer something of themselves.
- Buy each girl a special "Birthday Journal" that she can begin keeping for herself. Each year she writes things about herself and her life so that she can see her growth.
- Invite all of the Young Women to write kind things about each other. Create a special card for each girl so that she can receive her card on her birthday with all of the thoughts previously written by the other girls.
- Make one of those giant chocolate kisses for the birthday girl. Put it on the floor in her classroom and say, "We KISS the ground you walk on."
- Gather well wishes from the birthday girl's family, teachers, and friends and put them all in a pretty binder to present to her.
- Buy some clean, polished rocks and write some of her talents and qualities on each rock with a permanent marker. Present them to her in a velvet drawstring bag.
- With her parents' permission of course, sneak into her bedroom when she's not home and decorate her room with birthday balloons or flowers.

- Put hearts all over her bedroom, car, locker at school, or front yard with a note saying she has received a "heart attack" from people who love her.
- Put wrapping paper and a bow all over her locker at school or on her bedroom door.
- Hang a balloon from the ceiling with small notes from all the girls and leaders. When you sing happy birthday she gets to pop the balloon and get the letters.
- Make a necklace that spells out her name in cute beads.
- Fill a basket with different kinds of pretty lotions and sing her this song sung to the tune of "We Wish You A Merry Christmas":

*We wish you a happy birthday*
*We wish you a happy birthday*
*We wish you a happy birthday and an awesome new year!*
*Good lotions we bring to you and your skin*
*We wish you a happy birthday and an awesome new year!*

- If you're using a theme for the year, choose something that corresponds. For example, if your monthly or yearly theme is "Love bears all things" then present her with her very own bear. Oriental Trading Company is great for inexpensive, themed gifts. Before ordering on-line do a Google search for "coupon code" for the store and you can save on shipping or a percentage off your order. You can also order by phone at 1-800-875-8480 or 1-800-228-2269.
- Give each girl a charm bracelet when they first become Beehives. Add a special charm for each birthday, as well as other events such as New Beginnings, Girls Camp, or when they complete certain Personal Progress goals. You can find some very inexpensive charms on-line.
- During the year take pictures of the girls at activities, Girls Camp, youth conference, etc. On their birthday present them with a scrapbook page that has been created just for them with their pictures.

- Present her with her very own Prayer Bear and this poem:

  *I'm just a little Prayer Bear,*
  *I'll sit upon your bed.*
  *It's my job to remind you*
  *When your prayers should be said.*

  *When you put me on your pillow*
  *As you make your bed each day,*
  *Remember as you hold me,*
  *To take the time to pray.*

  *Then when you go to bed at night*
  *And put me on the floor,*
  *Remember to take the time to kneel*
  *And say your prayers once more.*

- Have an "Unbirthday Party" just for fun to celebrate everyone's birthday at once or just to break up the monotony of a long, cold winter. Have everyone bring either goofy presents or a nice gift under $5 to play the "White Elephant" game.
- Hang a giant poster at her school or home wishing her a happy birthday from all the Young Women in your ward.
- Send her a Happy Birthday text message.
- Create a cookie bouquet to give to each girl on her special day.
- Present each birthday girl with a "Temple Bag" filled with a white scrunchie, picture of Christ, white comb, white towel, etc that she could take to do temple baptisms.
- Put a picture of the birthday girl and another one of Christ between two pieces of glass and then framed. Add a quote, pressed flowers, lace, ribbon, etc.
- Give each birthday girl her own Young Women music book with sheet music and instructions on how to conduct songs.
- Give her a CD of Young Women music. You can even e-mail the artist and request that they autograph them or sign a note to the birthday girl.
- Make chocolate lollipops for all of the girls celebrating birthdays that month and present them all at once.

- Buy an inexpensive canvas bag that can be used to carry a change of clothes and other items in during temple baptism trips. Decorate the outside of the bag with a picture of your nearest temple and her name. Include a nice note and a challenge to wear out the bag with many temple trips!

- Decorate a canvas bag with the Young Women logo or value-colored items that go with your annual theme. Encourage her to bring her bag each week filled with her scriptures, Personal Progress book, Young Women songbook, etc.

- Have a combined monthly birthday party for all of the girls who are celebrating that month.

- Show her baby picture to everyone and have them guess who they think it is. Present her with a bag of Baby Ruth candy bars.

- Present her with toe socks with a "Faith in Every Footstep" note attached.

- Give her a special picture of the Savior.

- Create a photo album by starting her first page which includes a photo of her, the Savior and a nice display of the Young Women theme, motto, values, etc.

- Invite all of the girls to stand up. As you read things that describe the birthday girl tell the girls to sit down if that item does not describe them. The birthday girl will be the last one standing. Sing happy birthday to her and present her with a little gift.

- Invite the parents of the birthday girl to make cupcakes to share with all of the young women on the Mutual night closest to her birthday. Hey, who said YOU have to do all the work?

- Send an e-mail birthday card using free cards at www.dayspring. com which includes a nice, inspirational quote from scripture. Other free cards can be sent from www.bluemountain. com, www.123greetings.com, www.superlaugh.com, www. birthdaycards.com, and www.freewebcards.com

- Spotlight all of the birthday girls each month on a bulletin board or special poster, by displaying pictures and information about each girl during the month.

- Design a festive birthday poster that can be rolled up and stored each month. Take a picture of the birthday girl in front of the poster. Keep a copy for your ward scrapbook and present her with a copy for her scrapbook.
- Write about the birthday girl and put the paper in a balloon. Have someone pop it and then guess who it is.
- Present a birthday mug, basket, or some other decorated container filled with various items in it. She then, in turn, fills it with items and presents it to the next birthday girl.
- Photocopy a clip-art flower on brightly colored paper and cut them out. Cut out green leaves and tape them to straws, creating flowers with a stem. Have the young women write loving messages on the back of the flowers and present the special boquet to the birthday girl. You could even photocopy a picture of the birthday girl into the center of each flower.
- Give her a collection of Mormon Ad posters.
- Create a flower or candy lei for the birthday girl. Add notes to the birthday girl from each of the young women in between the flowers or candy.
- Invite the birthday girl's parents to come in and talk about how great their daughter is. Limit the time to five minutes. They can show baby pictures and brag about all of her accomplishments. Be careful to not let this spotlight time turn into an uncomfortable competition and be especially sensitive to the girls who do not have parents who could present a birthday message.
- Design Young Women "money" with clip art and award the birthday girl with some birthday bucks that she could cash in at the "Young Women's store" — a box with miscellaneous items to choose from.
- Be sure to have your Young Women's secretary mail the birthday girl a special card signed by the presidency!

"Breakfast in Bed." Make a shoebox look like a bed and fill it with non-perishable breakfast items that could be stored in a young woman's closet.

CHAPTER 8

## *New Beginnings*

*"How beautiful is youth! How bright it gleams
with its illusions, aspirations, dreams! Book
of Beginnings, Story without End, Each maid
a heroine, and each man a friend!"*

HENRY WADSWORTH LONGFELLOW
*1819-1892, American Poet*

The "New Beginnings" evening is a wonderful opportunity to officially welcome new girls and their families into your ward and revisit the purposes of the Young Women's organization together. Parents attend with their daughters to support and celebrate their daughter's accomplishments and learn more ways they can provide encouragement to their daughters' success in the Personal Progress program. It could be held during Mutual or another night and should be a special evening, highlighting each of the young women. While New Year's resolutions are still fresh on everyone's minds, holding this event towards the beginning of each year encourages both the young women and their parents to recommit to Personal Progress. Encourage the girls to help plan the New Beginnings program as a possible Value Project.

A sample program might include:

- Hymns or special musical numbers
- Opening & Closing Prayers
- Official welcome by Young Women's President
- Introduction of class presidencies
- Recognition of new young women

- Presentation of theme, motto, symbols
- Guest speakers
- Skits
- Explanation of Personal Progress program & awards
- Young Women values
- Refreshments
- Take home gift

## "ALL STARS"

Relate Personal Progress to sports: the manual is the playbook, the refs are the priesthood Church leaders, the Young Women are the players, the parents are the coaches. Explain that the Young Women leaders are the cheerleaders to encourage both the parents and their daughters to work together. Talk about different kinds of goals. Have the girls wear football jerseys or baseball attire. Include some entertainment during your "half time" and serve refreshments at the "concession stand."

## "PEARL OF GREAT PRICE"

Present each girl with a pearl necklace and talk about how each pearl represents some aspect of the Young Women's program. Compare how an oyster makes a pearl with how the girls will become women. You could decorate in an Asian style.

## "BECOME THE GIRL OF YOUR DREAMS"

Decorate with pillows, blankets, stuffed animals, and bedroom décor. Wear modest pajamas. Read a bedtime story and talk about how living the YW values will help the girls become the girl of their dreams. Present the PJ's program (Prayer, Journals, Scriptures) and give each girl a prayer rock.

## "STAND AS A WITNESS AT ALL TIMES"

Decorate with clocks and watches. Each speaker introduces one of the values by saying, "It's time to develop this value."

## "STAR"

"Stand for Truth And Righteousness" or "Standing Together Achieving Righteousness" or "Strong Testimonies Are Reachable."

PARABLE OF THE TEN VIRGINS

Using the Parable of the Ten Virgins, have the girls dress in costumes to represent both ancient and modern young women. If you would like to give each young woman a small oil lamp that resembles the ones made and used in Jesus' time you can find them at www.myweb.cableone.net/loupeck/  The creator, Judi Peck, is LDS! You can also purchase inexpensive oil lamps at Oriental Trading. Instead of lamps you could give each girl a small glass vial that could be put on a necklace to remind her to add drops of oil to her spiritual lamp. Because the parable describes a wedding, you could serve wedding cake for refreshments.

"HAND TO HAND"

Using the theme "Hand to Hand" blow up some latex gloves with helium for balloons. Have the girls perform a song using sign language. Bakery gloves can be filled with goodies for dessert. Show pictures of the Savior's hands and talk about different kinds of hands and what they mean such as clinched fists, hands in prayer, holding hands, thumbs up, pointing finger, peace sign, etc.

"PUT ON THE WHOLE ARMOR OF GOD"

Show the various items in armor and how they correspond to the various aspects of the Young Women's program.

"SAFE HARBORS" OR "SAILING HOME"

Use a nautical theme and talk about what safe harbors are in our lives and how we can create and maintain them. Spray paint paper hats in value colors for your Young Women sailors. Compare the Savior, parents or the leaders to a lighthouse that guides and directs through the storms in our lives.

"GO FOR THE GOLD"

Create gold plates out of metal or cardboard pages that have been spray painted gold. Focus on the scriptures and present each young woman with a Book of Mormon with her name engraved on it. Using "Art Emboss" have the girls "engrave" their testimonies on the gold sheets. Talk about things that are golden in our lives.

## "CELEBRATE THE LIGHT"

Decorate with rainbows, using the value colors (of course!). As you talk about each of the values shine a flashlight or spotlight in that color by placing colored cellophane on the light. Talk about the light of Christ and sharing our own light. Discuss Personal Progress in terms of the light at the end of the rainbow. You could also use snaplights or glow sticks.

## "HOPE CHEST"

Decorate with antique items and as you pull items out of a hope chest talk about how they apply to the Young Women's program. Have girls bring genealogy items to display and invite the parents to share some of their hopes for their daughters.

## "ASPIRE HIGHER"

An "Aspire Higher" theme could focus on value-colored kites or hot air balloons. Talk about things that lift us, how the Holy Ghost is like the wind, and the marvelous view we can see when we've reached spiritual heights.

## "BLOOM WHERE YOU'RE PLANTED"

Using the lessons we learn from flowers, talk about what the young women need to grow spiritually. Serve cupcakes in small clay pots for dessert.

## "KISS"

"Keep Inspiring Spiritual Sisters" or "Keep It Spiritual Sisters!" Present each young woman with one of those cute Hershey's kiss roses.

## "THE WORTH OF A SOLE"

Assign a different kind of shoe to represent each girl or aspect of the Young Women's program. There are some cute Relief Society skits on-line that could easily be adapted to a Young Women's theme.

## "HEARTS AFIRE"

Talk about how Personal Progress is the "heart" of Young Women's, how to have a "heart to heart" with the Savior, etc.

"STAR SEARCH"

Divide the girls and/or parents into seven groups that will receive a bag filled with various items in the color of one of the seven values. They are given five minutes to come up with a skit to represent that value, using their miscellaneous props. Have the host announce the winners of the "Star Search" contest. Talk about the various aspects of the Young Women's program that help each girl to shine. Decorate with lots of stars!

TAKE A TRIP

Decorate with travel items such as suitcases, airline tickets, train motif, etc. Have the girls and their parents actually travel through the Church building into different rooms that represent our journey here on earth from birth to childhood, adolescence, college, mission, marriage, grandparents, etc. Point out the wonderful foundation the Young Woman program will lay for the rest of the girls' lives.

"CNN"

(Church News Network). Create a news anchor feel and show video reports about the different aspects of the Young Women's program that the girls make ahead of time.

BECOMING A BUTTERFLY

Use a butterfly motif and compare the Young Women process to an earthbound caterpillar that slowly becomes a beautiful butterfly that flies heavenward.

"UNDER CONSTRUCTION"

Home Depot will probably give you some of their free kid-sized orange aprons to use. Talk about all of the things in the Young Women's program that help build a righteous woman and compare them to tools: HAMMER home the idea about Personal Progress, previous parents SAW great blessings in their homes when their daughter participated in Young Women, LEVEL-headed leaders will help add BALANCE to each girl's life, it's cool to be SQUARE when we follow the STRAIGHT EDGE, etc.

### "EWE ARE LOVED"

Talk about the Great Shepherd, how we can feed His sheep, and how each lamb (young woman) is counted and cared for. Serve mutton for dessert . . . no, just kidding.

### "PATTERN YOUR LIFE AFTER THE SAVIOR"

Create a "Pattern your life after the Savior" sewing theme.

### "COME HOLD YOUR TORCHES HIGH"

Use the Young Women torch motif, using value-colored lights to introduce the Young Women's program.

### "CHINESE NEW YEAR & BEGINNINGS"

Hang signs that say things like "Confucious say: New Beehive Girl Very Fortunate Cookie" or "Confucious say: Good Fortune In Store For Young Women", etc. Use Chinese décor and serve almond cookies and mandarin oranges. Have each new Beehive choose a fortune cookie from a tray and read the fortune aloud, telling her of one of the exciting "Yung" Women areas in her future (Mutual, camp, Personal Progress, friends, etc.)

### "FABULOUS FLAVORS"

Use an ice cream theme and introduce the new "flavors" (Beehives) to everyone. Using value-colored ice cream, talk about how sweet Young Women's is. Decorate with ice cream parlor tables and chairs, sundae glasses, and ice cream cones with value-colored cotton ball scoops.

### "SEEDS OF TOMORROW"

Using a garden theme introduce the new young women by giving them a new name such as "Hibiscus Heather" and describe her fragrance (great qualities). Serve punch from a watering can and put brownies or cookies in clay pots.

### "HATS OFF TO YOUNG WOMEN"

Use different kinds of hats to show off the personalities of the girls and describe the features in the Young Women's program.

## "IN TUNE"

Introduce each new young woman in a "This is your life" TV show format. Have the girls do "commercials" about various aspects of the Young Women's program. Make the room look like a family room with a giant TV set. Serve refreshments on TV dinner trays.

## "KICK OFF NEW BEGINNINGS"

Use a football theme and have the Bishopric dress up like referees. Set up the gym to look like a football stadium. Make up questions that have to do with Personal Progress, the scriptures, For The Strength of Youth, the Young Women values, etc. Play a game with the girls and their parents, letting them score yards and touchdowns as they answer the questions. Recognize the new Beehives as the Rookies and have a pre-game speech about the importance of playing the game, having good coaches (parents) and cheerleaders (Young Women leaders). Serve refreshments in the concession stand.

For more theme ideas look in the chapters on Young Women in Excellence, Girls Camp, and Youth Conference.

CHAPTER 9

## *Young Women In Excellence*

*"Excellence is an art won by training and habituation. We do not act rightly because we have virtue or excellence, but we rather have those because we have acted rightly. We are what we repeatedly do. Excellence, then, is not an act but a habit."*

ARISTOTLE
*BC 384-322, Greek Philosopher*

Young Women in Excellence is a celebration of Personal Progress! It's a great opportunity to give recognition to each of the young women for projects they have completed during the year as well as motivate them to continue working.

Invite the parents and let them see you slobber praises all over their daughters. Be careful not to turn the event into a talent show and watch out for a feeling of negative competition among the girls. Include them in the planning and encourage them to create an event that will allow ALL of the girls to shine. The projects that are set out on display should be an outward reflection of the inward growth of each girl and what she has learned about the seven Young Women values.

There are so many creative ways to design a memorable event that is fun and gets the girls excited to work harder on their Personal Progress. Here are just a few to get your own creative juices flowing again:

NEWSPAPER THEME

Cut out words from newspapers with the values. Write newspaper articles about each of the girls to hang up like posters. Have a roving reporter ask people to talk about their projects.

"HANGING AT THE MALL"

Set up "stores" to look like you're shopping in a mall. Display projects and accomplishments in each store such as the sporting goods store, hair salon, photo studio, book store, bath & beauty store, etc. Have refreshments set up in the food court!

"WAX STRONG IN THE GOSPEL"

Create a fun candle dipping event while talking about all of the experiences and opportunities in the Young Women's program that add layers to her strength. Use value-colored paraffin wax for dipping. Put a large metal juice can in an electric frying pan. Add 2 inches of water. Put paraffin wax in the can and melt it over low heat to a liquid. You can put pieces of old crayons in for coloring. Have another large juice can filled with water nearby. Use a wick out of 100% cotton twine or twill so that the wick will burn when lit. Cut a piece to the desired length, making sure it is not longer than the depth of the can holding the wax. Slowly submerge the string into the wax and then into the water. Go back and forth until the candle is the desired thickness. When finished, you may roll it on a table to make it smoother. Press the bottom of the candle on the table to flatten it. The first few times you dip, the string will curl, so run the waxed string through your fingers to straighten it.

"RECIPE FOR SUCCESS"

Decorate with cookbooks, chefs hats, aprons, and kitchen gadgets. You could even pretend to do a cooking show, teaching guests how to create the refreshments for the evening, but using the value names as the ingredients "Flour of Faith", "Dash of Divine Nature," etc.

"MEET THE MASTERS"

Hang posters of famous artwork and decorate with paintbrushes, canvases, art books, and those wooden modeling figures. Each value table should be "painted" in the coordinating color with displays from the girls. The audience gets to "meet the masters" as the young women give their presentations. Talk about how they add beauty to the world and their lives. You could also add a sculpture dimension and talk about how the Savior molds us into better people.

## PAPER DOLLS

Have the girls make life-size paper dolls of themselves and back them with cardboard or even strips of Luan to make them stand up. Have the paper dolls stand next to each of the girls' displays. Have the speaker use one paper doll to talk about the values and change her dress to match the color of value that is being discussed. Decorate with paper clothes and accessories around the room.

## MORE PRICELESS THAN RUBIES

Decorate with lots of gemstones on black velvet tables. Give each girl a crown. You could also use gemstones that match the color of each of the values such as Diamonds for Faith, Sapphires for Divine Nature, Rubies or Garnets for Individual Worth, Emeralds for Knowledge, Topaz for Choice & Accountability, Gold for Good Works, and Amethyst for Integrity. Check out www.aboutgems.org for information about gems and their meanings.

## "TITLE OF LIBERTY"

Decorate with value-colored flags. Have each girl design her own flag that represents who she is and what she has accomplished.

## "PRESCRIPTION FOR SUCCESS"

Decorate with medical supplies. Wear white medical coats, or surgical coats. Have a "doctor" give a prescription talk about how Personal Progress is good for the girls' spiritual health. Fill "GosPILL" bottles with candy and talk about Christ as the "Master Healer."

## "STAND AS A WITNESS AT ALL TIMES"

Showcase the history of the Young Women's organization by decorating with pictures and memorabilia from the 1860s through today. Talk about how the program has evolved and how the Young Women in the Church have stood as a witness through the ages.

## "THE LORD IS MY LIGHT"

Decorate with candles, torches, flashlights or even a lighthouse motif. Girls "let their light shine" as they present their projects. Talk about the Light of Christ.

## "SISTERS AROUND THE WORLD"

Share how young women all over the world are developing their talents. Have each girl's table represent a different country.

## "STAND IN HOLY PLACES" OR "IN HIS FOOTSTEPS" OR "STAND FOR TRUTH AND RIGHTEOUSNESS"

Cut footprints out of paper, making paths all over the floor. Have someone sing "I walked Today Where Jesus Walked." Decorate with different kinds of shoes and have speakers talk about the girls' soles (souls). Set up little signs on the display tables or make big posters with sayings like:

— "Don't let your goals sneak up on you!" (sneakers)
— "Being a Young Woman is uplifting" (high heels)
— "Buckle down and keep the commandments" (shoes with buckles)
— "Don't get tied up with unimportant things" (shoelaces)
— "Don't be a loafer – live the gospel!" (loafers)
— "Just open your mouth to share the gospel and converse!" (Converse shoes)
— "Never let your standards slip" (slippers)
— "Don't flip flop your values." (flip flops)
— "Get a kick out of Young Women's!" (cleats)
— "Keep on your toes with your Personal Progress goals" (ballet slippers)
— "Never let your testimony go flat" (flats)

You get the idea . . .

## TEMPLE NIGHT

Invitations could have a picture of the temple in velum placed over a picture of each girl. Present each girl with her own temple magazine. Have each girl display her favorite temple and show items that are helping her prepare to make and keep sacred covenants there.

CARNIVAL

Decorate with lots of balloons and red and white striped fabric. Set up a booth for each value where the girls and their families could play various carnival games. Guests are given tickets to play games and earn prizes, such as refreshments.

MISSION POSSIBLE

Wear secret agent attire and dark glasses. Play the music from the movie. Have a Tom Cruise look-alike introduce your secret agents (the Young Women), giving them a Code name and revealing their secret talents. Give families a mission: to go to various tables and complete certain Personal Progress tasks together. Have girls put their items to display inside brief cases.

OSCAR NIGHT

Everyone dresses up fancy and walks in on a red carpet. Have people taking lots of pictures like paparazzi (some cameras will allow you to use the flash without taking a picture.) Decorate with stars and have the young women make handprint stepping stones like in Hollywood. Award each girl some kind of Oscar-looking trophy on stage and have her give an acceptance speech. Have some Primary children sing "I Am Like A Star." Hang posters that say "S.T.A.R." which means "Stand For Truth And Righteousness."

"ANGELS AMONG US"

Decorate with angels holding signs that say "Thank Heaven For Young Women." Decorate the girls' tables with cotton to look like clouds. Leaders should dress like angels. Serve a heavenly dessert. Have someone play a harp for background music.

YOUNG WOMEN IS CHARMING

Present the girls with bracelets they can add charms to every time they complete a project. Check out www.angelicimpressions. com/simplycharming.htm#a

UNDER THE BIG TOP

Circus décor. Have chairs in a big circle where the young women come in to show their talents. Serve cotton candy.

COUNTY FAIR

Wear overalls and decorate with lots of denim and checkered fabrics. Set up tables to look like county fair booths and present blue ribbons to the girls. Play country music and teach square dancing.

HOME SWEET HOME

Make cardboard houses out of large appliance boxes. Each house represents one of the values. Paint or glue pictures of the girls looking out of the windows. Have a speaker talk about reaching our heavenly home. Talk about how Christ is building mansions for us.

WOMEN AT THE WELL

Construct a large well for the center of the room. Paint the outside to look like stones and decorate the area with urns, plants, and dippers. Wear Biblical clothing and talk about the women from the Bible who knew Christ and the lessons they learned, such as Mary of Bethany, the woman at the well, Martha, Mary of Magdala, Jesus' mother, the woman who sinned, the widow who paid her last mite, the sick woman who touched Jesus' robe. Each of the women could represent one of the Young Women values.

UNDER CONSTRUCTION

Decorate with tools, construction signs, blueprints and orange cones. Wear hardhats and overalls. The display tables could represent the YW values or the girls' efforts. Have the speaker talk about the YW values as tools to help build a girl into a woman. Show pictures of Jesus and Joseph as carpenters and talk about Christ as the master builder.

"SOUPER YOUNG WOMEN"

Design posters to look like soup labels and decorate like a kitchen with wooden spoon bouquets. Talk about the "recipe for excellence" and do a Julia Childs skit about the ingredients that help a young woman to succeed with her Personal Progress goals. Emphasize the things the young women "can" do. Serve soup and yummy rolls.

ROYALTY

Focus on the girls' divine nature and how they are princesses. Award the girls crowns and have each girl wear a queenly robe while she does her presentation. Paint a cardboard castle out of large appliance boxes. You could also make one of those cone princess hats with the flowing fabric. Read *The Paperbag Princess* by Robert Munsch.

BREAD OF LIFE

Set up a Boulangerie (French bread shop) with lots of different kinds of bread (rolls, French loaves, wheat, pita, white sandwich, breadsticks, etc). You could make an analogy of how the different kinds of bread are like the YW values or even the different kinds of girls. Talk about Jesus as the Bread of Life and how he molds us like dough to create something warm and sweet. Serve cinnamon rolls.

Use this Parable of the Bread:

*Just a humble loaf of bread,*
*But 'twas once a bowl of paste,*
*Which, if I left in that condition*
*Would have surely gone to waste.*

*But, when kneaded, it was changed*
*Into something good to eat.*
*By some kind and loving hands*
*And an interval of heat.*

*We, like that loaf of bread,*
*Must be "needed" to become*
*What the Lord desires of us*
*Ere we return back home.*

*But we cannot "Need ourselves"*
*We must all serve one another*
*With kind and loving hands,*
*Just like our elder Brother,*

*So that when we are subjected*
*To that interval of heat,*
*We'll be like the loaf of bread;*
*Warm and smooth, and smelling sweet.*

## "ADVENTURE IN EXCELLENCE"

Wear khaki and safari attire and decorate with lots of vines, bushes, and African stuffed animals. Give guests a map of the jungle (your building) where they have to hunt for the Young Women, who will be in various rooms with their projects. Play jungle music and have everyone eat refreshments in the watering hole. You might even recruit some of the Young Men to dress up like animals and walk around or chase stragglers.

## YOU MUST HAVE BEEN A BEAUTIFUL BABY

Decorate with baby blankets, toys, clothes, pacifiers, diapers, etc. Show baby pictures of the girls and have everyone guess who they are.

## "YOU ARE SPECIAL"

Based on the book by Max Lucado. You can buy discounted paperback versions through Scholastic Books. Use pictures from the book as ideas for decorations.

## FINDING COMFORT IN YOUNG WOMEN'S

Decorate with quilts and sewing objects.

## ASPIRE HIGHER

Use hot air balloons as décor using paper maché over balloons and painted soup cans as the base. Colored balloons could also be weighted to the ground with a painted rock that has the YW value printed with permanent marker.

## A WHOLE NEW WORLD

Based on Disney's *Aladdin* movie. Decorate with Persian rugs, genie lamps, Persian princess, etc. Play the movie soundtrack.

## "HEARTS KNIT TOGETHER"

Knitting is so popular now, so use lots of cute yarns and knitting décor. Talk about the "threads" that run through a young woman's life, such as the character traits espoused in the seven values. Perhaps you could demonstrate the young women's progress by teaching them how to display it with a cross stitch project, knitting, crocheting or some other art.

"IN HIS HANDS"

Make posters of hands doing different things. You could even present a slide of the girls doing different things with their hands. Superimpose a picture of each girl onto a picture of a hand so it looks as though she is sitting in the hand of the Lord. Sing the song "Created In His Image" which can be downloaded for free at www.defordmusic.com. (It talks about Christ's hands.)

"IN HIS HANDS"
*a poem for Young Women*
*by Shelly Young-Nichols*

*In His hands the power to form this mortal sphere*
*And tenderly He blessed and sent me here*
*To freely choose all for myself*
*The path of Truth and Righteousness.*
*In His hands, Heavenly Father's plan was clear*
*And at His birth did man and beast stand still to hear*
*Harold Angels proclaim the joy*
*The Son of God, this baby boy.*
*And the earth did turn and time did pass*
*His earthly ministry began at last*
*To free us all from sin and pain*
*That we might live with Him again.*
*In His hands the power to heal*
*The deaf to hear, the blind to see,*
*The dead He raised, made demons flee,*
*And calmed the storm on Galilee.*
*In His hands they drove great nails of pain*
*But they could not His power contain*
*For us He drank the bitter cup*
*That we might all be lifted up.*
*A daughter of God, of infinite worth*
*I know I have a mission on earth*
*Embrace and stand for truth and light*
*In His hands I'll trust my life.*

## "THE KEEPERS OF THE FLAME"

Use pretend torches and outline the great women who have gone before you in the Church. Share how the young women are now carrying on the tradition.

## "BORN FOR THIS DAY"

Hang baby pictures of all the girls and show how they have grown in the Young Women's program. Decorate like a baby shower.

## "HATS OFF TO YOUNG WOMEN"

Decorate a room with all kinds of hats and discuss them.

## "ON THE GOOD SHIP HEAVEN BOUND"

Show how the girls "stay afloat" as they choose the right! Decorate with a nautical theme and have parents visit different "ships" with the names of the girls such as SS Brittany.

## "EVENING WITH THE STARS"

Highlight pictures of the girls with value-colored stars around their head. Talk about our earthly mission and how the girls are heaven bound. You could also decorate with solar system images and use a planet for each of the seven values.

## "BY THEIR FRUITS YE SHALL KNOW THEM"

Fill the room with ficus plants decorated with white, sparkling lights. Hang decorative fruit ornaments on the trees that can be give to the young women by their parents who talk about their daughters "fruits" (accomplishments, good qualities). Have lots of different kinds of fruit for everyone to sample.

## "TALENTS TO TREASURE"

Send the invitation looking like a treasure map. Decorate with a pirate, island theme. Use treasure chests as centerpieces with value-colored jewels spilling out. Have the girls and their parents hunt for the girls' treasures (displays) in various rooms in the building by following a treasure map.

CHAPTER 10

## *Fun Traditions*

*"Youth is happy because it has the
ability to see beauty. Anyone who
keeps the ability to see beauty never
grows old."*

FRANZ KAFKA
*1883-1924, German Novelest, Short-story Writer*

Traditions create a feeling of unity and security. Some of the following ideas might not work in your ward or branch, but they may get you thinking about what special traditions you can begin to create continuity and wonderful memories.

MAILBOXES

You could use an actual mailbox to put little love notes, announcements for future events and handouts in. Open up the mailbox every Sunday or during the mid-week activity and pass out everyone's mail.

Another version of this is to get a big box and put file folders in it, one for each girl. Each week on Sunday or during activity night the girls can wander over to the box and retrieve their mail. At a quick glance the leaders can see who's folder is full to see who hasn't been coming very much lately. The young women can take turns being responsible for putting a surprise in the folders once a month. Keep some stationery and pens near the box to encourage the girls to write kind notes to each other or leave anonymous "love" letters to one another.

## PRAYER STICKS

Each girl writes her name on a pop-sickle stick and decorates it however she'd like. Of course, you can use something more clever and cute than a pop-sickle stick! Whenever you ask one of the young women to pray have her select a prayer stick out of a specially decorated can to include that girl's name in her prayer. The girls become more mindful of each other's needs and a sense of unity is developed when they hear other people praying for them!

## DOOR DECORATING

Decorate the Bishopric's door every month to remind them how important they are to the youth and teach them a little bit about your monthly themes. Put pictures of the girls on cut-out hearts for February, write the names of the girls on pumpkins for Thanksgiving—you get the idea. That simple act of surprise service will also draw the hearts of the young women to their priesthood leaders.

## PHOTO OPPORTUNITIES

Take lots of photos of the girls at every activity so that at the end of each year or for the graduating Laurels you can present a special scrapbook for them.

## YOUTH WALL

Mission Presidents hang pictures of all of their missionaries on one large wall where they can constantly be reminded of them. Make a board like that with pictures of all the youth for your Bishop to hang in his office.

## ROTATING CENTERPIECE

Create a lovely centerpiece for your table that can have elements that are switched each month to reflect the value you are focusing on. For example, you could create a flower arrangement in a basket where the colored flowers can be switched by simply lifting out smaller pots of flowers in a gardening basket. You could use different colored bears next to a honey pot or bunnies wearing different colored ribbons sitting in a carrot patch or a doll that holds a different colored flag each month.

GOOD NEWS

In a world full of terrible news headlines, it's nice to hear some good news! Once a month or even once a week, have the girls share with the group their good news. It can be anything from getting an A on a test to finally getting to Seminary on time. Be sure to cheer and applaud their successes and good news. Set the timer for only one or two minutes and when the bell rings everyone knows it's time for the lesson or activity to begin.

YOUNG WOMEN CHOIR

Rather than sing just any song for an Opening Hymn each week choose one song that the girls could work on and perform in an upcoming Sacrament meeting. The Young Women should be able to provide a special musical number about every other month. It's a great way for the rest of the ward to get to know your girls and it's a great experience for the young women to have the opportunity to be in a "choir." Your singing time together can be much more meaningful as well. If your group has a lot of talent and energy you could perform a value-oriented song each month so that the ward knows what the Young Women focus is each month. You could also offer to perform special musical numbers for the Relief Society and even Primary! Create a special Young Women Songbook.

YOUNG WOMEN'S NEWSLETTER

Present your girls with a newsletter each month with pictures of past activities, articles about the girls, fun polls, helpful information, announcements for upcoming events, poems about the value you're focusing on for the month, suggestions for cool websites to check out, birthdays, leaders' phone numbers, Personal Progress ideas, monthly lesson in review, and spotlights on girls who accomplish their goals or just need a little extra attention that month. Fill the pages with whatever interests your young women and encourage them to submit their own artwork, stories and photos. This could become a great service project for a young woman with computer skills!

## NEW TO YOU TABLE

Set out a table where the young women can bring any of their unwanted items from home and anyone is free to take whatever they want. The items that still remain at the end of the night can be delivered to Goodwill, Deseret Industries, Vietnam Vets, or any other organization of your choosing. You could also deliver items to your local Spanish branch or whatever special needs branch you have in your area. You can have the girls bring random items each month or designate a different theme each month such as perfume, toiletries, value-colored items, clothing, etc. This could be a one-time activity or held every month.

## OLD AND YOUNG SISTERS

Join the Relief Society for Opening Exercises once a month and have the sisters introduce themselves to the older sister sitting next to them. Have the Young Women stand to recite their theme and then have the Relief Society sisters stand and recite theirs! Simply being in the Relief Society room will help ease their anxieties once they get closer to their 18th birthday and will permanently join the Relief Society.

## CHIT CHAT

The Young Women always have so much to say to one another each Sunday and it's often frustrating to have to keep telling them to be quiet during the lesson. Once a week set the timer at the beginning of the lesson and allow the girls to chit chat as fast as they can until the timer goes off. Once they hear the bell they know their time is up and now it's the teacher's turn to talk.

## "QUILTING CORNER"

It would be fun to have a quilt set up somewhere each month that the girls could work on while they visit with one another. Quilts could be ongoing projects, made as gifts from your ward Young Women for new babies, graduating seniors, new brides, families in need in the ward or as an international humanitarian project.

The Young Women could be encouraged to work for a few minutes each week as a gathering activity while you wait for everyone to arrive and begin your official activity.

"S.O.S. TABLE"

S.O.S. stands for Seek Out Service. Each month one or two organizations are spotlighted so the girls can get ideas for service projects they can get involved in with their families or for their Personal Progress Value Project. This is an opportunity to introduce the girls to ways they can become more involved in their community and reach out to others. You can provide pamphlets or flyers with a contact phone number so the girls can follow through with their interest.

You could have one of the young women make a short presentation each month or simply provide the information on a designated "service table" so the girls can pick it up some time during the activity night. Organizations you might want to introduce to the girls could include: American Kidney Foundation, Second Harvest, American Cancer Society, Candy Stripers, local nursing homes they can visit or perform in, local hospitals they can volunteer in, etc. Be sure to have the girls check out the following websites that provide tons of ideas for service projects in your specific area: www.volunteers.baou.com, www.networkforgood.org, www. pointsoflight.org, and www.1-800-volunteer.org.

SECRET SISTERS

Have the Laurels be a Secret Sister to the Beehives. The Laurels could make cute gifts during Mutual and surprise their little sisters with things on Sundays.

FAMILY HOME EVENING PACKET

Have the young women create a Family Home Evening lesson for their families. Each packet could include visual aids, a recipe for the refreshments, songs that coordinate with the selected theme, and even a refrigerator magnet with the scripture for the week! The girls could choose what topic they would like taught and they could each bring copies of stories or visual aids to color. An easy way to start is to have them make a Family Home Evening packet each month based on the Young Women's value you are focusing on that month. Then move on to the *For The Strength of Youth* topics covered in the pamphlet, The Proclamation on the Family, or even subjects introduced in the *Proclaim My Gospel* handbook.

## YOUNG WOMEN SCRAPBOOK

A leader, young woman, or class presidency could be assigned to take pictures each week during activity night that highlight the event and the girls. A table could be set up where the girls could help create scrapbook pages using the photos from previous months. This could be a big activity once a year or quarterly and a real celebration of the past events. It could also be a gathering activity each week to give the early-birds something to do while you all wait for the others to arrive.

## YOUNG WOMEN PHOTO DIRECTORY

Digital cameras make putting together a photo directory a snap! An updated directory could be printed every six months or yearly. The directory could include phone numbers, addresses and e-mail addresses of the girls and leaders. Although this idea encourages increased communication among all those in the Young Women program, it could also be the source of security problems for the safety of your girls if placed in the wrong hands. You would need to stress the importance of the girls' safety before handing out such a list and you might even consider getting parental permission beforehand.

## DOOR PRIZES

Door prizes are fun to use to help solve any problems you might be having with activity night to reward positive behavior. For example, if your girls have a tendency to straggle in late every week you could award door prizes to all the young women who are there on time. If you want to encourage missionary work with the girls you could offer a little prize to each girl who brings a friend each month. Door prizes could also be offered randomly to add a little excitement for the evening. Prizes don't have to cost much and can even be donated by local vendors. All you have to do is ask!

## BOOK OF MORMON CHALLENGE

Each week or month the young women could be challenged to share a Book of Mormon with a non-member friend. Have the girls give a short report on her experience. Have a contest with the Young Men to see who can give away the most copies.

SISTER SPOTLIGHT

Each month a different girl is spotlighted and given a little gift. She stands in front of the group while someone tells all about her favorite things, her accomplishments and talents, and why she is so special to the Young Women's program in your ward. You could also tell the group all about her and have the sisters guess who they think it is and then present her to the group.

FRIENDSHIP BASKET

A friendship basket could be filled and presented each month to a girl whose name has been drawn out of a hat. The recipient then brings the basket filled with new items for the next month's Friendship Night. The basket could contain random gift items or things that are selected according to a theme such as coordinating with that month's Young Women Value, cute Young Women stickers and items, or things that describe the giver and her interests so that the girls can get to know each other a little better. The basket should not be a financial burden, but an opportunity to simply express friendship and sisterhood.

BIRTHDAY CAKE

Serve a special cake once a month to celebrate all of the girls and leaders who have a birthday that month. It might be kind of fun to include birthdays of current apostles, past prophets or other people in Church History.

RECIPE BOOK

The recipes for the refreshments served during the month could be given to the young women to add to their collection. A special binder or box could be given to all of the girls where they can keep all of the recipes together to remember their time in Young Women's. The girls could also submit their favorite family recipes to create a ward Young Women's cookbook. Another version of this activity is to have the girls create a simple cookbook that could be sent to the missionaries who are serving from the ward or to create one the girls could use when they go away to college.

## MISSIONARY MESSAGES

A table could be set out once a month with stationery, note cards, and markers so that the young women could write letters of encouragement to the missionaries who are serving from the ward. All of the letters could then be mailed either separately or together in a special care package from the Young Women. Similar packages of cards and letters could be mailed to any ward members serving in the military away from home or college students away for the school year.

## WALKING CLUB

Young Women could be encouraged to exercise each week before activity night by walking from a certain location to the chapel before the meeting begins. Participation awards could be given in addition to lots of applause for their healthy choices.

## GET TO KNOW YOU TABLE

Invite all of the young women to bring a few items to put on a table that describe themselves and their interests so that all of the other girls can get to know them a little better.

## CARPOOL AWARD

Everyone who arrives at activity night with another girl gets a little prize. Carpooling encourages the girls to bond, invite and remind each other every week, in addition to saving gas money and the environment!

## "LUNCH BUNCH"

This could be a huge hit or a terrible bomb, depending on your young women! Once a month the Young Women leaders could meet for lunch with the girls at their school or meet at a nearby park if the girls are allowed to leave campus during lunch. Give an award for the "Most tasty brown bag" or other goofy categories.

## "WALK AND TALK CLUB"

Girls and leaders who are interesting in walking for exercise could meet at a designated location and do it together.

PHONE TREE

Create a phone tree where the class presidencies are in charge of calling several girls who then, in turn, call other girls about upcoming activities, etc.

"WE ARE DAUGHTERS CLUB"

Create a special award for the girls who have memorized the Young Women theme. Be sensitive to any girls who may have special difficulty memorizing. This idea is meant to reward the girls' efforts rather than single out girls who haven't done this yet.

"ROSE" TOURNAMENT

If your Stake has basketball, volleyball or softball tournaments you can create the new tradition of calling them ROSE tournaments to represent "Remember Outstanding Sportsmanship Everyone!"

TEMPLE COUNTDOWN

Have a countdown for the next temple that will be built and dedicated, especially if there is one near you. Do special activities to prepare, find Pen Pals from a ward or branch in that area you can write to, make temple bags the girls can take to do proxy work.

FLORAL PRESENTATION

Have each girl choose a flower that best represents her. Create a bouquet of all the girls and use it as a centerpiece at Mutual, Sunday Opening Exercises, New Beginnings, and other special events.

"MEET ME BASKET"

Each week someone fills a basket with things that describe her. She presents the basket to the class and writes about her likes and dislikes in a special binder that remains in the basket.

"RAINBOW SUNDAY"

All of the girls and leaders choose a value and prepare a spiritual thought based on their selected value. Everyone could also be required to prepare a handout or small item to give to everyone to remind them of that value.

## "TEACHER APPRECIATION GOLDEN APPLE"

Each girl invites a teacher, coach or adult who has made an impact on her life to a special dinner. This can be an annual event that really encourages reaching out into the community.

## "TESTIMONY JOURNAL"

Pass around a testimony journal each week so that every girl gets an opportunity to write. Some girls will be able to express their feelings on paper better than if they were speaking in front of a group at a testimony meeting.

## "COLLEGE NIGHT"

Invite all of the young women who have recently returned from college to do a panel about their experiences. It's a fun way for the girls to touch base with their old friends, hear about their good experiences, and reinforce the idea of getting a college education.

## PEN PALS

Become pen pals with young women in another ward or branch far away. Join a discussion board for LDS Young Women leaders and you're sure to find someone in another state or country who would like to swap letters, ideas, and care packages with your girls.

## CREATIVE COUPONS

Award "Caught Being Good" coupons to girls when you want to reinforce good behavior (attendance, language, kindness, service, etc). They can turn in their coupon to the Bishop, who will have a special basket of treats waiting for them (which you provide him with). The Oriental Trading Company has "Caught Being Good" coins you could reward the girls with.

## SEMINARY SPOTLIGHT

Every week or month ask the girls to share one thing they learned in Seminary that week (Mia Maids and Laurels only).

## "LINGER LONGER"

The Young Women could begin a tradition in your ward to hold a monthly after-Church supper, complete with awards for best dishes.

TESTIMONY MEETING

Hold a special testimony meeting or combined meeting with the Young Men when there is a fifth Sunday in a month.

EMPHASIZE THE ARTICLES OF FAITH

Help the girls memorize the Articles of Faith. Take time each month to help girls "pass off" each one with a party to celebrate their accomplishments.

CONFERENCE BINGO

Get together during a General Conference session to watch it together. Play Conference Bingo. To help the girls prepare for conference you could play "Name That Apostle" and teach the girls a little bit about each of the men in the Quorum of the Twelve. Another fun twist to learning about the apostles is to make playing cards of them by making four copies of each picture and play "FISHers of Men" (like Go Fish where they have to collect four pictures to make a "book.")

WISE INVESTMENT

If you don't have them already, you just might as well invest in some value-colored tablecloths now! You will use them a million times and creative a festive atmosphere every time you do!

MAKE PUNCTUALITY MATTER

Start everything on time. When you tell the young women to be there at 7 p.m. they will know that they'll be missing something if they arrive late!

CHAPTER 11

*Youth Dances*

*"Dancing is a wonderful training for girls; it's the first way you learn to guess what a man is going to do before he does it."*

CHRISTOPHER MORLEY

*1890-1957, American Novelist, Journalist, Poet*

Music has a powerful pull on the youth. If the world offers them dances and music that are not appropriate, then we need to be able to provide them with some that are! Church dances can offer the youth a safe place to have fun, enjoy good music, and practice social skills. Dances can also be a traumatic experience for the "wallflower." Get involved in the planning so that the dances that are offered to your young women will be positive experiences. Here are a few tips:

- Have your Youth Committee plan the dances and give each ward a specific assignment. More people will feel involved and feel ownership over the dances' success.
- Make sure the following nine areas are included in the planning:
    1. Participants: how many, age span, leaders, proportion of male to female, dress
    2. Place: equipment, decorations, A/C, entrances and exits
    3. Time: Announce specific start and end times and then follow through
    4. Theme: Coordinate decorations, invitations, refreshments, activities, publicity, posters, music

5. Invitations and Publicity: Be clever, fit the theme, be inexpensive, announce time, place, dress, theme.

6. Decorations: Consider the walls, ceiling, entrance, exits, food area, halls, bathrooms.

7. Refreshments: Fit the theme, be creative, consider people with food allergies.

8. Clean-up: Assign specific people rather than hope everyone will just want to stay and help, make it a game.

9. Program: Opening & closing prayer, mixers, entertainment, games.

- Plan activities or games that will break the ice and get early-birds in the mood to get the party started, get people talking and mingling.

- See the chapter on Ice Breakers for tons of ideas!

- Don't forget to begin and end with prayer!

- Include opportunities for individuals to dance without a partner such as line formation dances.

- Provide breaks in the music so people can switch partners.

- Plan some kind of entertainment or floor show to add to the excitement and variety.

- Combine with other Stakes to share costs and ensure more people.

- Ask your Bishopric to call a Dance Specialist to represent your ward.

- Have all of your Young Women leaders take turns chaperoning at dances. That way they can get to know the youth better and the burden isn't on just one or two leaders.

- Borrow one of those chocolate fountains or beverage fountains so people have to linger longer at the refreshment table and talk.

- Have the youth decorate their own cookies so they stay and mingle longer.

- Avoid any music that is questionable. Do not allow the youth to bring music CDs to the dance unless they have it approved far in advance.

- If your Stake budget can allow you might consider investing in "Clean Dance" —a set of music CDs which consists of a wide variety of music—all of which is clean as well as enjoyed by the youth. About four times a year, for $16, they send an update of new songs at www.cleandance.com.

- Provide a "Request List" of approved songs on a table so the youth can look at what's available and choose what they like.

- Do a lot of mixer dances during the evening to expose the youth to more people.

- Check out the approved BYU music list at www.byu.edu.

- Offer a formal dance so that the youth who were not able to go to their prom can have a similar experience.

- Tie a heavy decoration to helium balloons to keep them anchored to the floor. Metal washers will do the trick too!

- Have a table set out where the youth can write letters to the missionaries who are serving from your ward or stake. Some youth will appreciate something to do other than dance.

- Set up a patriotic table with stationery the youth can use to write to LDS military soldiers and express their thanks.

- Set out those inexpensive cameras on each table or scattered throughout the room so the youth can take pictures of each other. Let them know you will develop the film and send the pictures to missionaries and/or post them on the stake bulletin boards in the building.

- Set up a digital camera station where you can print out pictures of the youth for them to take home and remember their fun evening.

- Open up a room in the building where you can show fun LDS movies during the dance. Some teenagers just don't want to dance but want to socialize with one another and be in the building during a dance. Others may want a safe place to hang when they're tired or intimidated by the dance floor.

- Ask your local radio stations what websites they recommend for their top twenty lists because different things are popular in different areas of the country.

- You'll laugh at this idea: have a Scripture Mastery Corner where Seminary students can pass off verses from Seminary and take a signed certificate back to their teacher as proof. Have fun activities, crossword puzzles, etc. to help them work on it.
- You can find lyrics to practically any song on the Internet. Check out lists of popular songs at www.billboard.com , www.mtv.com (total request live lists) , www.radiodisney.com.
- Have a bag of ties for the guys who forgot to bring theirs.
- Have a bag of girls' clothing they could wear over inappropriate clothing. That is nicer than turning away the girls.
- Have a corner of the room set up to make music videos to popular songs or to Church ones.
- Have an "LDS Musician Spotlight" where you introduce the youth to LDS performers and their music.

# THEMES

- Turn your cultural hall into a park by setting out park benches that can be borrowed from members. Make lamp posts out of used carpet rolls covered in black paper with flashlights in the top. Borrow silk trees and put clear Christmas lights on them. Most plant nurseries will loan you as many bushes and trees as you would like for the night if you just ask!
- "Holy-Wood: A Night of Stars." Use red paper on the entry floor to make it feel like a fancy red carpet entrance. You could even have "Paparazzi" youth take pictures of the people as they walk in. Black plastic or fabric could be hung over the door frames to make it look like a theater. Find or make Oscar-looking trophies by spray painting toy figurines on a base. Use spotlights, and signs that say "Hollywood", "Planet Hollywood" or "Dance with Oscar Tonight". Tape stars to the floor with the names of famous LDS members.
- "Formal Fun." Have the Bishops dress up in tuxedos and serve dessert to the people sitting at elegantly decorated tables. Inform the Young Men that they can only dance if they offer their arm to a Young Woman and escort her to the dance floor like a proper gentleman.

- "The Other Side of Heaven" Give everyone a plastic Lei as they walk in. Create a tropical feel with lots of raffia grass, palm trees (carpet rolls covered with brown paper and green paper leaves taped to it), paper-maché coconuts, an old boat, burlap, fishnets, blue cellophane waves, Hawaiian fabric, tissue flowers, and tiki torches. Serve umbrellas in the drinks.

- "Black and white." Everything is decorated in black and white, including food. Youth should be encouraged to wear only black and white. You could use the black & white keys of a piano as a theme, chess board motif, Dominos, black top hats and bow ties, newspapers, or cut out black silhouettes of people, buildings, and other images to post on walls. Hang signs that remind the youth of scriptures that teach us about opposition in all things such as 2 Nephi 2:11. You could also set up an area where people can have their silhouettes drawn by using a small spotlight. Tape black paper to the wall and have another person trace over the outline of the youth's head. The young man or woman could then cut it out and glue it onto a white poster board.

- Nerds

- Jamaican Me Crazy

- Almost Famous : Dress like a star

- Mad Hatter (everyone wears a hat)

- Dress Like a Rock Star

- Mexican Fiesta

- Pigskins and Pigtails: everyone wears football jerseys or cheerleading outfits.

- Barn Dance

- "50s Sock Hop." Put a Harley Davidson motorcycle in a corner with a photographer to take pictures of the kids posing on it. Fill tall soda fountain glasses with mint and pink tissue paper sticking up out of for table decorations. Scatter bubble gum on the tables for the youth to take. Serve root beer floats or cream sodas. Make life-size stand-up posters of 1950s celebrities.

- Check out the chapters on New Beginnings, Young Women in Excellence, Girls Camp, and even Youth Conferences to see if there are some theme ideas that could be tweaked into a great dance theme!

# ACTIVITIES AND MIXERS

- Have a "snowball" activity where one couple starts dancing (two kids who are enthusiastic about it and don't mind being watched for a few minutes). Then have the music pause after a few minutes and they grab a new partner so four people are dancing. After some music and a short pause each person already out on the floor grabs another person who isn't dancing yet. By the end of the song, everyone should be out on the dance floor!

- Teach them how to do the "Animal dance." Get everyone out on the dance floor and then play a song. Yell out different kinds of animals and everyone has to dance like that animal. For example, someone yells "monkey" and everyone starts dancing like a chimpanzee.

- Put balloons all around the gym as decorations, but in some of the balloons put slips of paper that have prizes written on them. At the end of the dance tell the kids to go pop a balloon and collect their prize at a certain location. Many local stores and fast food restaurants will donate prizes if you just ask them.

- Reverse dance or backwards dance.

- Ladies Choice dance.

- "Decade Dance." Choose songs from the 50s, 60s, 70s, 80s, and 90s and everyone has to dance in a style that was popular for that decade.

- "Waterfall." Everyone lines up on opposite sides of the room with both lines facing the front of the room. The lines come together in the middle where you pickup your partner and dance your way down the middle of the floor to the other end of the floor. Thank your partner and rejoin your respective lines. When you reach the front of the line meet and greet a new partner. Dance down the floor. This goes on as long as the music plays.

- "Chair Dance" You start by placing three chairs near the front center of the ballroom floor. Leave room behind the chairs for people who are not dancing to stand. Then you ask a gentleman to sit in the middle chair and two ladies to sit one on each side of the gentleman. All other dancers will be standing behind the chairs. The gentleman holds a rose and he selects one lady to present the rose to and he asks the other lady to dance. They take the dance floor and dance in line of direction around the dance floor. Once the couple stand up the remaining lady takes the center chair and two gentlemen sit down on either side of her. She now selects the gentleman to receive the rose and she asks the other gentleman to dance. They take the dance floor and dance in line of direction around the dance floor. And now the gentleman takes the center chair and two ladies join him. This type of exchange continues all through the music. The couples that are dancing around the floor rejoin the non-dancers behind the chairs once they have completed the circle of dancing around the dance floor. You can use different objects besides a rose. If it is April you may use a stuffed Easter bunny; or October you may use a mask or jack-o-lantern; February you may use a heart shaped box of candy; May a spring flower; June a beach ball; a Hawaiian theme dance a luau; a formal dance use a top hat, etc.
- Have everyone do the Hokey Pokey.
- "Spotlight Tag" The lights are turned down so that a shining flashlight can be easily seen. Two spot lighters (people with flashlights) stand in the middle of the dance floor with singles lined up behind them. You can use one person and have all singles enter mix and line up behind that person or you can use two people and have ladies behind one and gentlemen behind the other. As the couples dance by the spot lighter shines the flashlight on the couple and the person behind the spot lighter joins the appropriate dancer partner on the floor. If the single at the head of the line is a female, then the dancing female must go to the end of the singles line and the single becomes a couple with the man and continues to dance.

- Have all the girls put one shoe in the middle of the floor. The boys run to pick a shoe and find the girl whose shoe it is and they dance. Later have the boys take off a shoe and the girls find their shoes and dance partners.

- Give everyone a name tag when they first walk in. Post a list of twenty things on a big poster on the wall that says, "Someone who . . ." has a birthday in the month of April, has blue eyes, is taller than you, is in a different ward, goes to the same school as you, etc. After every slow song the youth have to find something about the person they just danced with that's written on the list. When they do, they go up to a chaperone, tell the leader one thing they learned and get a sticker to put on their name tag. The young man and young woman who have earned the most stickers by the end of the night receive a prize.

- Bring back the tradition of those old fashioned dance cards. After every dance the youth have to sign each other's cards and can't get refreshments until theirs is completely full.

- "Couple Match-Up"  When the youth arrive give them a card with half of a couple's name written on it. During the dance they have to find their other half. Fun combinations could include: Adam & Eve, Joseph & Emma, Mickey & Minnie, Sleeping Beauty & Prince Charming, Mom & Dad, Him & Her, Salt & Pepper, Sonny & Cher, peanut butter & jelly, Acne & Adolesence, etc. Sometime during the dance have the pairs go up on the stage and announce them so everyone can hear the funny combinations.

- Teach them the Bus Song, Cotton Eye Joe, or the Macarena.

- Have a floor show of ballroom dancing performers. There are many dance schools around who would be eager to do this for free.

- Invite couples to teach the youth how to ballroom dance.

- Get an old disco ball and teach them the Hustle and the electric slide.

- Have a karaoke contest at the end of the dance, during the first half hour to warm everyone up, or intermittently during the dance.

Church publications have printed several articles worth considering while preparing the youth for a dance. These articles can be located at www.lds.org.

ENSIGN ARTICLES:
"Satan's Thrust: Youth" by Ezra Taft Benson (Dec.1971)
"Inspiring Music-Worthy Thoughts" by Boyd K. Packer (Jan.1974)
"As a Parent or Youth Leader, What Should You Know About Today's Music?" by Larry Bastian (April 1974)
"I Have A Question" by Larry Bastian (July 1974)
"Do Not Despair" by Ezra Taft Benson (Nov. 1974)
"First Presidency Stresses Important Role of Music" (Dec. 1974)
"A Closer Look at Popular Music" by Lex de Azevedo (March 1985)

NEW ERA ARTICLES
"What About Pop Music?" by Lex de Azevedo (Jan. 1971)
"The Church's New Statement On Music Standards for Young Men and Young Women" (Jan. 1971)
"For What it's Worth" by Randall S. Chase (Feb. 1973)
"The Loudness Factor" by Randall S. Chase (March 1975)
"Guidelines for Church- Sponsored Dance Groups" (March 1975 )
"Some Thoughts on Song Writing" by Marvin Payne (Aug.1976)
"I Have A Question" by Newell Dayley (Jan. 1977)
"The Cream Of The Crop" (Feb. 1986)
"Mushrooms" (Feb. 1990)

CHAPTER 12

*Music*

*"Music expresses that which can not be said and on which
it is impossible to be silent."*

VICTOR HUGO
*1802-1885, French Poet, Dramatist, Novelist*

President Brigham Young has said: "We cannot preach the gospel without music." President J. Reuben Clark, Jr. declared: "We can get nearer to the Lord through music than perhaps through any other thing except prayer." President Harold B. Lee said that "the most effective preaching of the gospel is when it is accompanied by beautiful and appropriate music."

Young men and women are especially interested in music during their teenage years and can be highly influenced by both good and bad music. They are drawn to popular music more than any other kind, often because they haven't been exposed to other kinds. Good music can help the young women to behave more reverently during meetings, but more importantly, it invites the Spirit and opens our hearts and minds to be taught. Any time you use good music during lessons or activities, especially hymns, you will feel a great measure of the Spirit of the Lord accompany you in your efforts.

- Create a Young Women songbook, collecting appropriate songs in special binders that can be used during Opening Exercises or even during Mutual activities. Each girl could have her own binder to decorate or they could simply belong to your ward and be passed on to the new young women each year.

- While singing the song in Opening Exercises pass around a bag of "Friendship Fudge". The girls mix the following ingredients together in a gallon Ziploc baggie by gently squeezing the bag when it comes to them. Talk about how the rewards are sweet when we work together.

    4 cups powdered sugar
    3 ounces softened cream cheese
    ½ cup softened margarine
    ½ cup cocoa
    1 tsp. vanilla
    ½ chopped nuts

- Sing in Sacrament meeting quarterly. Your ward will love hearing the sweet voices and messages from the young women. Rather than sing a random hymn during your Opening Exercise time, practice a selected song for several weeks until you are ready to perform it.

- Play a Pictionary-type game to familiarize the girls with the hymns. Divide into teams and have the girls draw clues for each other to guess what the hymn title is.

- Have the young women go through the hymn book and create a list of hymns that correlate with the Young Women Values.

- LDS musician Michael Ballam gave a talk called "Music and the Mind" that can be purchased on cassette at most LDS stores. It has an excellent explanation of the powerful influences of music.

- Offer to have the Young Women sing to the Primary children during their Sharing Time for a special musical presentation.

- Offer to sing to the Relief Society, Elders Quorum, or High Priests during their meeting time. They'll love it!

- Have a "Meet The Mormon Musicians" night for Mutual where you introduce the girls to new and upcoming LDS artists. Listen to their music. Write the artist a letter or e-mail, thanking them for sharing their talents and musical testimony.

- Create a special certificate that could be awarded to the girls who serve as pianists and choristers each week or month.

- Have a "Meet the Masters" lesson where the girls learn about famous composers and musicians throughout history. Talk about why they think the Lord would inspire them to write such beautiful music. Discuss what they think are the elements for determining what beautiful music is.

- Invite your Bishop to extend a calling for a Young Women Music Director who can teach the girls about music, train them how to conduct, create a youth choir, organize special musical numbers during Opening Exercises, and arrange for times and places where all of the Young Women can perform.

- Teach the girls how to conduct music and provide opportunities during Opening Exercises and Mutual where they can use their new skills. To make it more fun, give each girl a glow-in-the-dark stick and then turn off the lights so they can see the pattern of 2/4, 3/4, 6/8, or 4/4 while they practice.

- Teach all of the girls how to play one Sacrament hymn. The Church Distribution has a very simple and helpful lesson book to learn how to play hymns called "Keyboard Course kit." You can even purchase an inexpensive keyboard if your Young Women's room doesn't have a piano.

- The hymnbook is often called "The Green Scriptures." Invite the girls to choose a hymn and share what gospel principles are taught by it.

- If your building doesn't have a piano to use you can purchase the hymns and even the Primary Children's Songbook on CD. It's one of the best bargains in town!

- Attend a temple pageant in your area or purchase the music from the show on CD through Church Distribution.

- Create your own ward's Young Women theme song.

- Learn to sing a church hymn or Primary favorite in another language.

- Listen to the songs that were created especially for the Seminary videos. Cassette tapes are only $1 and CDs are only $2!

- Learn to sing the Young Women song "Come Hold Your Torches High."

- Every year "Especially for Youth" creates unique songs for the youth and offers them on CD or cassette. Have the girls who attend EFY share the music and tell about their experiences there.

- Invite the Primary Chorister to come in and review some of the old Primary favorites, complete with hand motions and movements for old time's sake.

- Play "Name That Tune" using Church music for the contest.

- Teach the girls the history of how each hymn came to be. There is a wonderful book entitled "Our Latter-Day Hymns, The Stories And The Messages" by Karen Lynn Davidson that shares how each hymn was created, the inspiration that led to its creation, the gospel principles taught, information about the composer and writer of the text, and more! It can be purchased at most LDS book stores as well as on-line.

- Allow the girls to share what their favorite hymn is and why. Then have the girls sing one verse. This can be done as a "Music Spotlight" or even for an entire lesson. You will be amazed at how the spirit will touch their hearts by doing such a simple exercise.

- Instead of singing time during Opening Exercises, invite a guest from the ward or a young woman to play a musical instrument. Talk about why she chose to learn that instrument and how the spirit can be felt while playing it.

- Teach a lesson about the history of music and how it has evolved over the years and across different cultures.

- Before singing a hymn, read the scripture that accompanies it in the hymnbook.

- Make music videos to go with church music, hymns, or popular LDS artists.

- Learn the music that is printed in the *New Era* and the *Friend* magazines! Words, clipart images and sheet music can all be found online for free! There is a great index of all the songs from the years 1975-1989 at www.lds.about.com/library/clipart/blnewera_music_1975.htm

- Create a Mormon Girl Band that could perform at ward parties, Road Shows, or Girls Camp.
- Teach them sign-language motions to a favorite song.
- Invite all of the girls to share their musical talents one night in a talent show. If some of the girls don't know how to play an instrument, teach them a simple song they could learn that night.
- If you have a ward full of young women altos you could transpose some of the popular Young Women's songs and hymns into a lower key.

SONGS ABOUT YOUNG WOMEN BY LDS ARTISTS

Nearly all of these songs are available for download for a small price at www.ldsaudio.com. Check them out!

FAITH

"In Perfect Faith" by Janice Kapp Perry
"That Kind of Faith" by Hillary Weeks
"Eyes of Faith" by Hillary Weeks
"Still Believe" by Hillary Weeks
"In Whom I Have Trusted" by Charity Angel
"Faith Endures" by Alex Boyé
"Help Me Find The Way" by Afterglow
"Ask In Faith" by Jeanni Gould
"His Love Will Bring You Home" by Jeanni Gould
"Celebrate!" by Jeanni Gould
"Faith in Christ" by Lucie Gibbons
"In Quiet Faith" by Jeanni Gould
"Peace" by Jeanni Gould
"There Is A Light" by Jeanni Gould
"Life Is A Train" by Maren Ord
"Hiding Place" by Maren Ord
"Sacred Grove" written by Julie Keyser, arr. by Lindy Kerby
"Hold My Hand" by Colette Call
"Face To Face" by Kenneth Cope
"Seek The Truth" by Julie de Azevedo

"I Walk By Faith" by Janice Kapp Perry
"Faith To Find The Answers" by Cherie Call
"Faith" by Greg Hansen
"Plant The Gospel Seed" by Marilyn M. Linford
"I Believe" by Dustin Simpson

DIVINE NATURE

"My Nature Is Divine" by Janice Kapp Perry
"Come Take Your Place" by Hillary Weeks
"Lead Me Home" by Hillary Weeks
"Daughter of God" by Marilyn Linford
"Come To The Savior" by Jeanni Gould
"Child of Heaven" by Jeanni Gould
"Make Us Holy" by Jeanni Gould
"Power In His Touch" by Colette Call
"Clay In His Hands" by Jessie Clark
"Our Worth Is Great" by Julie de Azevedo
"I Am A Princess" by Natalie Martinez
"Children of Light" by Jenny Phillips
"Daughter of God" by Marilyn M. Linford (She also has bookmarks and posters with the beautiful words of this song available at marilynmlinford@yahoo.com )

INDIVIDUAL WORTH

"I Am Of Infinite Worth" by Janice Kapp Perry
"A Song To Sing" by Hillary Weeks
"When He Calls My Name" by Hillary Weeks
"He Came For Me" by Hillary Weeks
"Though I Stumble And Fall" by Charity Angel
"Gifts" by Jeanni Gould
"Sisters Across The World" by Jeanni Gould
"Song for My Daughter" by Jeanni Gould
"Bread of Life" by Jeanni Gould
"Your Love" by Lily Rubio
"Typical Girl" by Cheri Magill
"As I Do" by Cheri Magill
"The Lord Looks On The Heart" by Wayne Burton
"He is There" by Margo Edgeworth

"If Only You Believe In Yourself" by Michael McLean

"Celebrate Each Season" by Marilyn M. Linford

"She's My Sister" by Johanne Frechette Perry & Felicia Sorensen

KNOWLEDGE

"It's a Wonderful Time To Learn" by Janice Kapp Perry

"Women of Virtue" by Jeanni Gould

"Ruth's Love Story" by Jeanni Gould

"Teach A Child" by Stephen Kapp Perry

"I Seek For Truth" by Johanne Frechette Perry

"Seek the Truth" by Julie de Azevedo

CHOICE & ACCOUNTABILITY

"Choose You This Day" by Janice Kapp Perry

"Come In" by Hillary Weeks

"Gentle Touch" by Jeanni Gould

"Word of the Prophets" by Jeanni Gould

"The Journey" by Jeanni Gould

"Not Today" by Maren Ord

"Don't See You" by Lily Rubio

"Ready" by Cheri Magill

"Chasing Yesterday" by Cheri Magill

"If You Believe in Love" by Colette Call

"It's Too Heavy" by Michael McLean

"It's Up To Me" by Julie de Azevedo

"Keep Your Covenants" by Marilyn M. Linford

GOOD WORKS

"If You Love Me" by Jeanni Gould

"Feed My Sheep" by Jeanni Gould

"I Hear A Knock" by Jeanni Gould

"Believe" by Lily Rubio

"Father Forgive Me" by Lily Rubio

"The Power of His Love" by Margo Edgeworth

"Let Your Light So Shine" by Janice Kapp Perry

"Hands Of Heaven" by Julie de Azevedo

"Building The Kingdom" by Greg Hansen

INTEGRITY

"Integrity" by Janice Kapp Perry

"All My Days" by Hillary Weeks

"Sacred Promises" by Jeanni Gould

"Daughter of God" by Jeanni Gould

"Sarah" by Maren Ord

"Keep Walking" by Alex Boyé

"Build The World" by Alex Boyé

"Return With Honor" by Janice Kapp Perry

"Go And Do" by Marilyn M. Linford

"Hold Our Ground" by Julie de Azevedo

YOUNG WOMEN THEME

"Stand As A Witness" by Jeanni Gould

"Stand As A Witness" by Wayne Burton

"I Believe In Families" by Jeanni Gould

"House of Faith" by Jeanni Gould

"Sacred Promises" by Jeanni Gould

"Of One Heart" by Jeanni Gould

"Somewhere There's Somebody Waiting" by Margo Edgeworth

"I Will Stand" by Julie de Azevedo

"Arise and Shine Forth" by Jenny Phillips

"May I Stand, A Young Women's Prayer" by Greg Hansen

"My Rainbow of Values" by Johanne Frechette Perry

"The Temple Reminds Me" by Felicia Sorensen

"Come Hold Your Torches High" by Johanne Frechette Perry

"In Every Woman There Are Three" by Afterglow

"Worthy To Stand" by Jessie Clark Funk

"My Life" by Stephanie Smith

GREAT WEBSITES FOR YOUNG WOMEN MUSIC

- www.alexboye.com
- www.byubookstore.com
- www.byuradio.org
- www.charityangel.com
- www.cherimagill.com
- www.collettcall.com

- www.deseretbook.com/store/
- www.defordmusic.com. Free downloads, free sheet music!
- www.inspirationalldsmusic.com
- www.janicekappperry.com
- www.jennyphillips.com. Beautiful songs written for values and themes.
- www.juliedeazevedo.com
- www.joansowards.com. Sheet music and downloads for Young Women.
- www.latterdaysongs.com. Sheet music and downloads for Young Women.
- www.jenmagazine.com/lds-music/lds-music.asp. The site has free downloads, bios, reviews of LDS artists as well as popular Christian music.
- www.ldsmusicnews.com. Filled with reviews on LDS music, announcements, articles, links to LDS artists, and tons more! A great place to hang on a Sunday afternoon.
- www.lds.about.com/library/clipart/blnewera_music_1975.htm Great index of all sheet music offered in the *New Era* and *Ensign* magazines from 1975-1989.
- www.lds.org/churchmusic/
- www.ldsmusicworld.com. Tons of links to LDS musicians.
- www.latterdaysongs.com
- www.ldsmusictoday.com
- www.marenord.com
- www.margoedgeworth.com
- www.musicfreedom.com/ellishadlock
- www.musicfreedom.com/jeannigould
- www.markhansenmusic.com. Contains LDS rock music, downloads, firesides, and performances.
- www.sheetmusicplus.com
- www.stephaniesmithmusic.com
- www.threeofheartsmusic.com

# CHAPTER 13

# For the Strength of Youth

*"The strength of a man consists in finding out the way God is going, and going that way."*

HENRY WARD BEECHER
*1813-1887, American Preacher, Orator, Writer*

The Church pamphlet "For The Strength of Youth" is like a temple recommend interview for teenagers. If they wear out the pages in that small booklet they won't have lives that are worn out. The pamphlet was created in 1990 for the youth, but its guidelines will provide strength and protection for anyone who is trying to live in this world but not be of this world.

Sociologists with the National Study of Youth and Religion, based at the University of North Carolina at Chapel Hill, have found that religious teenagers are less likely to get involved with risky behaviors...you know, sex, drugs and rock and roll! Their studies show that the more involved a teenager is with any church the more successful they will be in school and the less likely they will be to drink alcohol, smoke or use drugs. None of that should be a shock to us, but it might be encouraging information when you share it with your youth! What a blessing it is to have a loving Heavenly Father provide us with standards that help us to live better lives.

A few excellent talks that were given about the standards we need to teach our youth and the impact this booklet has on teens, parents and leaders are:

—"The Lord's Standards Haven't Changed," *Ensign*, Sept. 1991, p. 7.

— "Navigating Turbulent Waters", *Ensign*, July 2000, p. 24.

— Earl C. Tingey, "For the Strength of Youth," *Ensign*, May 2004, p. 49.

— Thomas S. Monson, "That We May Touch Heaven", *Ensign*, Nov. 1990, p. 45.

— Vaughn J. Featherstone, "A Champion of Youth," *Ensign*, Nov. 1987, p. 27.

— Charles W. Dahlquist II, "Four Heavenly Helps", *New Era*, Aug. 2005, p. 44.

— Robert D. Hales, "Fulfilling Our Duty To God," *Ensign*, Nov. 2001, p. 38.

— Joseph B. Wirthlin, "Live In Obedience," *Ensign*, May 1994, p. 39.

— Thomas S. Monson, "The Lighthouse of the Lord," *Ensign*, Nov. 1991, p. 86.

— "Stronger Than Ever", *New Era*, Jan. 2002, p. 20.

— Harold B. Lee, "A Leader – The Champion of Youth" MIA June Conference 1968.

— Gordon B. Hinckley, "The Shepherds of the Flock", *Ensign*, May 1999, p. 51.

— Marvin J. Ashton, "Love of the Right," *Ensign*, June 1971, p, 30.

• Invite the youth to listen to John Bytheway's CD "Are Your Standards Fences or Guardrails?"

• Throw a fashion show with both the young men and young women, demonstrating modest fashions.

• Make a fun video of doing what is right.

• Invite a panel of young men to share what they like about "good" girls.

• Go to the temple and take pictures of the youth in front of the temple so they can, literally, picture themselves being worthy to enter it one day.

• "Project Runway." Have them design modest clothes with duct tape and newspaper. Choose a spokesperson to announce the model and describe the outfit being presented on the runway.

- Have each class prepare a skit about the different aspects of the pamphlet.
- Talk about how the Amlicites in the Book of Mormon marked themselves to look like the wicked Lamanites and how we mark ourselves to follow the world's fashions.
- Invite the girls to wear their mothers' wedding dresses and talk about bridal fashions and temple standards.
- Decorate the cultural hall like a wedding reception. Display wedding dresses and temples. Have a speaker, musical number, and serve wedding cake. Several weeks before the event invite each girl's parents to gather items for their daughter's wedding day and seal them in a #10 can (most Stakes have their own sealer for food storage). You can add a few things from your Young Women, including a ribbon and card that says "You CAN be worthy to marry in the temple by keeping the commandments."
- Have the girls compare the photos and articles in their favorite teen magazine with the *New Era* magazine.
- Teach the girls how to make one of those pictures of a young woman wearing a bridal gown that is made out of a handkerchief. Talk about how abiding by the principles in the "For The Strength of Youth" pamphlet will help them "make and keep sacred covenants."
- Invite a panel of college-aged kids to answer the youth's questions about dating, education, music choices, language, peer pressure, and other topics from the pamphlet.
- Set up stations that provide a short activity and handout about each of the areas addressed in the pamphlet. Have the youth rotate through the tables and conclude with a special musical number, speaker and refreshments.
- Offer workshops on all of the topics in the pamphlet that the youth can choose to attend. Use a strength-building theme by decorating with fitness signs that say things like "God's gym", "How strong are you today?" or "No weaklings allowed". Set up a table where people can arm wrestle, compare it to peer pressure and talk about how Enos "wrestled with the Lord".

- Focus on one of the topics in the pamphlet each month during all of your lessons and Mutual activities. Cover two each month if you want to finish all of them in a year.
- Visit stations to collect items that represent each of the topics from the "For The Strength of Youth" booklet such as:
  — **Agency & Accountability:** Now and Later candy. The choices you make "NOW" will determine the consequences "LATER" whether good or bad.
  — **Gratitude**: Thank you card
  — **Education:** Smarties candies
  — **Family:** Gum (to remind them that a family that "sticks" together stays together)
  — **Friends:** A gold thread. Friendship is the golden thread that ties together our hearts.
  — **Dress and Appearance:** small mirror
  —**Entertainment and the Media:** Lollipop to remind them to "lick temptations!"
  —**Music and Dancing**: a CD of some nice Church music
  — **Language:** Breath mints to remind them that their words should be refreshing to others
  — **Dating:** Hershey's Kisses
  — **Sexual Purity:** Soap
  — **Repentance:** An eraser
  — **Honesty:** A penny to remind them of "Honest Abe"
  — **Sabbath Day Observance:** A pen so they can write letters to missionaries or in their journals
  — **Tithes and Offerings:** A tithing slip and envelope
  — **Physical Health:** An exercise towel or Trail mix
  — **Service to others:** A list of websites where they can learn about service opportunities and sign up such as www.volunteermatch.org
  — **Go Forward with Faith:** Socks so they remember to have faith in every footstep.
  — **The Living Christ:** A picture of Christ
  — **The Family: A Proclamation to the World:** A letter from their parents that has been prepared for them before this event.

- Offer an "Amnesty Program" where girls can turn in clothes that are not modest. In exchange the girls could earn money, coupons, or discounts to stores that sell modest clothing.

- During each class presidency meeting have the girls take turns reading out of the "For The Strength of Youth" booklet.

- "Bishop's BBQ". Invite the girls to bring their clothes that are not modest and burn them in a big bonfire. Have a farewell ceremony and celebrate their new standards.

- It's a jungle out there! Talk about how we shouldn't "monkey around" or "go bananas" for bad media, etc. Use jungle décor and animal themes.

- Each girl is given X amount of dollars and is taken to a discount store. They have to purchase the outfit within the parameters of the budget they are given. Then, they have a fashion show. The clothes they purchased and modeled are donated to a youth in need.

- Have the girls create modest prom dresses out of duct tape. They can even enter a national contest and win quite a bit of money by doing so! Check out www.ducktapeclub.com/contests/prom/

- Family Feud about *For the Strength of Youth* pamphlet – download online at www.sharingwithyw.com

- Using a theme about kites, talk about the importance of the kite tail and string and how they relate to the church's standards.

- Encourage the girls to sign up to receive uplifting e-mails from www.ldsgems.com as well as other websites that send daily inspirational messages.

CHAPTER 14

*Youth Conference*

*"Every youth owes it to himself and to the world to make the most possible out of the stuff that is in him."*

ORISON SWETT MARDEN
*1850-1924, American Author, Founder of Success Magazine*

Youth conferences provide a unique experience for the young men and young women that they can't get any other way. The youth feel they are a part of something bigger than themselves and they gain strength as they associate with other teenagers who are trying to do what's right. Under the direction of your Stake President, design a conference that meets the specific needs of your youth. It could be an event that spans an entire weekend or just a few hours on a "Super Saturday."

Successful elements of a youth conference could include a dance, keynote speaker, workshops, service project, get-to-know-you games, testimony meeting, and lots of great food. Check out the chapter on Young Men/Young Women Combined Activities as well as the one on Ice Breakers; you might be able to incorporate some of those ideas into your conference. The main purpose is to provide a fun atmosphere that allows the youth to feel the Lord's spirit and strengthen their testimonies.

- "Road Show In A Day" Select a theme and divide the youth into small groups. You could provide props, scripture verses, songs or even certain lines they have to incorporate into their skit. The youth practice and prepare for a few hours in the day, have a potato bar or a quick meal of some kind, and then perform at night to your adoring stake audience. A great resource for tons of road show ideas is www.ldscn.com/roadshow/

• Make Mormonads.

• "Carnival of Life" Play carnival-type games, trying to win as much "money" as they can to buy prizes. At the end of the carnival, they all "die" and must be judged. They learn that it doesn't matter how much money they have or prizes they won. Another twist is to award blessings or prizes at the booth and when they die they can only take the blessings with them.

• "Skit In A Box": Divide the youth into groups and provide them with a box full of props they have to use in a skit they put together. Choose a theme, scripture or lines they must use in their skit.

• "The Amazing Race" Develop tasks small groups have to complete in order to move on to another area. This could be done in different rooms of a church building or actually out in the community. Some tasks could include a service project, memorizing scriptures, writing a skit, eating at a particular location, visiting someone, listening to a speech, etc.

• Design T-shirts the youth can wear during the conference with the theme and a special logo.

• Read the entire Book of Mormon! You can add variety by taking turns reading, listening to it read on CD, reading silently, projecting the words up on a screen, small group readings, etc. Find a cozy cabin, fill them up with great food and snacks and just keep reading!

• Go camping and do lots of group-building games where they learn the importance of communication, working together, and patience.

• Have the young women spend the night together at several local houses and the boys in separate houses. Gather during the day time for various activities.

• Along the lines of "Survivor" divide into groups and compete for "Eternity" (Immunity). As they win various challenges they can earn luxury items or even some of their own items back that you have confiscated at the beginning. Plan team-building activities rather than fiercely competitive ones.

- Pioneer Trek. Entire books and web pages have been dedicated to the details that go into planning an amazing experience for all of the youth in your stake! This should definitely be put on your "To Do" list!

# THEMES

- The Hero Within (Be sure to serve Hero sandwiches!)
- A.R.M.Y. = A Righteous Mormon Youth
- B.O.O.T. Camp (Build On Our Testimonies)
- Stand As A Witness
- Got Scriptures?
- "Seek To Thrive, Not Just Survive"
- Circle of Friendship
- Under Construction
- M.A.S.H. = "Modern Armies Standing High"
- Heaven- Don't Miss It for the World
- Stand In High Places
- M.A.P.S. "Mormons Always Progress Shiningly"
- It's a Jungle Out There
- Becoming
- Be All That You Can Be (military theme or Pres. Hinckley's Be's)
- Celebrate the Light
- One Heart, One Mind
- Fight For What Is Right
- S.T.A.N.D - Stay True And Never Doubt
- Turn Your Heart to Home
- No Empty Chairs
- Unsung Heroes
- You Are Special (book by Max Lucado)
- Bloom Where You're Planted

- Strengthen Your Stride
- Heaven, Don't Miss It For The World
- Like a Lighthouse
- Win the Race
- See Us Shine
- Feed the Spirit, Nourish the Soul
- Enduring it Well and To the End
- The Best Things in Life Aren't Things
- The Lord Is My Light
- State of the Heart
- Hold to the Rod
- The Rising Generation
- Let the Holy Spirit Guide
- The Whole Armour of God
- Making a Difference
- Beyond This Moment
- Something Extraordinary
- Fly United
- No Story, No Glory
- The Ties That Bind
- The Possible Dream
- Can't Judge a Book By Its Cover
- The Light Within
- Earth And Beyond
- Treasures in Heaven
- Got Testimony?
- Armor of God

CHAPTER 15

*Reinforcing the Young Women Values*

*"Try not to become a man (or woman) of success, but rather try to become a man (or woman) of value."*

ALBERT EINSTEIN
*1879-1955, German-born American Physicist*

When Sister Ardeth Kapp, a former General Young Women President, presented the values to the First Presidency she explained that the first three values have to do with our identity. The next four, our direction in life. Their order suggests a natural progression.

The first value is the same as the first principle of the gospel, "Faith". You can't do anything in this life if you don't have faith in Jesus Christ and His plan. All that we do is predicated on faith in the Savior.

Once you understand that, you can better comprehend "Divine Nature", that you really are a child of God. Then you are prepared to grasp your "Individual Worth" and once you understand your identity, you are ready to receive direction. You are prepared to cultivate "Knowledge." The more you know, the more "Accountable" you are for every "Choice" you make. Then you are ready to nurture others, build the kingdom, and bless the lives of others through "Good Works." Finally, when you live what you know, you have "Integrity."

Sister Kapp went on to explain that the colors used to represent the values have no significant religious meaning, but are simply used as reminders.

White is symbolic of purity and Faith. Divine Nature seems to suggest creation, the big blue sky, and all that is divine. Individual Worth should be bold and confident; red fit that feeling. Knowledge is symbolic of green and growing. Choice and Accountability, two values together, is represented by putting two colors together; red and yellow make orange. Good Works bring sunshine, happiness, and light; yellow seemed to fit. Integrity is purple, the color of royalty and righteousness.

Here are just a few ideas to help the Young Women you serve remember the values every time they see the colorful world around them:

- If you don't have them already, you just might as well invest in some value-colored tablecloths now! You will use them a million times and creative a festive atmosphere every time you do! Go ahead and make some value-colored flags while you're at it! Hmmm . . . do I hear "Value Project"?

- Use value-colored gumballs, MnM's or skittles and pick out the color for the corresponding value you're working on. Present them to the girls each week to carry out the theme or to award to girls who have completed a Personal Progress item.

- Have "Value Sunday" where the girls are supposed to wear clothes in the color of the value you are focusing on that week or month.

- Decorate a table in the classroom with a value-colored tablecloth and display other items that match the value you're focusing on during the month.

- Have the Young Women make flags or pendants to go with each value that can be displayed during the month you're focusing on them.

- Have the girls create posters representing each value that can be displayed in the room during the corresponding month.

- Invite each girl to create a collage either for each value or one that represents all of the values together. Display them in the room on the walls or spotlight one of them on an easel in front of the room each week.

- Invite the girls to listen on CD to John Bytheway's talk *Whose Values Do You Value?*

- Create a "bouquet" of pens or pencils that can be kept in a special clay pot so the girls can use them when marking scriptures, taking notes, or doing a writing activity in class. To make the "flowers" attach a silk flower in a value color by using florist tape and wrapping it around the pen or pencil to secure the stem.

- Work on a value quilt that can be given to each graduating Laurel.

- Have the girls split into groups to find scriptures and quotes by Church leaders about each of the values. Then have the groups make presentations about what they found. Have them create a visual aid to use with their presentation.

- Invite a guest to speak on one of the values each month and give ideas for Personal Progress projects that relate to it.

- Rotating Centerpiece. Create a lovely centerpiece for your table that can have elements that are switched each month to reflect the value you are focusing on. For example, you could create a flower arrangement in a basket where the colored flowers can be switched by simply lifting out smaller pots of flowers in a gardening basket. You could use different colored bears next to a honey pot or bunnies wearing different colored ribbons sitting in a carrot patch or a doll that holds a different colored flag each month.

- As a group, focus on one value each month. Help the girls to ask themselves "What do I want to become?" not "What do I want to do?"

- Create a Values Binder where she can collect handouts from lessons and organize them according to the values. When she gets ready to choose a Value Project she can refer to the handouts.

- Include a Values article in a monthly newsletter to spotlight some of the girls' Value projects and accomplishments.

- Take pictures of the girls representing the different values. Display them on your table during Opening Exercises. For example, use the pictures that focus on faith when your ward is studying that value and so on.

- Invite everyone to bring refreshments to Mutual that are a value colored food.

- Go "grocery shopping" in a pretend store and buy "values" at each booth. For example, each girl could get a cute pea-shaped handout that says "You can be a PEAcemaker in your home" or receive a small book to represent Knowledge.

- You know those fabric covers they put on seats in the Primary room to identify the children who are going to give talks and prayers or to mark where each class is supposed to sit? How about making some value-colored ones like that? I'm fully aware this is a "fluff" item. No, they won't strengthen the girls' testimonies one iota, but if you have the sewing skills, time, inexpensive fabric and desire to create a festive environment, then go for it!

- Have the Young Women choose which value they identify most with. Each girl selects a scripture, song, and makes a poster to share with the others about why she chose that one.

- Plan a "Value Pageant". Prepare a bag with random value-colored items in it that can be worn on the "runway." You could also take the girls to a thrift store to find crazy clothing for the pageant. Each girl has to pick a silly name that somehow goes with the value she's representing and prepare a talent to show off in that part of the competition. Have a Masters of Ceremony announce each girl as she models the outfits and describe the value she's representing. Add some cheesy music and a few "Miss America" type questions for the contestants to answer so the girls can really ham it up.

- "Value Scrapbooks" Invite the girls to bring Church magazines and other publications that can be cut up to create collages on a poster that represent the Young Women values to them.

- Learn how to do pedicures. Use value colors to polish the girls' nails. Talk about standing in holy places, "how beautiful are the feet of those who spread the gospel" and discuss what we can learn from when the Savior washed the disciples' feet.

- Make calendars using one of the values for each month and the Young Women's theme for the other months.

- Teach the girls how to cross-stitch a design using all of the Young Women values and create a pillow, wall hanging or picture to be framed and used in their bedrooms or in the Young Women's room.

- Teach the girls how to make a quilt using the Young Women colors and a design that highlights the values.

- Have the girls decorate pillow cases with the Young Women values so that they will think of them every time they wake up and go to bed.

- Each week present someone with a "Caught Showing Values" award.

- Instead of the regular kind of "Spotlight" on Sunday where you invite one of the girls to talk about herself or you do it for her, try having a "Value Spotlight". Each week invite a different young women to choose a value and tell how she is trying to learn about it and live it.

- Make a Value Fruit Salad using value-colored fruit held together by faith (whipped cream).

- Invite the young women to rotate through different stations that represent each of the values. Offer a short activity at each table and give them some kind of momento to remind them about what they learned as well as ideas for Value Projects that could be done for each value. Items could include such things as

  —**Faith**: A picture of the temple or a girl praying, Articles of Faith card, scriptures bookmark

  —**Divine Nature**: A crown or a mirror

  —**Individual Worth**: A cookie because they are so sweet

  —**Knowledge**: An apple, Smarties candies

  —**Choice and Accountability**: Now and Later candies

  —**Good Works**: A little shovel, a list of websites to let them know about projects they could sign up for such as www. volunteermatch.org

  —**Integrity**: A penny to remind them of "Honest Abe"

# CHAPTER 16

# *Christmas Activities*

*"Christmas waves a magic wand over this world, and behold, everything is softer and more beautiful."*

## NORMAN VINCENT PEALE
*American Christian Reformed Pastor, Speaker, Author*

The Christmas season is magical and allows for special activities that bind and create lasting memories like no other time of year. It's also an extremely busy time of year, so remember to be mindful of the hectic schedule your leaders, young women and their families have. Be careful to not over plan during the holidays, but to choose activities that are meaningful and draw the young women closer to the Savior and the "reason for the season."

# ACTIVITIES

### NATIVITY
Have the girls help plan a special nativity show by inviting everyone in the ward to bring their nativity sets to display. The young women could decorate the cultural hall or another room and pass out special invitations or flyers to invite the community. This could become a huge community event or just a fun tradition for your ward members to enjoy. Provide a written card next to each display identifying what country the crèche is from or whose it is. One ward painted backdrops to go behind the displays, played Christmas music and had people walk by Christmas paintings in between the nativity sets for a longer show.

## "BETHLEHEM EXPERIENCE"

This would be a great combined activity or even a ward activity because it requires a lot of work, but can be such a powerful experience. Turn your cultural hall into Bethlehem , complete with village shops, Roman soldiers, an inn, and a stable. Guests visit booths, taste samples of food of the day, learn how to make a craft, hear music, fill out a census for taxing, pet sheep, etc.

## FRANKINCENSE, GOLD, MYRRH

Learn about the nature and symbolism of the gifts that were brought by the wise men and show samples. Talk about things that we love, need, and want. Discuss gift-giving customs and have the girls prepare a gift they could give the Savior by creating a special box where they and their families would write a goal they will try to meet the next year or a bad habit they will "give away."

## JOY

Present a lesson about JOY:  J= Jesus, O=Others, Y=Yourself. Decorate the room with Christmas decorations that say JOY. Have the girls create two ornaments with the word JOY on it."

## KRIS KRINGLE MINGLE

Share Christmas stories and provide copies for each girl to put in a special Christmas binder she can then share with her family. Some families read one story each night while a candle burns down to another mark as a type of advent. For tons of stories check out:

—www.allthingschristmas.com/stories.html

—www.joyfulheart.com/christmas/

—www.infostarbase.com/tnr/xmas/

—www.inspirationalstories.com/christmas-1.html

## CALENDAR CREATOR

Give each girl a collection of Young Women stickers for her to put on her calendar for the new year to remind her what dates activity nights will be held, including combined Young Men/Young Women events, firesides, girls' camp, and stake events. The girls can design their own calendars or you could provide copies of photos that have been taken of the girls during the past year.

## MY FAVORITE THINGS

Everyone brings a favorite Christmas decoration to show and then tells a favorite Christmas story. Top off the night by eating everyone's favorite Christmas goody.

## GIVING TREE

If your stake or ward sponsors a Giving Tree project then you coud provide gifts to needy families as a Young Women's group. If no such project exists, then you could be the ones to start it! Get a list of needy children from your Bishop or Stake President and coordinate donations by hanging information about each recipient on a paper ornament on a "Giving Tree." Information should not include a name, but instead the age, sex, clothing size, and possibly the wish of each child. When someone wants to buy a gift for that person he takes the ornament to remind himself of his commitment and then fills out a donor card with his own contact information and puts it into a specially decorated box. That way you can remind him, collect the item, send a thank you card, etc.

## GIFT SWAP

A few weeks before your chosen activity night pass out brown lunch sacks to all of the young women to decorate at home. The girls will then fill their bags with whatever gifts they would like to give. On your activity night or Christmas party every girl who brings a filled, decorated bag then gets to select another bag to take home. Every bag will be different so its contents will be a fun surprise. The giver remains anonymous unless you want each girl to include a little note inside with a special Christmas message that identifies who she is. You might want to suggest a maximum budget to be spent on the contents.

## CHRISTMAS CARDS

Share ideas on Christmas cards the young women can make that center on the Savior and their families. Collect old Christmas cards and mail the front to your local Ronald McDonald House. They remake them, and use the profits to help sick children. This can also be a great project to start in January.

## "SECRET SISTERS"

One month before the Christmas activity night have the young women pick each other's names out of a hat to determine who will be a "Secret Sister" for whom. During the next few weeks the girls can do all kinds of anonymous service and make little gifts for the young woman or leader whose name she picked out of the hat. You may want to establish certain guidelines that limit the dollar amount of spending to encourage the girls to be more creative and so it won't be a financial burden. At the Christmas party all of the Secret Sisters will reveal themselves to each other. Often times there will be girls who go all out while others don't do very much. Be sure that it is a voluntary experience so that only the young women who really get excited about this idea will participate, while others who don't want to do it can gracefully slip out.

## "KEEPING CHRIST IN CHRISTMAS"

In all your preparations for the holidays, help the young women focus on the birth of Christ and encourage a more spiritual celebration during the holidays. Make costumes for families to recreate the Nativity story in the scriptures.

## BOOKMARKS

Have the girls make special Christmas bookmarks that identify the story of Christ's birth and can be placed in their families' scriptures during the holidays.

## PROGRESSIVE DINNER

If your ward boundaries include your church building you could either begin or end at the building. Hopefully you'll get lucky and find some girls who live within walking distance to one another so you can have them walk to each house after each course. You can have separate houses for hors'deourves, soup, salad, entrée, and dessert. You may want to limit house visits to just three homes if they're located farther away. If none of the sisters live close enough to each other to make it practical you could host a traveling dinner by using and decorating different rooms in your church building.

## TRAVELING DINNER

This is a traveling dinner that spotlights several holidays during the year. For example, the first home could celebrate New Years Eve with appetizers, the next home could focus on Easter and serve salad. The following home could serve soup or fruit and spotlight Independence Day. The main course could be at a Thanksgiving home and the final home that serves dessert would be decorated for Christmas.

## "CHRISTMAS STATIONS"

This could be a progressive event where each activity is held in a different home or else in a different room of your Church building.

Station 1 – Christmas stories

Station 2 – Musical presentation

Station 3 – Christmas candy-making demonstration

Station 4 – Gift ideas

Station 5 – Focus on Christ, sing Christmas carols

## "CHRISTMAS AROUND THE WORLD"

Focus on international décor, food, music and learning. Have returned missionaries tell about the foreign country where they served, and display items. Don't forget to include the United States!

## CAROLING

Choose several homes or neighborhoods the young women could visit together and sing a selection of Christmas carols. Bring plates of cookies to give away and have everyone wear Christmas colored clothing and Santa hats. Give copies of music selections so the girls can take them home and plan a caroling evening with their families in their own neighborhoods. Have them invent new words to familiar tunes and call them "Cracked Carols."

## "HEY, HEY, HAY!"

Create a hay wagon for outdoor caroling. Drive by peoples' homes while singing Christmas carols.

## "SUB FOR SANTA" OR "ELFING"

Arrange special service projects related to the holidays.

"TINSEL TOUR"

Choose three or four homes to visit. At each home the hosts share Christmas stories and treats.

"IT'S THE THOUGHT THAT COUNTS"

Offer a fun workshop full of mini-classes on how to make attractive gift baskets, cookie bouquets, inexpensive gift ideas, gifts from the kitchen, card making, how to ship presents so they don't break in the mail, home-made wrapping paper ideas, how to show gratitude, teachers' gift ideas, and thank you card ideas. Be sure to offer a lesson that all of the girls can attend that encourages them to focus their holiday efforts on Christ.

MEANINGFUL CRAFTS

Have the girls make a wooden nativity set they could keep for their future children and families.

"SWEET DREAMS"

Sew holiday pillow-cases for the whole year by using fabric with holiday designs.

"CHRISTMAS KIDNAP"

Kidnap the young women early in the morning by singing Christmas carols to them and taking them to a special breakfast in someone's home. Be sure to arrange this with the parents ahead of time! Only pajamas are allowed. Share Christmas stories, sing carols, make and/or exchange gifts.

FESTIVAL OF TREES.

Attend a local festival or create your own! Invite families in the ward to enter a decorated, themed tree in a competition. Coordinate with your Ward Activity Chairman to use the trees as decorations for the Ward Christmas party.

"TREE OF LIFE"

Make special decorations that represent stories and people from the Book of Mormon to hang on a Christmas tree.

## "SNOWFLAKE ATTACK"

Cut out a bunch of snowflakes to hang on someone's door anonymously and leave a plate of goodies too! The girls will get the thrill of playing ding-dong-ditch, but they'll really be spreading Christmas cheer!

## HELPING OUT THE PARTY

Help your Ward Activity Director make backdrops, props, Santa gift bags, table decorations, or anything else that is needed for the Ward Christmas party.

## WHITE ELEPHANT GIFT PARTY

Everyone brings a wrapped gift and sits in a circle. Draw numbers. The first person chooses any gift to open. The second person can "steal" that gift or open a new one. Keep going until everyone has had a turn. It's fun to make the rule that no gift can be "stolen" more than three times.

## PHOTO SWAP

If you've been taking pictures all year long you could have a scrapbooking party, slide show presentation, or photo swap.

## END OF THE YEAR WRAP UP

Invite the girls to bring all of their unfinished crafts and other projects and finally finish working on them!

## TWELVE DAYS OF CHRISTMAS

Choose a family to do the "Twelve Days of Christmas" to by dropping off little Christmas items at their house each night. You could also wrap 12 items in a basket with a note telling them to only open one item each night. Include a scripture reference for each day.

## CHRISTMAS SITTERS

Have a Babysitting Night so all parents can go Christmas shopping while you provide a "Santa's Workshop" for their children at the church building. Show Christmas movies, play games, and help the children make a craft they can give to their parents for Christmas.

- Have a cookie exchange.
- Make decorations for the Ward or Stake New Year's party.
- Make thank you gifts for the Stake Presidency, High Councilmen, and Bishopric for all of their service during the past year.
- "Are You Part Of The INN crowd or one of the stable few?" When the Young Women walk into the room drape Biblical fabric swatches around them and have them sit on cushions on the floor. Cover tables with burlap, beads, oil lamps, gords, etc. to create a feeling of being in Bethlehem. Talk about what life must have been like for a teenage girl back then.

## GIFT IDEAS

For Young Women Leaders, Young Women, or for the girls to learn how to make as gifts for others:

- "In His Footsteps" Tie fuzzy socks with a pretty ribbon and attach the following quote by Thomas S. Monson: "What will you and I give for Christmas this year? Let us in our lives give to our Lord and Savior the gift of gratitude by living His teachings and following in His footsteps. It was said of Him that He went about doing good. As we do likewise, the Christmas spirit will be ours."
- Decoupage a picture of Christ on an ornament and attach this note:
  *"As you hang this ornament on the tree, remember*
  *the man who walked the shores of Galilee."*
- "People Feeder" Buy inexpensive chicken feeders and fill with small candies.
- "Clearly See Christ" Buy clear, glass ornaments that you can insert a picture of Christ inside.
- Make candy cane bath salts by placing one cup of Epsom salt and 1/4 cup sea salt into a Ziploc baggie. Add 3 drops of peppermint oil and squish around. In a second container mix 1 cup Epsom salt, 1/4 cup sea salt and 3 drops of red food coloring. Layer the red and white salt mixtures in a clear bottle and decorate with ribbon and a candy cane!

- Using clean, dry soup cans or those big food storage cans, paint holiday designs on the outside and fill with treats.
- Create an ornament by attaching this poem to a card that has a nail on it:

"THE NAIL"

*It's Christmas time at our house*
*and we are putting up the tree.*
*I wish I could find one simple way*
*to remember Christ's gift to me.*
*Some little sign or symbol*
*to show friends stopping by*
*The little babe was born one day*
*But he really came to die.*
*Some symbol of his nail pierced hands,*
*the blood He shed for you and me...*
*What if I hung a simple nail*
*upon my Christmas tree?*
*A crimson bow tied 'round the nail*
*as His blood flowed down so free*
*to save each person from their sin*
*and redeem us for all eternity.*
*I know it was His love for us*
*that held Him to that tree*
*but when I see this simple nail*
*I know He died for me.*
—*Author Unknown*

- "Cookie Cutters" Tie ribbon to a Christmas cookie cutter and attach a note that reads, "In order for a COOKIE to come out right you need to use a pattern. We, too, in order to turn out right, need To use a PATTERN—The Savior's."
- Place a picture of Christ and an inspiring poem or quote in between two pieces of glass. You can use two inexpensive frames for the glass, using one of the frames to hold it all together. Add ribbon, lace, pressed flowers or whatever else you would like, using only a few glue dots to affix each item to the glass.
- Attach a note to a can of soda that says, "We soda-lighted to wish you a Merry Christmas!"

- Have the girls decorate bookmarks with their photo on it. Laminate them to give as Christmas gifts to friends and family.

- Nativity Set: Drop off one piece of a nativity set each night until the set is complete. Include a scripture reference with a note about that particular piece and the part it plays in the Christmas story.

- Create "Magic Reindeer Dust" by mixing some dry oatmeal with glitter in a small baggie tied with a ribbon. Include directions for the user:

  *On Christmas Eve night, when it's dark and still*
  *And Santa is on his way.*
  *Sprinkle this magic food outside*
  *And it will guide his sleigh.*
  *Rudolph will smell the oatmeal*
  *As they hurry across the sky*
  *And the sparkle of the glitter*
  *Is sure to catch his eye.*
  *So say your prayers and jump in bed*
  *As softly as a mouse,*
  *so Santa and the reindeer*
  *Can visit every house!*

- Wrap a little box or block of wood to look like a present and attach this note:

  *"This is a very special gift*
  *that you can never see.*
  *The reason it's so special is*
  *It's just for you from me.*
  *Whenever you are lonely*
  *Or even feeling blue,*
  *You only have to hold this gift*
  *And know I think of you.*
  *You never can unwrap it.*
  *Please keep the ribbon tied.*
  *Just hold the box close to your heart*
  *It's filled with love inside!"*

- Fabric boxes. Cut holiday fabric into squares or rectangles with pinking shears. Dip fabric melted wax with tongs and quickly place over a mold such as a loaf pan or bowl that has been lightly sprayed with oil. Crease the corners so they will fold nicely. Let sit until cool and stiff. Cut a piece of cardboard to fit the bottom, fill with treats and wrap with cellophane or tissue and a ribbon.

- "Let's give her a hand!" Roll out skin-colored polymer clay and then trace the shape of your hand with a pencil, cutting with an exacto knife. On the bottom write the name and date in pen, pencil or a thin permanent marker. Shape hands upside down over a custard dish and cook for about 10 minutes in a 275 degree oven. After cooling, varnish with two coats. Put treats or anything in the opened hand and wrap!

- Box of Christmas lights or flashlight: "May your Christmas be radiant and bright!"

- Create brown antlers out of pipe cleaners to root beer bottles. Add little eyes and a red nose for Rudolph.

- Make flavored oils and vinegars and put them in decorative bottles. There are tons of great recipes and instructions online.

- Strainer: "We couldn't restrain ourselves from wishing you a Merry Christmas!"

- Eggnog: "Have an udderly MOOvelous Christmas!"

- Whoppers: "We hope you have a WHOPPER of a Christmas!"

- Cookie Dough: "We think you're a smart COOKIE! Here's a little extra DOUGH for Christmas!"

- Bubble gum or bubble bath: "May your holidays BUBBLE OVER with the spirit of Christ."

- Bell: "With each chime of this festive bell may a Christmas wish come true, and bring you peace and happiness to last the whole year through!"

- Ice scraper and brush: "May you learn from the SCRAPES of this past year and allow the Savior's love to BRUSH away your tears."

- "Last Year's Snowman": A small carrot with two buttons floating in a jar filled with water.

- Music CD: "May the sounds of Christmas put a song of love in your heart!"
- Hershey's kisses in a wire whisk: "We WHISK you a Merry Kissmass!"
- Package of sewing needles: You're just SEW sharp! Merry Christmas!"
- Pencils and notepads: "Merry Christmas from our pad to yours!"
- Make cinnamon dough ornaments by mixing 1 cup of apple sauce with 1 cup of cinnamon. Add 1 teaspoon of both nutmeg and cloves. Roll out like cookie dough and cut into shapes, remembering to put a little hole towards the top to tie a ribbon through. Dry at room temperature for about a week, turning them over every other day.
- Can of Sprite: "May your Christmas be merry and SPRITE!"
- Jar of Jam: "We hope your holidays are JAM packed full of good cheer and the spirit of Christ!" Or "We just wanted to SPREAD some holiday cheer and wish you a Merry Christmas!"
- Angel ornament, pin, decoration: "We think you're just an ANGEL! May your Christmas be HEAVENLY!" Or "May you always have an angel by your side."
- Box of gloves: "This is the HANDiest Christmas present we could find!"
- Frozen pizza: "Warm up to a great holiday season, TOPPED with Christmas cheer and lots of PIZZAz!"
- Heart ornament or pin: "May the joy and love you give away come back to you on Christmas Day!"
- Measuring Cup or spoons: "Wishing you a joy beyond MEASURE!"
- Candle: "May your days be happy, your heart be light, your Christmas merry and your New Year bright!"
- Grate and cheese: "We don't want to sound CHEESY, but we hope your Christmas is just GRATE!"
- Can of soup or dry soup mix: "We hope your Christmas is SOUPer!"

- Homemade frozen rolls: "Here's a little holiday treat. rise and bake, it can't be beat! Warm fresh rolls just for you. Top with butter, that's all you do! Warm holiday greetings from us to you."
- Attach the poem 'Twas The Night Before Christmas" to a wooden or sliver spoon and write a note saying: "Not a creature was stirring . . ."
- Spiced apple cider, Wassail, or Christmas spices: "We just wanted to SPICE up your holidays!"
- Jolly Ranchers: "Have a JOLLY Christmas!"
- Joy dishwashing soap: "My your Christmas be full of JOY"
- Bag of microwave popcorn:
    *"We thought for hours what to give you for*
    *Christmas and then suddenly this idea POPPED*
    *into our heads! Merry Christmas!"*

    or

    *"Christmas comes but once each year,*
    *And always keeps us hopping!*
    *Running around here and there*
    *Christmas wishes dropping. So,*
    *When your feet are tired and sore,*
    *And you feel you should be stopping,*
    *Sit right down and have a rest*
    *While this corn is popping!"*
- Paint holiday designs and add ribbon to sisal door mats for a festive and practical gift for the home.
- Check out www.organizedchristmas.com for tons of fun ideas!

CHAPTER 17

*Combined Young Men & Young Women*

*"Today you are beautiful, choice, sweet, and pure, but tomorrow is up to you. Your future is bright and full of blessings. Youth is power. The greatest single resource that the Church has is youth."*

GEORGE P. LEE

The youth are our modern "Sons of Helaman." They are preparing to fight on the front lines of the battle for the souls of men. Our Mutual activities must have more substance than ever before. Combining the Young Women and the Young Men for Mutual activities, conferences, service projects, and other events provides them with important experiences for them to grow spiritually and emotionally, as well as develop their leadership, communication and social skills.

The poem on the following page was written by one of my Seminary students, a wonderful young man named Ammon O'Connor.

About this poem he wrote, "Dedicated to the lovely Young Woman of the LDS Church. Remember that you are a sacred daughter of your Heavenly Father and a pure example of love and kindness. Be a light not only to the world but to the Priesthood holders who look up to you to be worthy hand-maidens and loving mothers to their children. You are so special in every way because you are the key to life. Praise to the Young Woman!"

## A YOUNG WOMAN'S VALUE

*A girl is not just a growing, delicate flower.*
*She is the daughter of her sacred Heavenly Father.*
*A girl is not just warm and soft like the silken sand;*
*She is every boy's dream and vital for the life of man.*
*A girl is not just a gleam in the suave, blue sky;*
*She is a rising star that nurtures every fruit and vine.*
*A girl is not just a precious honorable mention.*
*A girl is beauty all around as she becomes a Young Woman.*

*Through Faith, Divine Nature, Knowledge, and Integrity,*
*Individual Worth, Good Works, Choice and Accountability,*
*She not only becomes a light that shines to every eye,*
*but the tear of love and joy from young men's pleading cries.*
*Oh, how a young man loves these great and marvelous examples*
*to soften their prideful hearts and make their lives so simple.*
*A Young Woman is not just an exciting expedition.*
*She is the mother of righteous warriors, as she becomes an angelic*
*Woman.*

*Through the pureness of her heart that she longs to expand*
*To share with one who's worthy to take her golden hand*
*She raises up her children mighty, bold, and strong*
*to fight through faith and knowledge, to choose the right from*
*wrong.*
*Through her humble prayers and blessed heart of humility*
*she dedicates her life towards Christ to the best of her ability.*
*Put on Earth to aid and assist in Heavenly Fathers plan.*
*Without worthy woman today, there could be no Man.*

*A girl is not just the gorgeous flutter of a butterfly's wing*
*A girl is the light for every man. A girl is everything.*

Include the youth in your planning. The more you include them the more successful your activities will be. Include your class presidencies or the entire Bishop's Youth Counsel in a brainstorming session and encourage them to identify what the ultimate goal is for each activity. After creating a big list of combined activities, have them list their top 12 (one for each month) and then determine which class will be in charge of each activity, as well as how much of the budget should be spent on each one. In a very short amount of time your entire yearly calendar can be planned, the youth will be excited, and they will have a lot of time to work out the smaller details to prepare for better activities.

There is an activity planning sheet on the Church website that is a great tool for you to use. It can be found at www.lds.org/pa/images/ym/activityplan.pdf

The following are some ideas to get your own creative juices flowing. Be sure to check out the chapter on ice breakers and games. Have fun!

### "MORMON MINIATURE GOLF"

Create your own miniature golf course in the cultural hall or even going down the hallways in the building, using various supplies from your local hardware store, giant cardboard boxes from appliances, and miscellaneous items such as sleds, rain gutters, and sports equipment. Divide into groups and have each group create their own hole. Ask your local miniature golf center to let you borrow some of their putters to use. A golf store may even have some damaged ones they'll let you use. Provide a short lesson on how to hold a golf club correctly, a gentle reminder about treating the building with respect, scorecards, a trophy for the winning team, and then let the game begin! Decorate a cake with green frosting to look like grass and with a small dab of frosting attach a donut hole to a golf tee to put in several places on the cake.

### "PICNIC BLANKET"

The Young Women each bring a picnic basket with a dinner or snack for 2. The Young Men each bring blankets and have to perform a task (shoot a basket, recite a scripture, etc.) in order to choose a basket, not knowing who brought which basket. The youth eat together with their basket partner, sitting on blankets. After they are through eating, form teams of 6-8 people who must sit on one blanket and turn the blanket over without letting their body touch the floor. Have each group perform a scripture skit, using their blanket. Talk about how the Holy Ghost is like a comforter.

## "CHARLIE AND THE CHOCOLATE FACTORY"

Teach the youth that Mutual is truly "sweet." Have a Scrumdidilyumptious Dessert Contest and invite the missionaries or Bishopric to judge. Hold an Agustas Gloups chocolate pudding eating contest, Violet Beuregards Bubble Blowing Contest, Veruca Saltz Golden Egg relay, Mike Teevee's LDS movie trivia, and an Oompa Loompa dance off. Award winners with Wonka candy.

## "RADICAL RELAYS"

Form teams and have them compete in a variety of relay races, making sure they include tasks which are a mixture of physical, scriptural, intellectual, and just plain goofy in order to benefit from everyone's talents. Be sure to include trophies and a short review on the apostle Paul's analogy about running the race of life.

Various actions from point A to point B could include:

- —riding on a broom
- —singing a patriotic song
- —reciting a scripture
- —putting on crazy clothes
- —carrying fragile items like eggs or water balloons
- —blowing up balloons until they pop
- —sticking life savors to their face
- —squirting whip cream in their mouth
- —transporting marshmallows on their nose
- —put a dangling chopstick in a donut hole without using hands
- —Put on a tie and missionary nametag
- —find their shoes in a pile of everyone's
- —put a puzzle together
- —move ice cubes from one bowl to another with toothpicks
- —pass a pretzel to all team mates using only a straw
- —crabwalk
- —sing a verse from a hymn
- —wheelbarrow walk
- —suck Jello through a straw
- —Fill out a tithing slip
- —Oh, the zainy tasks are endless . . .

## "FROLF" (FRISBEE GOLF)

Set up flags, construction cones or vertical markers of some kind in a park, parking lot, or inside the cultural hall. Teams have to see how many throws it takes to hit the flag on each "hole." It's scored just like golf. Include a short lesson on how to reach our goals and aim at what's most important in life.

## BIBLE BOWLING

Use 2-liter plastic soda bottles or plastic water bottles as bowling pins. You may want to put a little liquid in the bottom to weigh down the bottles. Line them up as bowling pins. You can use a Frisbee or any kind of sports ball to knock them down and score points. Here's where the Bible comes in (or you can use Book of Mormon verses): If someone knocks down only a few pins he/she can earn another pin by answering a scripture question that has been written down on a card and selected from a hat.

## "HOLLYWOOD SQUARES"
*(or insert the name of your town instead of Hollywood)*

To create the look of the game show in a cultural hall, set up three chairs on the floor, three more on a very steady table behind them, and three more on the stage above them all. The "celebrities" could be parents, Bishopric, youth leaders or even the youth themselves. Each "celebrity" is given a giant, paper "X" and an "O". Ask questions about the Book of Mormon or "For The Strength of Youth" pamphlet. The celebrities can give true or false answers or come up with funny answers. The players are then asked if they agree or disagree and the X or O is marked. The first team to win a Tic Tac Toe wins.

## HUMAN FOOSBALL

Cut some PVC pipe into different lengths to make it as much like a foosball table as possible. Put some masking tape on the floor to mark the lines where players need to stay, moving only side to side and not forward or backward. Put marks also on the PVC pipes where the players' hands need to stay in order to keep the spacing right. Use a soft kick ball or beach ball so that no one gets hurt. Include a short lesson on teamwork.

## ICE CREAM SCULPTING

Divide the youth into groups and provide each team a half gallon of vanilla ice cream, as well as a variety of edible décor such as pixie sticks for color, licorice, candy, coconut, pretzels, chocolate chips, jelly beans, sprinkles, etc. Give each team a large tray where they will create their masterpiece and sculpting tools such as straws, melon ball, spoons, scissors, etc. Award certificates and serve ice cream for dessert. Talk about how the Lord can sculpt us into magnificent creations if we are moldable and teachable. If you want to be able to serve the sculptures for dessert have the budding artists wear those clear, plastic gloves.

## "IRON CHEF CHALLENGE" OR "BAM!"

Divide into teams and, if possible, have the groups cook in homes near one another. Their task is to create an appetizer, a drink, a main dish or a dessert while using a "secret ingredient." The secret ingredient is given to them in a brown paper bag, which they are not to open until they begin. It could be peanut butter, lemons, or anything else you want it to be. Have everyone meet at the biggest house in one hour for judging and awards. Include a short lesson on how we are all sent to earth with "surprises" in our bag (such as handicaps, fears, dysfunctional families) and we need to make the best life we can with what we are given.

## PINEWOOD DERBY

Each class can enter an agreed upon number of cars in the Derby. You'll need a week or two before this combined event to prepare the cars. You could even invite some Cub Scouts to be the judges or to offer some tips on how to build the best car. Borrow a track from your Cub Scout Pack and provide car refreshments made by adding cookies to a Twinkie to look like wheels and candy to decorate the car. Award certificates and include an "Anything Goes" category where there are no restrictions on weight or design and any car can compete. Have a short lesson on what we need to do to prepare ourselves well to compete and be successful in this life.

## VIDEO ROAD RALLY OR VIDEO SCAVENGER HUNT

Divide into groups and provide a video camera, adult driver and car for each group. Give each group a list of scenes they are to record on their camera, assigning a particular amount of points for each one. The more they film the more points they get! Time-tested rules you may want to enforce include:

1. Only adults can use the camera.
2. A predetermined amount of points will be deducted for teams who return after the assigned time.
3. Drive safely
4. Include all team members

Ideas for things to include on your list of scenes are:

—Singing a patriotic song with a citizen
—Doing a Chinese fire drill at a stop light
—Asking someone for directions to the nearest Mormon church building
—Jogging alongside a jogger
—Pumping gas into someone else's car
—Singing a nursery rhyme with a child
—Asking a fast food place for a single French fry or katsup
—Teammates sliding down together on a slide
—Going 55 miles per hour in your car (videotape the speedometer)
—Building a pyramid in front of your school
—Driving through a car wash
—Giving away a Book of Mormon
—Talking to someone who is walking their dog
—Standing next to a headstone with the date before 1900
—Running around a track
—Making a free throw basket
—Wearing a hat that belongs to a fast food restaurant employee
—Dancing to music
—Climbing a tree
—Reading books in a library or book store
—Wrapping someone with toilet paper
—A picture of the team with the Bishop

—A picture of the whole team in a telephone booth or a Volkswagen Bug

—Sliding at home plate on a baseball field

—Hugging a fireman

—Asking someone in the meat department at a grocery store which kind of steak is better

—Someone in the group holding their favorite candy bar

—Picture of someone sitting inside a grocery cart

—Form a word using only the team's bodies

Provide a short lesson on how the Lord is always watching us and we are earning "points" by our daily deeds. After watching the videos, present awards and a bag of candy bars to coordinate with the category:

—**Silliest Video Clip:** Laffy Taffy

—**Most Fun:** Almond Joy

—**Best Teamwork:** Three Muskateers

—**Most Helpful:** Life Savers

—**Hollywood Film Award:** Lemonheads

—**Extra Effort Award:** Extra Gum

—**Highest Number of Points:** Treasures

FLOUR SOCK WAR

Fill old socks with about a cup of flour and close tightly with a rubber band. Remind the youth to wear dark clothes so that when they're hit it's more noticeable. Separate into two teams and let them go! You could play it like Dodgeball, Capture The Flag, or do several timed sessions like Paintball. When you get hit you are out. If you can play at a park that has playground equipment, trees and bushes the players will have some shelters and can create strategies. Enforce the rule that no one can aim at another's head or he is out for good. Ask the youth to come up with gospel applications to this game! There are many!

MARSHMALLOW GUNS

Using PVC pipe, make marshmallow guns and have two teams play against each other like Dodgeball, Paintball, or Capture the flag. Have a short lesson on the "fiery darts of the adversary" and how we can protect ourselves against them.

## HOLD A LIP SINC OR AIR BAND CONTEST

Some areas actually have large competitions your youth could compete in! Amazing, I know. Talk about how we shouldn't "fake it" in the Church, but live the gospel completely.

## "THEN AND NOW"

Invite the older people in your ward to play a Trivia Game based on how life was then and now. Form teams of two, pairing up an older player with a younger player. It would be fun to create a slide show that compared then and now, such as pictures from American Bandstand and American Idol. Share a short history of how the Church has grown since then and where it is now.

## "CRAZY CUISINE"

Serve a dinner but assign crazy names to the food, utensils and dinnerware. The youth can only choose 5 items and have to dine on what they are given. They can "earn" more items by passing off Seminary Scripture Mastery verses, reciting Articles of Faith, singing Primary songs or performing some other task.

## GOLDEN APPLE AWARD OR CRYSTAL APPLE AWARD

Some wards and stakes have a tremendous tradition of presenting high school teachers, Seminary teachers, or favorite coaches with this award at a fancy dinner. The evening could include guest speakers, slide show, entertainment, and youth choir. It's a wonderful tradition that creates goodwill in the community and helps the youth to express their gratitude while representing the high standards of the Church.

## KARAOKE NIGHT

Invite groups or individuals to perform. You could add another fun element to the evening by having the youth make music videos to their favorite songs.

## MYSTERY DINNER

There are many scripts you can find on-line as well as purchase in game stores. Check out www.groups.yahoo.com/group/lds-youngwomen/files/

## SPEECH FESTIVAL

Some Stakes have a great tradition of an annual speech competition. The youth are taught the elements of how to write and deliver a great speech. Then they are given a certain amount of time to prepare before they compete in the tournament. This could be quite a serious event or else the youth could speak on lighter subjects but still practice the elements of public speaking. Invite the local high school's Speech and Debate coach to share some pointers. Categories for the competition could include:

1. Expository – informational speech using visual aids and props
2. Impromptu – Speaker prepares for two minutes, then speaks for five minutes on a given subject
3. Persuasive – Speaker tries to influence how judges would vote on a particular issue
4. Dramatic Interpretation – Reading from a script
5. After Dinner Speaking – Stand up comedy format
6. Duo Interpretation – Two people read from a dialogue

## "SCRIPTIONARY"

Same rules as Pictionary, but all the clues are based on the scriptures. To add a twist, have the youth use finger paints or pudding to draw. Talk about how youth could prepare as missionaries to teach subjects using visual aids.

## "ANYTHING ON WHEELS"

The youth are allowed to compete on an obstacle course or through various relays, transporting themselves on anything with wheels (roller blades, tricycle, skateboard, unicycle, scooter, etc) Invite someone from "Meals On Wheels" to talk to the youth about their national service organization and how they provide food to the hungry.

## "DRIVE-IN THEATRE"

Have the youth make cars out of cardboard and watch a short movie in their cars. There are some great old Church movies you could watch ("What is Real", "The Mailbox") as well as some fun clips on the Family Home Evening videos.

## "WHAT'S MY LINE"

Divide into teams and give each person an identity from Church History or the scriptures or whatever you want to teach the youth or reinforce for Seminary. You could also have the youth choose who they want to be, making sure there are no duplications. The teams take turns answering yes/no questions in order to guess who their players are. The answers can often be enlightening!

## DATING PANEL

Invite parents, Bishopric, or have youth leaders answer questions about dating, creative invitations, inexpensive activities, keeping standards.

## "TREASURE HUNT"

Using all of the rooms in the church building, hide clues that require the use of scriptures. Include a short lesson on how the scriptures are a true treasure in our lives.

## "WOULD YOU LIKE FRIES WITH THAT?"

Have the youth make cars of out cardboard and then go to a fast food drive-through to order snacks. Share pass-along cards with people you drive past.

## ETIQUETTE NIGHT

Invite the Bishopric and their wives to do skits that illustrate both the wrong and right way to eat at a fancy restaurant, introduce someone, and behave in various situations. Whenever they do something wrong have the youth yell "STOP" and then the actors have to correct what they were doing.

## BOXES

Provide the youth with tons of boxes, all different shapes and sizes. Group the youth into teams and have a contest to see which team can build the most creative thing. Give prizes for "Strongest", "Most Creative", "Best Foundation", etc. Talk about what we need to build our lives, what makes the best foundation, etc. Decorate with a construction theme.

## PROGRESSIVE DINNER THROUGH THE KINGDOMS

Have a guide explain to the youth that they will be dining in the 3 kingdoms of glory tonight. The youth follow the guide who holds up a light to direct them from room to room. Teach the youth what each kingdom will be like as they experience the different rooms. To progress to each room have the youth pass some sort of test such as memorizing a scripture, singing a song, etc. In the Telestial Kingdom, a darkened room with no tables or chairs, serve crackers and cheese with no beverages. The Terrestrial Kingdom should be a room that is a bit brighter, with no tablecloths on the tables and where a soup or salad is served. The Celestial Kingdom should be a room that can be beautifully decorated with music playing and lovely table decorations with fancy china. Serve the main course and then invite a guest speaker to inspire the youth while they eat dessert. Hang pictures of the youth with their families to reinforce the idea that the Celestial Kingdom is where they can be together forever with their families.

## "WHERE'S WALDO?"

Youth have to find various members of the ward who are hiding in the church building or in a shopping mall. Disguise the identities of the hiding members and have the teams get their signatures on a card when they are successful in locating them. Talk about how we often judge people by their appearances.

## NAPOLEON DYNAMITE NIGHT

Hold a costume contest, dance contest, teach a sign language song, eat "dang quesadillas," see who can sound the most like characters from the movie and watch clips from the movie. Talk about other Mormons who have been in movies or done famous things.

## MTC NIGHT

Have contests that reinforce things the youth need to do to prepare for their missions such as sewing on a button, making a peanut butter & jelly sandwich, packing, cleaning, ironing, finding something on a map, etc. Read in Alma 17 how the sons of Mosiah prepared for their missions.

SKIT IN A BOX

Put a bunch of random props in a box. Each group could have the same items or different ones. Choose a theme they have to stick with. They have to come up with a skit using each of the props and a theme that has been selected for the evening. Award prizes for best skit, most creative, funniest, etc.

MISSIONARY COOK-OFF

Have a cooking contest where the ward missionaries are the judges. Everyone eats and then the Elders give a spiritual message about how to "feast upon the words of Christ." (2 Nephi 32:3)

"POINTS PLAY"

Divide into groups and provide everyone with a list of items they have to incorporate into a skit such as a particular scripture, Primary Song, missionary phrase, random props or talk a Bishopric member into performing with them. Award points for how many of the items they used and present awards.

SCRIPTURE DATES

Play the Dating Game but the participants have to answer questions as if they are a particular person from the scriptures. Include music from the old TV show and blow kisses at the end.

"WHOSE LINE IS IT ANYWAY?"

Play games from TV's "Whose Line Is It Anyway?" such as:
1. Alphabet Conversation
2. Scenes from a hat
3. 3 headed Broadway star
4. Skit with only talking in questions
5. Skit with only talking in song titles
6. Party where host has to guess identity of guests
7. 5:00 news with two anchors, sports caster, weatherman
8. Crazy Props
9. Hoe down
10. Greatest hits: two salesmen and two singers
11. Green screen guy has to guess what's behind him
12. Stand up, sit down, lean over skit

## "FOOD WARS"

Talk about spiritual nourishment for the soul and then have different kinds of competitions such as

1. Pie eating contest (whip cream-filled pie tins)
2. A person puts whip cream on his face while his partner tries to throw as many Cheerios on his face to stick
3. Banana eating contest
4. Lemonade squeezing contest
5. Cake decorating contest
6. Peanut butter & jelly sandwich-making race
7. Put a penny on top of a pile of flour and see who makes the penny fall when each team has to cut a slice of flour off the pile
8. Carry ice cubes across a room using toothpicks or chopsticks

## "RANDOM ACTS OF KINDNESS"

Have a contest and see which team can perform the most service in an hour. They need to return to the building with actual signatures from people they have served. Their tasks could be recorded on video or photos as proof.

## "GRATITUDE DINNER"

There are several variations on this popular event which basically divides the youth into three groups: a poor group that sits on the floor and is only given rice to eat; a second group that sits at plain tables and is served simple food; and a third group that sits at beautifully decorated tables and is offered a wonderfully lavish dinner. The evening is intended to illustrate how blessed we are and how much of the world goes hungry every day. Leaders have to decide how far they will let the youth play out the natural reactions such as complaining, begging for more food, etc. There is a great Power Point presentation that could be shown during the evening at www.groups.yahoo.com/group/lds-youngwomenfiles2/files/

## "DANCING WITH THE YOUTH"

Teach the youth different kinds of ballroom dance styles from the most formal Viennese waltz to a Latin salsa.

## "STONE COLD"

Form teams and have a contest to see who can create the most unique ice cream concoction, providing a variety of flavors and mix-ins. They have to also make up a unique name and present it to the judges in a creative way.

## "FOREIGN EXCHANGE"

Invite a family from another country or the foreign exchange students from school to share the food, music, language and culture with the youth.

## GLOW IN THE DARK VOLLEYBALL

Use black lights in the room to make everything glow. Give everyone glow-in-the-dark bracelets to wear. Spray a beach ball with glow in the dark paint or squirt some of the glow-in-the-dark liquid from those sticks inside the beach ball.

## "SOUND SCAVENGER HUNT"

Provide each team with a tape recorder, blank tape, adult leader, vehicle, and a list of sounds they have to find in a certain amount of time.

## SNORKEL AND SWIM

Go snorkeling in a pool. Plan activities that include both beginners and talented snorkelers. Hide prizes at the bottom that the youth have to find.

## PHOTO NIGHT

Teach a short lesson on photo tips, composition and light. Give each group a digital camera so that pictures could be shown that night on a big screen or printed out. Give awards for "Most Creative" and other categories.

## "CAPTURE THE FLAG"

Play the game, then talk about capturing the missionary spirit.

## BROOM STICK HOCKEY

Play on a wood floor wearing socks and use an eraser for the puck. Have a short lesson on goals and teamwork.

## "AUTO SHOP"

Teach the youth how to shop for a car, compare financing, look for safety records on-line, sell a car, and maintain the vehicle. Divide into groups and learn how to change a tire, check the oil, etc.

## "HOME IMPROVEMENT OLYMPICS"

Set up various tasks such as changing a lightbulb, changing a tire, decorating a cake, sweeping up a pile of balloons, etc.

## AMAZING RACE COMPETITION

Divide into groups and provide each one with an adult leader, car, and first clue. Set up clues around town and end up at an ice cream shop. Allow time for everyone to share their experiences and what they learned.

## "MUSIC APPRECIATION"

Invite all of the youth to share their musical talents by performing a song of their choice. Talk about the effect that good and bad music have on us physically and spiritually.

## BOARD GAME NIGHT

Set up several tables with board games. Play some music and have all the youth run to the table of their choice and start playing the game when the music stops. When they hear music playing again (after 10 or 15 minutes) they have to pick a winner and run to another table to play a different board game.

## "WEDNESDAY NIGHT FEVER"
*(or whatever night you have Mutual)*

Teach the youth different kinds of disco dances from the electric slide to the hustle. Have them dress up in 70s clothing and hold a dance-off.

## "WAX STRONG"

Teach the youth how to make different kinds of candles such as in sand, candle dipping, and in molds. Share examples in the scriptures of how people waxed strong in the gospel.

GENEALOGY FAIR

Invite your ward's Family History Consultants to teach everyone how to find an ancestor on the computer. See who is related. Create a ward family tree.

"SCRIPTURE STATIONS"

Divide into groups and have the youth rotate through various stations such as

1. Memorize Scripture Mastery verses for Seminary
2. Write letters to the missionaries or military members who are serving far away and including one scripture in the letter
3. Making cake or cookies using ingredients from the scriptures (many recipes online)
4. Highlighting certain passages in copies of the Book of Mormon that could then be given to the missionaries to give to investigators
5. Listening to songs based on scriptures
6. Creating a skit based on a scripture

"SERVICE AUCTION"

Everyone has to donate an item or service that can be auctioned off. When the youth arrive they will be given a list of all the items they can bid on. They earn bidding dollars or points by answering a questionnaire that awards them a certain amount of points for things they have done that day such as praying, reading the scriptures, hugging a parent, attending Seminary, doing homework, etc.

"OLYMPICS"

Create a new tradition in your ward by holding an annual Olympic event where youth compete as countries in various tasks and games. Hold opening and closing ceremonies, torch lighting, award medals, etc.

"A GAME OF CLUE"

Just like the board game. There are several versions of scripts on-line or you could make up your own. Check out www.groups/yahoo.com/group/lds-youngwomen/message/41

## "PIONEER TREK"

Build handcarts that could be used on a pioneer trek. Invite a guest speaker to share his experiences while participating in one. Shake cream in baby food jars to make butter. Make hot dog sticks by putting a wood block on the end of a rod. Milk a cow by filling a glove with milk and attaching it to a cardboard box cow.

## "SEMINARY APPRECIATION"

Hold a special evening in honor of the Seminary teachers the youth have.

## "SUPER SIZE IT"

Turn any board game into a human-sized version by creating giant play money and using youth as game pieces. Games that work well are Monopoly, Tic Tac Toe, Jenga (cut up 2x4s), and Aggravation.

## "ELBOW TAG"

Everyone is given a number of 1 or 2 and two volunteers are needed to start the game as "It" and "Not It." When IT tags someone they are frozen until NOT IT tags them. If a 1 and a 2 hook elbows they are "safe." Take turns being IT and NOT IT. Share a short lesson on the symbolism of the game in our life.

## "TIME WARP"

Encourage everyone to dress in time period costumes. You could choose a particular era to focus on or cover the history of the world. Talk about how the gospel was presented on the earth during those times. Sample food, music and games from each dispensation.

## "HE SAID/SHE SAID"

The Young Men plan a short "girly" activity for the girls and then the Young Women plan a short "macho" activity for the boys. Then switch!

Here are some other ideas:

- Play basketball and tie one hand behind everyone's back.
- Ice skating or roller skating at a local rink
- Hold a gratitude dinner in honor of the parents of the youth.
- Flashlight tag. Talk about the importance of light in our lives.
- Pumpkin Carving Contest, Corn Maze, Hayride
- BBQ cooking contest.
- Hold a Passover dinner and teach the youth about the special foods, customs, ceremony and symbols that point to Christ.
- Go Rock climbing for real or in a sports store that has a rock wall.
- Learn self-defense. Talk about spiritual defense as well.
- Invite an ethnic branch to share its culture with yours such as a Spanish branch, Vietnamese branch, deaf branch, etc.
- Wash car windows at the temple, leaving nice notes and thanking the patrons for attending that day. Be careful of car alarms!
- Career Night
- Play "Flashlight Tag"

Visit these websites for more fun activity ideas:
    www.egadideas.com
    www.christianteens.about.com/od/activityideas/
    www.simplyouthministry.com
    www.teambuilding123.com
    www.teenlifeministries.com
    www.pastor2youth.com
    www.thesource4ym.com

we miss "ewe"!

Beth  Taylor  allison
  Amy  Sister M.

CHAPTER 18

# Finding the Lost Sheep

*"I believe that every active member of the Church knows a lost sheep who needs the attention and love of a caring shepherd."*

ELDER BEN B. BANKS
*Quorum of the Seventy*

Class presidencies should be taught to care for each class member. In fact, the handbook tells them their first responsibility is to help each girl feel needed and loved. Help them to see all of the young women as Christ does. Be sensitive to each girl's situation. Some of the following ideas might be just what one girl needs to feel welcome and desire to reactivate while it may offend another. Sometimes you can gently press and other times you have to step back and allow more time and space. As a leader you have been given the right to receive inspiration for your calling. Ask Heavenly Father what approach to take since He knows and loves each daughter more than anyone.

"L.A.M.B."

Prepare a LAMB (Less Active Members Back) evening for all of the young women or just your class presidencies. Decorate your room with lots of lambs and pictures of the Savior with sheep. Prepare a paper lamb or a nice craft one that provides the name, phone number, address and birthday of each less active young woman in your ward that will then be given to an active girl. There is a lovely Church movie called "Feed My Sheep" that could be shown.

Talk about the parable of the lost sheep, Christ's admonition to "Feed my sheep", how the Savior shepherds us and how we can be like shepherds as well in finding His "lost sheep." Explain that each active girl will be a shepherd to the assigned girl for a designated amount of time and can do several things: invite her "lamb" to church on Sunday and to Mutual, offer to help with transportation if necessary, call her to chat, send her friendly notes, remember her on her birthday, and visit her if appropriate. Give each active girl a little lamb with a note saying "Ewe can make a difference." Make little sheep out of cotton, marshmallows or pom poms.

- Have each class Secretary write a note to each girl who is not at Church on Sunday, letting her know she was missed.

- Have class presidencies take turns visiting less actives and bringing them handouts each week.

- Ask the Ward Council to help.

- Plan a surprise party for each less active girl.

- "Baskets of Love" Fill a basket with simple things like candy, quotes, bookmark, picture of Christ, Pass-along cards, etc. Have each class presidency deliver one to the less active girls.

- Get a picture of each less active girl (from friends, family, yearbook) and paste it onto the back of an empty milk carton with the words "MISSING" in large black letters above the picture and "Have you seen me?" below. Serve milk and cookies at an activity to see if the girls even notice the pictures. Talk about how it's important to put names with faces and that when we pray for the less active we need to know who we're really including in those prayers.

- "Attendance Bingo" Make a special Bingo card for each girl and stamp it or put a Young Women's sticker on each square when she attends Church on Sundays or Mutual. Award prizes for attendance. Sometimes all girls need is a little extra motivation.

- "Star Search" Sing the Primary song "I Am Like A Star Shining Brightly" and find out which stars are missing in your class. Focus on how each star (Young Woman) shines and makes the class brighter.

- Hide a bead somewhere in the room where you meet on Sunday or during Mutual. At the beginning of the meeting show the girls a box of beads and tell them that you want to make something special with them. Look at the beads and note that one is missing. Set out in search of it. The girls will naturally join in. When the missing bead is found thank the girls for their help. Tell them that the beads represent them. Whose bead was lost? Identify the names of the girls who are less active. What you want to make with the "beads" is a loving Young Women's group. Invite the girls to make a bracelet and pick out one bead to remind them every time they see it to think of the less active girls.

- "Stuffed Chairs and Animals." Invite each girl to bring a stuffed animal that represents them and share why they chose the one they did. Attach a name tag to each animal. Each week set up as many chairs as there are young women. Whenever a girl isn't there set her stuffed animal on the chair to represent her. That way everyone can really "see" who isn't there. You could also use little lambs for each of the girls.

- As a Young Women presidency, try to make in-home visits to all of the girls, bringing them a little treat. Sing a song, chat, share a short devotional, or just "hang" with them for a few minutes.

- "Some Body Is Missing" Create a life-size Young Woman and talk about her different body parts, pointing out such things as how her HEAD should be filled with the words of Christ, her EYES should focus on her goals, her HEART should feel love towards others, her ARMS should reach out with service, etc. Talk about how some BODY is missing in your class and how we can use those body parts to help.

- "Charlotte's Web." Watch a part of the movie *Charlotte's Web* or read the story. Talk about how strong a spider's web is. Throw a ball of black yarn to one girl in the circle and tell what she contributes to your class. She then throws the yarn to another girl, holding a piece of the yarn in order to create the look of a web. Talk about how strong your class is because of all the girls' talents and love. Decorate cupcakes with spider web frosting.

- "Bedroom Inspections."  Have Young Women leaders make appointments to do "bedroom inspections" at each of the girls' homes. Wear a white glove as if you're testing for dust. Tell them something is terribly wrong and that they are missing something—Church! Invite them to attend, give them a calendar of events and a little treat, handout, picture of the Savior, etc.

- "The Lord's Vineyard." Taste different kinds of grapes and talk about how we have the privilege and responsibility to work in the Lord's vineyard. Share the allegory of the Olive Tree in the Book of Mormon or how our faith can grow like a seed into a plant.

- Create a monthly report that the class presidencies can fill out that records what types of contact were made with each girl. That will serve as helpful information as well as an opportunity to remind the girls of their stewardship.

- Recruit the help of the less-active girl's Home Teachers and Visiting Teachers (if there are some going to the home.)

- Find out if the less active girls are receiving a copy of the *New Era*. If not, consider buying her a subscription or leaving last month's issue at her doorstep when you are through with your copy.

- Teach the girls to know the details about all of the girls: WHO is not attending, WHY aren't they able to come, and HOW we can help them.

- "Paper Dolls." Create a life-size paper doll to represent each less active girl and have her "sit" in a chair each week she isn't there so the other Young Women will really think about her.

- Visit the less active girls at their places of work, their athletic tournaments or musical performances. Your presence and support can say more than your words.

## IDEAS FOR "LOVE LETTERS" AND "WE MISS YOU" GIFTS

- Attach a note to a can of soda that says "We soda-lighted that you're in our Young Women's group!"

- Box of crayons: "Add COLOR to your life! Join us next week in Young Women's!"
- Popcorn: "We just POPPED by to see how you are." or "Feel free to POP into Mutual any time!"
- Popcorn ball: "We think you'll have a BALL at church with us!"
- Dollar Store Calculator: "We're COUNTING on you to join us next Sunday in Young Women's!"
- Can of Rootbeer: "We're ROOTING for you and hope your day is going well!"
- Loaf of bread: "No matter how you SLICE it, we miss seeing you at Young Women's!"
- Basket of bath items or treats: "When you feel like a BASKET case, just remember we love you!"
- Cute little lamb: "EWE are missed!"
- Pace Picante Sauce: "Take a break and slow your PACE. We miss your face!"
- Angel pin, ornament, decoration: "We think you're an ANGEL and when you join us at Mutual it's just HEAVENLY!"
- Oven mitt with treats: "We have to adMIT you're a great young woman!"
- Toy airplane: "It's PLANE to see you mean a lot to us in Young Women's!"
- Cookies: "We think you're a real smart COOKIE!"
- Bananas: "We go BANANAS when we don't get to see you at Young Women's!"
- Squeeze-It juice box and Hershey's kisses: "Here's a SQUEEZE and a KISS so you'll know you are missed!"
- Bear-shaped honey: "Hi HONEY! We think you are BEARY sweet!"
- Gummy Bears: "We can't BEAR it when you're not with us at Church!"
- Sweet Tarts: "We think you're a real SWEETART!"
- Sparklers: "You add SPARKLE to our Young Women's group! We hope to see you SHINING brightly again soon!"

- Emory board/nail file: "It's ROUGH when we don't see you for awhile!"
- Musical note or CD: "Just a NOTE to let you know we're thinking of you!"
- Mug with hot chocolate mix: "Just sending you a chocolate hug in a mug!" or "To our friend who is so dear, we wish you this big cup of cheer!"
- Can of soup or dry soup mix: "We think you're SOUPer!"
- Heart candy: "You're in our mind and our HEART!"
- Smiley stickers: "We missed your SMILE at Young Women's!"
- Donuts: "DONUT you know that we miss you when you're not with us?!"
- Grater & cheese: "We think you're GRATE!"
- Lifesaver candy: "Be a LIFESAVER! Come help us have fun at next week's Young Women's activity!"
- Flowers: "If friends were flowers we'd pick you!"
- Lightbulb, Highlighter pen: "You LIGHT up our class when you come to Young Women's!"
- Frozen pizza: "We think you're the TOPS with lots of PIZZAz!"
- Aim Toothpaste or a target & arrows: "We hope you'll AIM to be with us at Mutual this week!"
- Pretty tray with goodies: "We TRAYsure your friendship."
- Nuts: "We're NUTS about you!" or "We have some fun to SHELL out at Mutual this week!" or "In a NUTSHELL, we miss you!"
- Starburst candy: "You're a STAR in our Young Women's class!"
- Body Glitter: "You just SPARKLE when you come to Young Women's!"
- Gum: "By GUM, we miss you when you're not at Mutual!" or "We hope you CHEWS to go to Mutual this week!"
- Bouncy ball or gumball: "Mutual is a BALL when you're with us!"
- Toffee or brittle: "Any way you break it, we miss you!"

- Cupcake or cake: "We think you're just great! You take the CAKE!"
- Mounds candy bar: "Our activity next week would be MOUNDS of fun if you were there!"
- Candy: "Everything is SWEETer when you're with us!"
- Bread: "We KNEAD to see you at church again so we can RISE to our potential!"
- Key or paper cut into the shape of a key: "You are the KEY to our having a great Young Women's class!"
- Toy watch: "Watch the time, don't be late. Remember in YW you really rate!" or "We'll be WATCHING for you in Young Women's on Sunday!"
- Leaf: "We beLEAF you will love our next Young Women's activity!"
- Basket of fresh strawberries: "You're BERRY special to our Young Women's class!"
- Picture of a radio or TV: "TUNE in for next week's Young Women activity! Enjoy the gospel in STEREO!"
- Lion stuffed animal or picture: "No LION, we missed you this week!"
- Yarn: "We're YARN'n to see you again in Young Women's!"
- Toy sailboat or picture of the ocean: "Long time no SEA! We missed you!"
- Grapes: "We miss you a BUNCH!"
- Stuffed dog: "Doggonit! We miss you in Young Women's!"
- Balloon: "We'll be DEFLATED if you don't join us next Sunday!"
- Doll: "We think you're just a DOLL!"

CHAPTER 19

## *Girls Camp*

*"The best remedy for those who are afraid, lonely or
unhappy is to go outside, somewhere where they can be
quiet, alone with the heavens, nature and God. Because
only then does one feel that all is as it should be and that
God wishes to see people happy, amidst the simple beauty
of nature."*

ANNE FRANK

*1929-1945, German-Jewish teenager during Holocaust*

Camp should be fun!! I have wonderful memories of the Girls
Camps I went to as a young woman. In fact, that's where I had my
own "Sacred Grove" experience and learned for myself that the
Church was true. God loves going to the mountains. That's where
he has talked often with His prophets and revealed wonderful
doctrinal truths.

There is definitely something about spending time up in the
mountains that allows us to hear Him better. Teach the young
women what He sounds like. Give them time to practice listening.
Being up in the mountains the air feels cleaner, the sun is brighter,
and the sky is clearer. Isn't it interesting that while we are up there
we also feel cleaner, brighter and clearer? No wonder Heavenly
Father likes to visit us there!

Often times we leaders spend so much energy planning
"spiritual experiences" for our young women that we forget to give
them time to just "be" in the mountains. Plan time for the girls to
wander around the hills and trees. Let them sit and reflect. Allow

them to do "nothing." Make sure they have time to be still and find an appreciation of God's creations. In those moments of doing "nothing" they will hear the whispers of the Lord. Did I mention the word fun? Remember to have lots of it!

# PRE-CAMP

Part of the fun of Girls Camp is the anticipation! Start talking about camp months in advance so the families of the young women can plan their summer calendar and the girls can get excited! If your ward does pre-camp certifications and trainings try to really capture the feel of Girls Camp with some of the following ideas:

- Have "Psyche Night" before camp to get everyone excited! Introduce the theme, leaders, and show a video or pictures from last year.

- Set up one of the classrooms with a mock campfire (logs and red cellophane paper with a flashlight tucked inside. Turn off all the lights and put glow-in-the-dark stars on the ceiling. Play music in the background or even sounds of the night such as howling wolves, rain, wind, crickets, etc. Set up a tent and create a fun atmosphere that makes everyone remember the thrill of camp and look forward to going again.

- Make a poster of a Young Woman camper with a pocket where flyers and updates can be put. Set it out for all of the young women and their parents months before camp starts so they will be able to plan and get excited about it.

- Refresh the rules for fire safety in the minds of the girls by making edible fires. Have them place round candies to create a "fire ring" and then place shredded coconut for the tinder, pretzel sticks for the kindling, and Cheetos for logs. Using different kinds of food review how to build different styles of fires.

- Include all of the girls in the Stake in a "Name That Camp" contest. Let them help choose a theme for your next big event. The more they feel a sense of ownership in Girls Camp the more fun it will be for them. You'll be impressed with how creative they can be!

- Have a contest to see which ward can create the best Camp Song for your next camp. Choose a theme and let them come up with a melody and lyrics. Have each ward present their song on the first night of camp and award the winners with something special.
- Sing camp songs and eat S'mores to get everyone in the mood. Try this recipe for fake S'mores

    8 cups Golden Grahams cereal (one 13-oz box)

    1½ cups Milk Chocolate Chips (or half that much semi-sweet)

    6 cups mini marshmallows (10-oz bag)

    5 T butter or margarine

    1 t vanilla

    ¼ c light corn syrup

    MELT 5 cups of marshmallows, chocolate chips, butter and corn syrup in 3-quartpan over low heat, stirring occasionally. Remove from heat. Stir in vanilla. Butter a rectangular pan, 13"x9"x2".

    POUR Golden Grahams cereal into a large bowl. Pour marshmallow mixtureover cereal; stir until evenly coated. Stir in remaining marshmallows.

    PRESS mixture into buttered pan. Cool at least 1 hour or until firm.

    Makes 24 bars. Store loosely at room temp.

- Have an early morning meeting and teach the girls how to make "Omelets In A Bag" to get in the mood for camp. Crack no more than two eggs in a gallon-size Ziploc bag and have everyone add whatever ingredients they would like in their omelet: ham, cheeses, green peppers, onions, tomatoes, salsa, etc. Place the bags into boiling water and cook for at least 13 minutes.
- Invite the girls to bring their camp items and attach cute nametags on them or use permanent markers to identify what belongs to whom. The girls could also make or sew name plates to use. If everyone's things are properly marked you'll waste less time in "Lost and Found" during and after camp.

# FUN TRADITIONS

- Design luggage tags with your camp theme on it for all of the girls to put on their bags and suitcases before they pack to go to camp.

- Make a life-size "Priesthood Pal" that could be hung in a prominent place in camp to let the girls know who the priesthood leader will be visiting the camp that day. Enlarge copies of photos of the brethren who will be visiting and change the face on the "Priesthood Pal" each day. The girls could even receive a bead or small award each time they spot the "real guy" in camp that day.

- Have a camp mascot! It could be the same one every year with a tweak to make it fit a new theme or it could be something completely different whose identity is a big secret until its unveiling at the first day of camp.

- Every hour on the hour have a bell chime that signals to the girls to hug the girl they're standing the closest to.

- Create a big poster with drawings of only the bodies of a few young women. Each day tape photos of real girls who are attending camp that year onto the bodies. Have a sign that reads "Have you seen me today?" Include their names on the poster and throw in a few photos of celebrities' faces once in awhile just to shake things up. Provide each of those spotlighted girls with some candy so that whenever anyone sees them during the day she can reward them with a piece. It's a fun way to get the young women to go out of their way to find and meet new girls.

- Have a suggestion box set out during the week so the girls know you're always trying to make camp the best it can be!

- Have a box set out for the girls to drop their daily surveys in. Surveys could include questions such as: "The highlight of the day was..." or "Someone I want to get to know tomorrow is..." or "The kindness I saw someone perform today was..." Share some of the answers with everyone the next morning at Flag Ceremony or breakfast.

- Upon arrival, each girl receives a leather necklace, lanyard, or chain of some kind where she can hang various beads or charms that she earns during the week when she gets up on time, passes off a certification, goes out of her way to be kind and helpful, does chores, sings you a song, or whatever behaviors you want to reward.

- Invite each ward to provide a motivational poster that will be hung each day somewhere in camp. It could include a quote, drawings, photos and the name of the ward that designed it.

- Pass out coupons for a free extra helping of dessert, an extra craft, or some other reward for good behavior.

- Induct members into the "Polar Bear Club" when they can swim in the pool, lake or whatever body of water you have near your camp at 6:00 in the morning.

- Award "Caught Being Good" coupons whenever you catch a girl being particularly helpful, obedient, kind, cleaning up the camp, or doing whatever behavior you want to reinforce. Create a "store" where the girls can spend their coupons on fun treats and momentos.

- Rotate groups to take turns presenting a spiritual thought before each meal.

- Create a camp song that is unique to your ward or Stake.

- Organize "Secret sisters" so the young women can be serving one another all week.

- Hold a "Let Your Hair Down" contest to see who can do the coolest braids, funniest hair-dos, and most creative styles. You could present one girl each day with the "Hair Today, Gone Tomorrow" award.

- Have a "Pillow Fairy" leave "Pillow Ponderings" (spiritual thoughts) written on scented paper and left on the girls' pillows each night.

- Design those Lance Armstrong silicone bracelets with your camp's theme written on them.

- Decorate special bathroom flip flops, visors, T-shirts or canvas bags that can be given to the girls before they come to camp.

- Bring a dancing Elmo or some other cute moveable creature and begin a tradition that when it comes out the girls have to dance with it.

- Play lots of Ice Breaker games.

- Plan a Post-camp fireside to share pictures, show a video or slides, and a time for all the girls to connect with their new friends from the Stake and relive the magic of camp.

- Create a D.E.A.R. time (Drop Everything And Read). For example, at 3:30 every day, everyone stops what they are doing and reads the scriptures for 10-20 minutes. You could also sound a horn or ring a bell randomly throughout the day to make it a daily surprise for the girls.

- Design special walking trails that have assigned stopping spots where stories, quotes, and pictures are posted. You can leave it up the whole week or set it up for one special day or time.

- Create a "Festival of Trees" where each group of girls or ward gets to decorate a tree along a pathway. Choose an overall theme or let the decorators really get creative and come up with one on their own. There could be awards for the various trees.

- Supply each girl with daily journal sheets and a writing time so she can record her thoughts and experiences before she goes to bed each night.

- Have a "Value walk" where value-colored stones are placed on a pathway and quotes and story handouts could be collected by the girls who visit.

- Provide lots of choices for the girls and time to rotate through stations.

- Choose some scriptures the girls have to memorize each day. When they pass it off they get to have a fingernail painted in a value color. By the end of camp, if they have memorized all the scriptures, all of their fingernails will be painted in the Young Women value colors.

- Have the girls make a Memory Book. Each day your camp photographer can take photos and print out pictures they can add to their pages.

- Hold a Nephite/Lamanite battle. Invite the girls to wear costumes or the camp could provide inexpensive Indian headdresses. The girls could bring or else you could provide them with water guns, shaving cream, silly string, etc. Divide the group and have the Nephites line up on one side of a large, outdoor field and put the Lamanites on the other side. Let the girls loose and enjoy the battle! Before the battle have certain adult or youth leaders assigned to incur battle wounds that all of the other girls have to take care of in order to learn or review first aid skills.

- Invite each girl to paint her name on a rock and create a special path for everyone in the camp that leads to the mess hall or the campfire ring at night time. It could even be a fancy opening and closing ceremony as the girls place and remove their rocks from the walkway.

- Make hand print cement stepping stones to always keep at the camp or else as a momento for the girls to take home and use in their own garden.

- Create a pinecone necklace tradition that includes a ceremony where someone talks about seeds of faith and likens them to the seeds left in the ground by pinecones and how both can become quite large when planted in fertile soil. Have the girls create their own necklace or award them with one when they have completed a particular task.

- Girls may be suffering withdrawals from their computers and text messaging phones, so you can offer "GIRLS ONLINE." Each girl gets a clothespin with her name on it that will be hung on a clothesline. They can clip notes and Secret Sister surprises to the clothespin any time during the week.

- Provide special recognition awards to the girls and leaders either at the end of Girls Camp or soon afterwards.

- "New News" Create a special chalkboard, poster or Dry Erase marker board where updated news can be posted during the day. Include information on weather, meals, classes, daily schedule, guests visiting the camp that day, Lost and Found, etc.

- Make a list of specific things each counselor, leader, Camp Mom, and parent is supposed to do before, during, and after camp so there is no misunderstanding of what is expected.
- Give lots of daily awards!
- "Secret Ward" If your camp consists of several wards in a Stake, then have them draw names to be a Secret Pal to each other, doing special and anonymous things for one another during the week.
- Invite each ward to create their own flag and cheer.
- Create the "Golden Peach" award by providing a written test or physical tasks any camper can participate in during the week. The information could be about nature, attitude, kindness, cleanliness or anything else you want to reinforce. The reward is a peach pit spray painted gold and strung onto a necklace.
- Another award could be called "Mother Nature" and is aimed at rewarding campers who go the extra mile to learn about the nature around them. The award could be a wreath made out of flowers and leaves.
- "Good Deed Beads" Have girls earn value-colored beads for things they do during the week.
- Give each leader a basket, bucket, or "bag of tricks" filled with scripture crossword puzzles, lanyard crafts, stories, stationery, etc. to help fill constructive time with the girls, if needed, and possibly serve as a back-up plan in case something goes wrong with the group's original plans.
- Offer a station where girls can wander by any time to work on crossword puzzles, actual puzzles, write secret notes to each other, etc.
- Give each girl a lanyard craft or something simple they can keep in their pockets and pull out during the week to work on.
- Help the girls prepare a 72 hour emergency "kit in a can" they can take home.
- Provide first aid supplies the girls can assemble to create their own emergency first aid kit that they can take home and keep in their cars or at home.

- Create a Girls Camp scrapbook that can be set out on display each year.
- Video tape as many girls as possible during the week. Show it during the Closing Ceremony or leave it running in a corner somewhere when parents come to pick up girls on the last day and everyone is gathering their belongings.
- Present the "Golden Plunger" Award to the group of girls who maintains the cleanest camp site each day.
- On a hot day provide big bowls of soapy water so the girls can have fun making different kinds of bubbles. Mix 1/2 cup of Joy or Dawn detergent with 5 cups of water. Adding 2 tablespoons of glycerine to the water makes stronger bubbles. Give them metal coat hangers they can bend around to create interesting shapes and sizes. Be prepared for it to turn into a water fight!
- "Camp Value Snakes" Have leaders carry a plastic or fabric snake (or frog or whatever creature fits into your theme) all week where you can fit gumballs or other value-colored treats in its mouth. Girls are invited to earn a gumball by popping out the candy and then doing something that corresponds to the value color. They must return and report on what they've done before they can earn another one.
- Offer a sunrise service or devotional.
- Have an annual Pajama Fashion Show. Shine flashlights on the girls as they model their PJ's down a makeshift runway. Have someone read the description of the sleepwear that each girl has written ahead of time. The goofier the better.
- Give every girl a disposable camera she can use during the week and encourage her to post her pictures on your camp website after she develops the film when she gets home from camp.
- Hold an evening "Debriefing" for leaders to share what they learned that day, what they would do differently, highlights, and things to remember for the next day.
- Create a tradition of using the Laurels to be the camp leaders, giving them lots of perks so the younger girls will look forward to it when they get older.

- Provide a journal, a snack, and water to each girl so she can have a "solo" experience. Encourage them to read about Enos' "solo experience" in the Book of Mormon. Make sure the girls are far apart from one another, but also safe.

Remind her to bring her scriptures. You might even supply them with a list of questions to ask themselves as they have a conversation with God such as:

  —One improvement I'll make in my life:
  —The important role I play in my family is:
  —I feel the most important thing I can be doing in my life right now is:
  —A spiritual lesson I learned at camp:
  —What I enjoyed most today:
  —Things I am grateful for:
  —My mission in life is:
  —Today I noticed:

- Pair up two girls to become "Good Buddies" all week and let them take care of one another. Provide them with Good Buddy bags and miscellaneous items they can give to one another when needed.

- Meet every morning for devotional and instructions and every night for singing and group prayer.

- Having individual and group scripture study in tents before bed is a good way to settle the camp down.

- The daily flag ceremony can be a wonderful patriotic and spiritual experience for the girls. Have them listen to this incredible recorded story and music about our nation's flag: at www.tecenv.com/thompson/entertainment.htm

- Give each girl a small bag they can loop onto their shorts and carry with them all week. Each time they go to a class, workshop or evening presentation they are given some small token to remember it by and keep in their bag.

- Pass out awards such as "Most Cooperative Camper", "Miss Congeniality", "Early Bird", etc. They could be certificates, trophies or some other award that stays with the girl or gets passed on to another set of girls next year.

- Give each girl a vest, belt, hat or something they can wear all week. When they memorize scriptures or do whatever else you want to reinforce they earn a patch or pin to add to their attire.
- Hot chocolate sampling event in the early morning or after the evening campfire program.
- Set up a trail-mix tasters table.
- At the end of the week have all campers nominate and vote for "Mosts" award recipients: Most Friendly, Most Mosquito Bites, Most Spirited, Most Enthusiastic Singer, etc.
- Be sure to have a Staff Appreciation Party before, during or after camp to let them know how truly valuable they are.
- Make a stuffed camper and change her outfit to reflect the activities and theme for each day.
- If your stake does all of the planning, you can still arrange a few surprises of things you know your girls especially love, such as an extra craft they can keep in their pockets and work on during "bored" moments, a smaller ward testimony meeting, or special awards.
- Make camp fun!

# THEMES

Be sure to let all of the campers know weeks before camp starts what the theme will be so they can begin working on their skits and gathering items from home that coordinate.

- Catch the Spirit (sports)
- Change of Heart
- Celebrate the Light (spotlight, highlight, flashlight, candles)
- A Year of Values (value colors that match certain holidays)
- Road Trip – On the Way to Eternity (vehicles, traffic signs)
- Fly United (airplane)
- Camp O-Lot (Camelot theme)
- By Their Fruits Ye Shall Know Them (Fruits, tropical)
- Superheroes

- Cartoons
- A Royal Army (military, missionary, or queens)
- Our Royal Family (medieval queens)
- Round Up (cowgirls)
- A League of Our Own (baseball)
- Sailing Home (nautical)
- Got Worth? (milk, ads, TV)
- Go The Distance (Field of Dreams, baseball)
- The Reel Life (movies)
- Out of the darkness and into the light
- Boot Camp (military theme) 1-888-864-9105 for personalized dog tags
- Build On Our Testimonies (BOOT Camp or construction theme)
- The Church around the world (different countries)
- It's a Jungle out there!
- In Tune (Broadway musicals)
- BUGS = Building Up Girls' Standards
- Sweet is the work (candy)
- Leave No One Behind (military theme)
- SOS = nautical (Save Our Sisters or Source of Strength)
- Stripling Warriors
- Anchored to Christ (nautical)
- Quest for the Best or Quest for Christ (medieval)
- Crowning Glory (medieval)
- Survivor (like the TV show, complete with buffs, torches, etc,)
- Hold Your Torches High
- A Season of Joy (winter, spring, fall, summer)
- Angels Among Us
- Check out other theme ideas in the chapters for New Beginnings, Young Women in Excellence, and Youth Conference.

- University of Eternity (collegiate theme)
- Stand As A Witness (missionary)
- All Times and All Places (around the world or history of the world)
- Circle of Friendship
- Song Of The Heart
- Hands of Heaven
- Reach For The Stars
- Olympics
- Fairy Tale Princesses
- Field of Dreams (baseball)
- The Promised Land

# HIKES

- Do an "Amazing Race" where they have to hike, raft, climb, canoe, etc. to gather clues and reach a final destination.
- Have the girls carry a hike journal and answer various questions as they go, such as locating certain items, reading a scripture that relates, describing a particular rock formation, etc. If they answer all of the questions they earn a special reward.
- Give each girl an egg to carry on her hike and tell her it represents something really important. During the hike have various people try to get the girls to drop their eggs, give them away or toss them into the woods. Take note of all the interesting things the girls will say and do. At the end of the hike tell them the egg represents their testimony and talk about all of the influences in the world that try to make us give up or lose our testimony. Use all kinds of analogies about cracked eggs, Humpty Dumpty, staying "sunny side up", etc.
- Provide a ripe, juicy piece of fruit after a long, hot hike. Talk about Lehi's dream and how delicious that fruit was. Teach the symbolism of the vision and how sweet the love of God is.

- While the girls walk they can be learning songs for the evening campfire such as this one to the tune "In Our Lovely Deseret":

*In our lovely summer camp, where the ground is always damp*
*We have pitched our little pup tents all around.*
*There's a beetle, and a bug,*
*Here's our TV. Where's the plug?*
*We can watch it, but it doesn't make a sound.*

*All the Young Women are camping,*
*See our fire burning bright.*
*We can hike and swim and play,*
*We can eat three meals a day,*
*And we never, ever go to sleep at night.*

*All the cooks in camp are lean, every thing we eat is green*
*Full of little critters, red and green and brown.*
*We can eat it if we try,*
*But it makes us want to cry,*
*So we slip and fall and spill it on the ground.*

*All the Young Women are camping*
*See our shower over there.*
*We have water, cold and hot,*
*Cold is cold and hot is not!*
*But we use it, then we dry ourselves with air.*

*In the morning we arise with our sleepy, bloodshot eyes*
*And they take us on a fifty mile hike.*
*Then our backs, they start to ache,*
*And our blisters start to break,*
*How we wish we had our good old mountain bike.*

*All the young women are camping.*
*See our fire burning bright.*
*We sing camp songs by scores*
*Then we go and eat the S'mores*
*And we never, ever get to sleep at night!*

- Here is an idea to help the girls think about something better on their hike than how hot or miserable they are. Give each girl a slip of paper with a short poem or quote on it. Periodically throughout the hike have the girls stop and read one. Talk about it and then move on.

- Hide "dinosaur eggs" along a path that the girls have to find, using their compass and orienteering skills. The dinosaur eggs could be watermelons that can then be eaten and enjoyed at the end. Be sure to include a watermelon seed spitting contest!

- The First Aid Hike is a strong memory that stands out in my mind. Older girls are scattered along the path with various injuries, complete with fake blood and torn clothes. The younger girls must treat them with first aid techniques as they find them, using their compass and orienteering skills.

- Give each girl a camera so she can take pictures of things she sees during the hike. Develop the film and have everyone vote for the most creative, inspiring, amusing, etc.

- "Experts" Before the hike assign each girl to be an expert over a certain area such as water, bugs, trees, flowers, clouds, etc. Provide each girl with a card that has information about her expertise that she can read to the group at a designated time. Encourage the girls to be on the lookout for insights they can include during their teaching moment.

- Include "Mother Nature" on your staff of leaders. Have her wear a wreath of leaves and help girls to focus on the beauty of the nature around them. She could go on hikes, teach nature classes, give environmental awards, etc.

- "One Liners" Give each girl several jokes written on slips of paper that she can pull out of her pocket to read to the other girls at assigned times. Hikes should be fun!

# EVENING PROGRAMS

- If your stake is too large and your gatherings are losing their intimate appeal you could separate into smaller groups to play games and participate in skits. Call it "Fun At The Fireside."

- "Singing Trees." Before camp starts, each ward chooses a spiritual song to practice and perform that goes with the camp theme for that year. On the night of "Singing Trees" everyone gathers at a grove of trees with flashlights. When it is time to begin, everyone turns off their flashlights except for the ward who sings. Those girls shine their flashlights up into the trees above them. When they are finished singing they quietly turn their flashlights off and the next ward takes their turn. Have everyone sing a song they all know together at the end.

- Give each group of girls a big garbage bag to be used as a ball gown. Each group must select a beauty contestant to represent them and enter her in the contest. Have them decorate the garbage bag with whatever they can find. The beauty contestants have to do a talent and tell how they will create world peace or answer some other goofy question.

- "Skit in a box" Put a bunch of props in a box. Each group has to choose 3-5 items they must use in their skit. They could all have the same props or completely different items.

- While singing and doing skits have the girls make ice cream in a bag for dessert. Use two sizes of zip-lock storage bags. Pour whipping cream, sugar, a pinch of salt, and vanilla into the smaller bag. Place the smaller bag inside the larger bag. Add ice cubes and rock salt. Close the bag and shake, shake, shake.

- When the girls arrive and leave the evening campfire have the girls sing the Seven Dwarfs song "Hi Ho" but change the words to remind them that "Happiness Is Helping Others."

- While singing songs or doing skits have the girls make "Friendship Fudge" by mixing the following ingredients in a gallon Ziploc bag:
    4 cups powdered sugar;
    3 ounces softened cream cheese;
    ½ cup softened margarine;
    ½ cup cocoa;
    1 tsp. vanilla;
    ½ chopped nuts

- A wonderful resource for skits and road shows is www.ldscn. com/roadshow/
- For a great place to look for silly skits go to www.macscouter. com/Skits/BBSkits_Contests.html
- Ask the Cub Scouts and Boy Scouts to teach you some of their fun songs such as the "Beaver Song", "Backwards Song", "Hands Up", etc.
- Begin each evening program with every group doing a cheer or singing a song they have made up to represent themselves.
- Play "Ooga Booga." Three people need to know how to play, but keep it a secret from everyone else. Tell the group that one of those three people is the Ooga Booga champion and no one has beat her yet. Ask for volunteers to try and dethrone her. The "champion" is seated on a chair, bench or log. The challenger sits next to the champion. The Ooga Booga person sits in front of them. Close behind the challenger is a bucket of water with a sponge inside of it, and a person who should remain inconspicuous. You can use the camp fire bucket since it's supposed to be next to the fire anyway.

    The Ooga Booga person explains the rules to the challenger: "In order to beat the champion, you must both do exactly what I do and the one who does it the best, and with the most enthusiasm will win. The audience picks the winner by their cheers. Whoever they cheer loudest for will be the champ." You really play this up reminding them that the champ has never been beaten. The Ooga Booga person says "Okay, we will do a couple of practices so the challenger can better understand how to play." The person then holds a stick in both hands high in the air and yells loudly "OOGA BOOGA!!" The champ and challenger do the same at the same time...the crowd cheers loudly. The person asks "what do you think? Should we give her another practice try?" Everyone yells. This time the person holds the stick and when she raises her hands she also raises one leg and shouts OOGA BOOGA!!! Everyone goes wild! "I think she's getting it! Champion, you may have to step down! Okay, this is it...this will determine the champion! Everyone get ready to decide!" (Really play this up.) This time the person holds the stick in both hands and as she yells OOGA she stands up and when she yells BOOGA she sits down. Now as the 2 do this, the person by the bucket puts the wet sponge on the challenger's seat . . .

• Play "The Rest Of The Story." Have someone begin telling a story. Everyone takes turns adding to the story until you get to the last person. Another twist is to have everyone take a strip of paper with a random sentence on it that they have to weave into their part of the story.

• "Indian Princess" (or queen or whatever works with your theme) Tell the story of the young princess braves who were sent from the tribe to search the world for the qualities of an Indian princess. Each young woman brings back her value (colored water in a jar) and talks about how each of the colors is found in nature and how they represent a value. Each value jar is then poured into a small pot inside a larger pot on the campfire that actually has dry ice in it to create a dramatic effect. After all the values are added the narrator reaches into the pot and pulls out special camp flag, young woman torch or something else that represents your theme.

• "Let Your Light So Shine" Provide the girls with some glow-in-the dark necklaces, bracelets or light sticks to wear on their hats or clothing. Talk about the light within and how they can be good examples. Have them chew Wintogreen Lifesavers with their mouths open and they'll see sparks from within!

• "The Iron Rod" Re-create Lehi's vision of the tree of life by setting up a special trail the girls will follow. Set up a long PVC "rod" which the girls are told to hold on to during their journey while blindfolded. Using lots of cardboard, Styrofoam and imagination, have the girls walk past the river of filth, the spacious building, and other aspects of Lehi's dream. Recruit some of the older girls to try to tempt the girls to let go of the rod, while others read scriptures and encourage them to continue. Once the girls get to the end of the "rod" they can take their blindfolds off and enter a beautifully decorated room where they see a tree lit up and small white bags (fruit) filled with special gifts. There is a song called "Hold On" that has been created especially for this kind of activity. You can order detailed instructions and a CD with the song by writing to Gina Prisbrey at prizz@mstar2.net or websters@infowest.com or write to her at 2432 Scenic Drive, Santa Clara, UT 84765.

- Have a special Girls Night Out where the mothers of the girls join in on the fun for the evening dinner and campfire.

- Have parents write to their daughters ahead of time and then present the letters to the girls during a special program.

- To reinforce the idea of Heavenly Father's love and reading the scriptures, have the girls' fathers write them a letter, expressing their love. Compare letters from home to the scriptures.

- If you'd like to purchase a Girls Camp songbook that includes over 180 songs you can contact Gina Prisbrey at prizz@mstar2.net or write to 2432 Scenic Drive, Santa Clara, Utah 84765.

- "The Flame of Young Women" Show how the Young Women each create a "spark" in their ward by tossing granulated sugar into the flames. Fireplace stores often have items that can be thrown into a fire to create interest and variety. Using different chemicals you can change the color of the flames in a fire. Create a program about the value colors and try creating these colors:
    Calcium - red
    Copper - green
    Sodium- orange
    Lithium - pink
    Potassium - purple
    Barium - light green
    Lean - blue

- Awards can be given each night to allow more girls an opportunity to receive something. The can be a certificate, ribbon, bead, pin or whatever the girls are collecting for your theme. They can be serious awards or silly ones (or both!) such as:
    Rubber Ducky Award – longest shower
    Spiderman award – most afraid of insects
    Miss Congeniality – friendliest

Songbird Award – always singing or sings with the most enthusiasm

Pig Free Zone – cleanest camp

Plates of Nephi Award – keeps her daily journal

CTR Award – Someone who made the right choice

Early Bird – First one up in the morning

Amor of God – demonstrated courage

Captain Moroni – showed good leadership

Night Owl – last one to bed

FSOY Award – demonstrated qualities from "For the Strength of Youth" book

Helping Hand – gave service

# CONTEST NIGHT

- "Speaker Stations" Rotate the girls through smaller campfires hosted by each ward where they hear a speaker and get a small treat or momento to remind them of the topic.

- Recreate "living" masterpieces of some of the Church's great artwork. Paint a background and then merge live girls into the scenes.

- Spend the evening fireside talking about our Heavenly Parents. Talk about all they have given us, how much they love us, and what we need to do to return home. Present each girl with a special letter written by their earthly parents.

- Attach a note to a small package of tissues that says "Your testimony is like this package of tissues: if they stay in the package they do no one any good, but if they are taken out and shared then who NOSE the growth that can happen!" or "Testimony Tissues: Share your testimony – don't let it dry up and blow away!"

- Do I need to remind you, again, that camp should be fun! Don't force the spiritual moments.

- "Chin Puppets" If you haven't seen this done before, trust me, it's a crack-up. Have several girls lie on a table on their backs and hang their heads over the edge of the table so their face is upside down. Draw eyes and nose on their chin with eye pencil so it looks like their mouth goes with this new little face. Cover their real nose and eyes with a scarf or hat. Have the girls sing a song, tell jokes and make funny facial contortions or do a simple skit such as Little Red Riding Hood and you will see your audience rolling in the aisles. I promise.

- Present an award each night to the girl who can find the most interesting or disgusting bug that day.
- Have the girls make ice cream while they sing or listen to a speaker. Divide the following mixture into 4 quart jars that will then be placed inside #10 (the food storage kind from the Bishop's Storehouse). Don't fill the jars to the top since the contents need to move around.

### VANILLA ICE CREAM

1 pint cream
½ gallon milk
1⅓ cup sugar
1 tbl vanilla
dash salt
2+ cups rock salt
crushed ice (large cubes not as good)

Pour crushed ice around the bottle inside the can. Dump ½ cup rock salt on top of the ice. Put on the lid. Put on gloves and roll the can back and forth on the floor. It should take about 50 minutes for the ice cream to be done. Scoop out and serve. Toppings and cobbler are optional, but highly recommended! Enjoy!

# CRAFTS

It's important not to do certain crafts just because you think they're cute, but to find things the girls will actually use, can give as gifts, or remind them of gospel principles and their positive experiences at camp. Try to coordinate the projects with the camp theme and even introduce the activity by tying it in with a scripture story.

A fun tradition that involves crafts is "SWAPS." They are little craft items that the girls make and exchange with one another. They can either make and bring 20-30 of the same item with them to camp or else the girls could be provided with craft supplies and a time set apart when they can make them there. As the girls meet one another they trade crafts throughout camp. Help them discover the joy of creating something lovely to share with others.

The following are some ideas for projects to be done in a craft class setting, while sitting around a campfire, as an ongoing project that is set out on tables throughout the week or as a kit given to each girl to keep in her pocket to be worked on at her leisure:

- Build a bow and arrow out of a piece of hardwood (not pine), string, and dowels. See "Boys Life" magazine, June 1999 issue for detailed instructions. Talk about Nephi's bow experience and the lessons he taught us. Have the girls practice knocking over cups and shooting targets set up on bales of hay.

- Memory boards to hang their camp photos on.

- Make marshmallow blow guns out of PVC pipe and then have a Lamanite/Nephite battle.

- Make twig pencils by drilling a thin hole about 2 inches in depth where you will glue in the lead.

- Friendship bracelets.

- Homemade lip gloss (lots of recipes online)

- Homemade bath salts (lots of recipes online)

- Create leaf prints on paper or fabric from sun exposure. Talk about the imprint of the Savior on us (image in his countenance).

- Stone rubbings. Talk about how this skill could be helpful with genealogy research, especially on tombstones.

- Invite a real art teacher to teach the young women how to draw, sketch and paint. Have them work on a real piece of art that could hang in their homes. Have a "Museum Grand Opening" where their works are hung and everyone can walk around drinking sparkling cider.

- Make rope and cedar berry necklaces. Tradition says that the cedar berries will ward off bad spirits when worn.

- Handkerchief dolls. Share the story about how these were made from the fathers' handkerchiefs for the young girls crossing the plains because they didn't have enough room for dolls on the wagons. They are small and could be put in a pocket. Fold a handkerchief in half diagonally and stuff some cotton batting as a head. Tie the neck off with a ribbon bow and sew. Knot each of the two top corners close to the ends. This makes it look like a pair of puffed sleeves and hands. Sew or glue lace around the bottom of the "gown" and across the top of the head to look like a bonnet.

- Make Tye Dye shirts or some other kind of camp shirt that can later be used as the girls' basketball or volleyball team shirts to save the wards money!

- Make Kazoos out of a hardwood and have the girls practice a song they could perform at the evening campfire. See "Boys Life" magazine, January 2000 for detailed instructions.

- Prayer rugs

- Beaded bracelets with CTR, FSOY, WWJD or other written spiritual reminders.

- Glow-in-the-dark necklaces for campfire time.

- Decorate or make scripture totes.

- Decorate photo albums or make those puffy album covers.

- Counted cross stitch scripture bookmarks.

- Make Indian dream catchers and teach them about the Indian legend.

- Set up a quilt the girls could work on throughout the day that can be given to a homeless or women's shelter.

- Set up a candy-gram area where the girls could send each other notes and candy. They make the candy-gram and then have the "Camp Sweetie" deliver them to the chosen recipient.

- Create a "Last Chance" station on the last day of camp where the girls can make the craft items they missed or make another favorite item as a gift for someone.

- Teach the girls how to make roses and other designs out of palm leaves.

- Metal tin can punch.
- Corn husk dolls.
- Friendship necklace.
- Camp scrapbook pages.
- Find "knotty" angels at www.mistral.co.uk/42brghtn/knots/42ktmenu.html.
- Pioneer necklaces and toys.
- Keychain with a reminder about what is "key" in their life.
- Pillow treats for each others' tents.
- Make stepping stones that could be donated to the camp or taken home. Talk about "standing as a witness". The girls could use stones, twigs, handprints, and other items to spell out words or make designs.
- Hot dog roasting sticks! These can be donated to the camp afterward or taken home by each girl. Buy 1" dowels cut to 6" in length. You can buy the metal part from a welding supply store. Drill a hole in each of the handles, then push the metal rod in. It needs to be a very tight fit. Decorate the handles or attach a yarn ribbon through it to hang.

### "LIQUID SUNSHINE"

You need:

  1 dozen lemons (or half as many lemons as you have making the candles)
  1 lb. of beeswax
  ½ t. lemon oil
  Wicks

Cut lemons in half lengthwise and squeeze out as much of the juice as possible without tearing the skin. Hollow out the lemon halves with a spoon or gently pull with your hands. In a double boiler, heat beeswax until melted, about 180 degrees. Turn off the heat, and add ½ tsp. lemon oil. Dip the wick and holder with wax until coated. This will stiffen and straighten the wick. Press the wick holder into the bottom of the lemon half and pour the wax into the lemon half almost to the edge. Use a small paintbrush to coat around the edges. After they cool they can be carried in a girl's hand while lit. The lemons start to go bad after a few days, so these could be incorporated into an evening camp fire program or special testimony meeting where each girl lights hers after sharing her testimony until the whole group is glowing with light.

# FUNDRAISERS

Fundraising is an aspect of camp that is always hotly debated by parents, leaders and girls. Refer to the Young Women's Handbook and get your Bishop's counsel before proceeding. If it is determined that your ward needs to do a fundraiser for Girls Camp then be sure to get your Bishop's approval on the specific fundraiser of your choice. Here are a few suggestions:

- Have ward members create a list of services they would pay for and a contact phone number so that any of the girls can choose to do that work and get in touch with the "employer" directly. For example, Brother Long will pay $20 to have his lawn mowed or Sister Duncan will pay $30 to have her windows washed, etc.
- Recycling project. This could be one event or an ongoing project. Not only are you earning money for Camp but you're also teaching the girls about our environment and helping the community.
- Deliver pre-ordered Valentine's Day cakes, flowers, corsages, candy.
- Deliver pre-ordered holiday treats and gifts such as Mother's Day dessert, Father's Day cinnamon rolls, Easter cupcakes, etc.
- Set out a large jar in your Church's foyer where members can "deposit" all that noisy loose change in their pockets before entering the chapel.
- Car wash.
- Make balloon bouquets for Mother's Day.
- Work with your Ward Activity Director in providing an evening of dinner and entertainment for a certain price.
- Make and sell frozen pizzas.

- Encourage the ward to hire the Young Women to do projects around their houses like painting, raking leaves, mowing lawn, moving boxes, babysitting, etc. Provide a list of girls and their phone numbers so the jobs could be set up privately and personally.

- Spaghetti Dinner and Auction. Each of the young women offers various services they will provide that the ward can bid on.

- Pre-order and sell corsages or giant Hershey Kisses for Mother's Day.

- Make and sell baked goods at Stake sports events.

- Teach the girls how to make cinnamon rolls. Provide samples during Mutual to parents as they drop off and pick up their children. Take pre-orders, make and deliver the next week.

- Garage sale. Collect donated items from ward members.

- Find out if a grocery store or hardware store would let you sell cooked hot dogs & hamburgers outside their entrance.

- Make homemade rootbeer to sell with frozen pizza.

- Find out if you can sell concessions at a local park, playground, parade, or other community event.

- Clean peoples' homes.

- Wash windows.

- Pressure wash peoples' driveways.

- Ask your city if there is a service you could provide for a fee.

- In some parts of the country Pine straw is laid as a ground cover seasonally. Offer to deliver or lay it outside residential homes or businesses.

- Some stores will pay to have help with their annual inventory.

- Wrap presents at Christmas time. (Think early!)

- Deliver phone books.

- Sell those "Entertainment" books, See's candy, Krispy Kreme donuts or other products that have a company fundraising program. Be sure to get the OK from your Stake President when dealing with other companies.

- Group babysitting.

- Silent Auction. Distribute a list of items and services in Relief Society and Priesthood quorums so people can bid and then outbid each other on them.
- Make and sell frozen cookie dough.
- Offer to can and deliver food from the Cannery.
- Create and sell a Ward cookbook.
- Scrapbook for individuals.
- Make inexpensive gifts or cards that Visiting Teachers could purchase to give as gifts.
- Collect pennies. They add up!
- Check with your local contractors. They are always looking for people to clean the houses after they are built and sold.
- Some businesses will pay to have their parking lots cleaned.

## BOOKS

- For additional ideas, ready Vicki Hacking's *Young Women Camp Suggestions* series. It includes recipes and instructions.
- Linda Dastrup has compiled books filled with handouts and ideas.
- Dian Thomas wrote *Roughing It Easy at Girls Camp* that has tons of great ideas, recipes, supply lists, and instructions.

## CONVERSATION GROUPS

www.groups.yahoo.com/group/LDS_GIrlsCamp_Leaders/
www.egroups.com/group/YW-girlscamp

## WEBSITE RESOURCES

www.hometown.aol.com/CWS38/camp.html (ideas)
www.mormonchic.com/gospel/girls_camp.asp
www.idos.com/ (International Dutch Oven Society recipes)
www.inspirationalstories.com (devotionals)
www.angelfire.com/tx/DrPepperPhD/stories.html (devotionals)
www.chickensoup.com (devotionals)
www.motivational-messages.com (devotionals)

www.maths.tcd.ie/~catherin/campfire.htm (camp songs)

www.geocities.com/EnchantedForest/Glade/8851/ (songs)

www.scouting.org.za/songs (camp songs)

www.backyardgardener.com/loowit/janeellen.html (songs)

www.cjnetworks.com/~kwood/scouting/menus/cooking.html

www.gorp.com/gorp/food/main.htm (cooking)

www.dir.yahoo.com/Arts/Crafts/ (Craft sites)

www.mormonchic.com/gospel/girls_camp.asp

CHAPTER 20

# *The Young Women Theme & Motto*

*"Give me a young woman who loves home and family, who reads and ponders the scriptures daily, who has a burning testimony of the Book of Mormon. Give me a young woman who faithfully attends her church meetings, who is a Seminary graduate, who has earned her Young Womanhood Recognition Award and wears it with pride! Give me a young woman who is virtuous and who has maintained her personal purity, who will not settle for less than a temple marriage, and I will give you a young woman who will perform miracles for the Lord now and throughout eternity."*

PRESIDENT EZRA TAFT BENSON

The Young Women theme answers life's most crucial questions "Who am I?", "Why am I here?" and "Where am I going?" Every time a young woman recites it those important answers sink into her soul and will, hopefully, guide her throughout her life. The Young Women motto is "Stand for truth and Righteousness" and one of the tasks of a Young Woman leader is to teach the girls how to do that and what it means in practical terms. The torch represents the light of Christ in all of us, inviting us to "come unto Christ." By standing for what's right we will hold up the light of Christ for all to see.

I remember when one of "my" young women tearfully shared an experience that strengthened her testimony of the inspired Young Women theme. She was at school one day when her teacher told the class they needed to write a graded essay about who they were and what they stood for. At first she was surprised and panicked about what she could possibly write in the given amount of time. The entire class slumped down in their seats, struggling for ideas and words to fill their blank paper. Slowly, a comforting assurance overcame her as she remembered the Young Women theme. She calmly wrote it down, word for word, and then sat back and relaxed. She realized it really did represent who she was and what was important to her in her life. She was proud to report that she earned an A on that assignment!

The following are just a few ways to help Young Women leaders reinforce those ideals during Mutual, Sunday lessons and special events:

- Teach the girls how to do counted cross stitch and have them make a picture or pillow using the theme and/or Young Women's torch for the design. Jenni Gould has created two different designs that are easy enough for the girls to learn how to make in her books "Midweek Treasures for Young Women" and "10 Terrific Programs for Young Women". You can learn more about them at www.JeanniGould.com

- Make crafts that have star designs to remind them that STAR = Stand for Truth & Righteousness.

- Ask the Bishop to invite the girls to do a musical presentation or give talks about the them during Sacrament meeting.

- Make crafts that involve a STAND = Stay True And Never Doubt.

- Talk about what it means to "Accept and Act Upon the Young Women Values to Come Unto Christ". Have the girls make a list of things they can DO to demonstrate their acceptance.

- Teach different memorizing techniques to help the girls memorize the Young Women's motto. For example, one method is to write the theme in small sections on a chalkboard. After repeating it several times, erase a few words or sentences at a time until they can say it without word clues.

- Cut out wood in the shape of a torch and have the girls paint and decorate it for their bedrooms, placing parts of the theme or motto on it.

- Decide how your young women will recite the theme each week. For example, they could stand facing a picture of Christ. Will one girl hold a poster with the theme to help girls see it while they are still memorizing it? Will class Presidents lead the group?
- You could create a melody you can sing using the Young Women's theme or motto.
- Ask the girls why they think it's important to have a theme. Why is it important to memorize? How does it fit in with the 3-Fold mission of the Church? Have the girls pick it apart, analyzing each word and meaning.
- Teach the girls how to say the Young Women's theme using sign language.
- Have the girls make posters reflecting all or parts of the theme and motto to decorate their bedrooms and the Young Women's room.
- Make bookmarks, light plates, doorknob hangers, pillows, and other decorative items the girls can keep in their bedrooms that will remind them of the Young Women motto and theme.
- Decorate pillow cases with the theme and logo so that the young women will think of it every time they wake up and go to bed.
- Teach the girls how to do calligraphy. Have them write the Young Women theme in fancy lettering and frame them nicely.
- Talk about how doing genealogy can strengthen their families. Create genealogy crafts, using the girls' family names on them. You could create a family tree wood cut-out, coat of arms wall-hanging, fancy pedigree chart poster, or decorate a frame designated for a family photo. Check out the book *Climbing Family Trees, Whispers In The Leaves* by yours truly (shameless plug) for tons of genealogy craft ideas!
- Create a Family Home Evening lesson about the Young Women values, theme, and motto that the girls could teach to their families. Include visual aids, refrigerator magnet and recipes for refreshments.

CHAPTER 21

# The Wonderful Worldwide Web!

*"Ideas are refined and multiplied in the commerce of minds. In their splendor, images effect a very simple communion of souls."*

GASTON BACHELARD
*1884-1962, French Scientist, Philosopher, Literary Theorist*

No need to reinvent the wheel, especially when you're using that wheel to drive on the Information Super Highway! The Internet is an endless resource of ideas, recipes, downloads, crafts, lesson material, music, and instructions for almost anything you'd like to do in your Young Women's program.

However, let me give you a serious word of caution about doing on-line searches. If you enter "Young Women" into a search engine you will get suggestions for links to all kinds of horrible pornographic websites. You must type in LDS Young Women, and even then, look at the description of the site before you click on it!

Oh, that the world were as clean and pure as our sweet young sisters. The safest way to avoid such websites is to type the following addresses directly into your Internet browser, rather than using a search engine.

## YOUNG WOMEN WEBSITE RESOURCES

www.lds.org
*The official website of the Church of Jesus Christ of Latter-day Saints. Click on "Serving in the Church" then choose "Young*

*Women." There are all kinds of great resources for Personal Progress, Mutual and other events, General Young Women Broadcast information, gospel instruction for Sunday teachers, guidelines for teaching Church standards, interest surveys, parental permission forms, activity planners, manuals, and so much more!! This should be your first stop on the Information Superhighway!*

www.lds-yw.com
   *Great ideas, links, recipes, downloads, leader info, products and lots more by Vickie Hacking*

www.jennysmith.net
   *Wonderful resource for everything!*

www.ywconnection.com
   *Tons of ideas, discussion board, links, Blog, handouts*

www.theideadoor.com/YoungWomen.html

www.sharingwithyw.com

www.youngwomen.faithweb.com/yw_container.html

www.lds.about.com/od/youngwomenyoungmen/

www.lds.about.com/od/activitiescommittee/a/act_ideas.htm

www.mormons.org/ywc/activities/whatkind.htm

www.sharingwithyw.com

www.of-worth.com/yw/

www.angelfire.com/ut/ldsyw/

www.hometown.aol.com/cws38/page6.html

www.geocities.com/ywlds/ideas.htm

www.ywsuggestions.tripod.com

www.mormonfind.com/Auxillary_Organizations/Young_ Womens/

www.christysclipart.com

www.home.earthlink.net/~ajandbj/

www.debanae.net/ Ideas, clip art

www.lds-yw.com/html/yw_files.html

www.angelfire.com/ut/ldsyw

www.scoutsoft.net/sbf.htm

www.ascol.net/~gwyder/

www.ldstoday.com/organizations/young_women.htm

www.ldsbrainstorm.com/yw/ywhome.htm

www.ldsabout.com/cs/youthprograms/index.html

www.geocities.com/jilladair-yw/

www.geocities.com/ywlds

www.primarypage.com/2000/ldslinks.htm

www.lightplanet.com/mormons/ywc/index.htm

www.yw-princess.ldsweb.net/index.htm

www.mormonmomma.com/gospel/callings/yw/s_yw.psp

www.ce.byu.edu/yp/efy/

www.cafeshops.com/germtwerm

www.hedgemom.net/tothe.htm

www.sharingwithyw.com/

www.primarypageetc.com/ywlinks.html

www.wmyw.org
    *Great tool for keeping track of Personal Progress and Duty to God requirements.*

www.ldsworld.com/churchorganization/youngwomen/values/
    main/values

www.lds-living.com/links.html

www.lds-living.com/yw

www.members.tripod.com/~1Molly/Mormon.html

www.lds.npl.com/

www.wanfear.com/hroper/

www.softcom.net/users/westra/youth.htm

www.ays.org

www.JeanniGould.com

www.ldschurch.net/f/gifford/

www.mormontown.org

www.LDS-YW@onelist.

www.sugardoodle.net

www.ldscn.com

www.valor.net

www.members.xoom.com/L.Blake

www.i.am/lds-youngwomen.com

www.ldsteach.com

www.geocities.com/perudol1/vt.htm

www.hedgemom.net/id108.htm

www.homeholidaysfamilyandfun.com/404.html

www.lightplanet.com/mormons/ywc/pp/morelaurel.htm
   *Personal Progress ideas*

www.jenmagazine.com
   *Fun, free, on-line magazine for LDS girls that your young women will actually like and that will help you know what's "in" and what's not.*

www.promoms.org/activitease.htm
   *Fun ideas for holidays and activities*

www.mormonchic.com

www.ldssplash.com

www.rev-fun.gospel.com

www.thoughts-for-talks.com

www.ldstoday.com

www.shire.net/mormon/humor

www.ce.byu.edu/yp/efy/
   *CES Youth Programs "Especially for Youth"*

www.makingfriends.com crafts

www.familyfun.com crafts

## LDS SEARCH ENGINES

www.ldsresources.com

www.lds.npl.com

www.zionsearch.com

www.ldslibrary.com

www.ldsmedia.com

www.ldsabout.com

www.mormon-lds-gateway.org

www.ldstoday.com

www.mormonlinks.com

www.ldsvoices.com

www.users.olynet.com/mkathj/lds.html
*A list of LDS links on the net*

www.thoughts-for-talks.com/tforldsyouth.htm
*Resource links*

www.younglds.com
*Discussion board for teens by Ben Bytheway*

www.ldsprinciples.com
*A catalog of books, music, and videos that teach gospel principles*

# MERCHANDISE

www.lds.org order church materials

www.ldscatalog.com

www.lds-yw.com

www.hometown.aol.com/jrlowman/myhomepage/business.html

www.orientaltrading.com

www.my-personalized-gifts.com

www.1on1.net/1valor/

www.ctrcreations.com

www.byubookstore.com

www.ldscharms.com

www.ldsweb.org

www.deseretbook.com

www.seagullbooks.com

www.ctr-ring.com

www.greatlengths.com

www.mormon-t-shirts.com

# LDS BLOGS

www.trudystuff.blogspot.com

www.ldsyoungwomen.blogspot.com

www.enrichmentideas.blogspot.com

www.happyjellybeans.blogspot.com

www.xanga.com/groups/group.aspx?id=46435

www.climbingfamilytrees.blogspot.com

www.sisterthrifty.blogspot.com

# INTERNET GROUPS

I highly recommend that you join a Yahoo Group. It's free to join and you'll meet some of the nicest people around! People share helpful ideas and tips in a real-time setting. You can receive e-mails individually or as a daily digest. Some groups are more active than others so the quantity of e-mails will vary.

There is no reason for you to reinvent the wheel when another great Young Women leader has already done it out there somewhere!

www.groups.yahoo.com/group/lds-youngwomen

www.groups.yahoo.com/group/LDS_GirlsCamp_Leaders

www.groups.msn.com/LDSYMYW/

www.groups.yahoo.com/group/GirlsCamp/

www.groups.yahoo.com/group/ywactivities/

www.groups.yahoo.com/group/lds-yw/

www.de.groups.yahoo.com/group/HLT-JD/
  *German speaking YW Leaders!*

www.groups.yahoo.com/group/ywleaders/

www.egroups.com

www.netwizards.net/~btphelps/mormon/lds1.htm

www.ldsyoungwomen.proboards74.com/ Young women message board

## MUSIC

www.ldsaudio.com

(See Chapter 12 on music options.)

## CLIP ART

I'm thankful for talented artists who share their wonderful creations with me, since I have trouble drawing decent stick people! Here are some of those generous artists:

www.christysclipart.com

www.graphicgarden.com/

www.debanae.net

www.designca.com/lds/

www.coloringbookfun.com

www.ldsweb.org/yw_art/yw_clips.html

www.davejennings.freeserve.co.uk/clipart/clipart.html

www.primary_art.tripod.com/yw.html

www.jennysmith.net

www.stums.org/closet/html/index.html

www.oneil.com.au/lds/pictures.html

www.lds.about.com/library/gallery/clipart/blclipart_gallery_
subindex.htm

www.free-clip-art.net

www.ldsfiles.com/clipart

www.coloring.ws/coloring.html

www.apples4theteacher.com

www.dltk-holidays.com

www.happytulip.com

www.lds.org/gospellibrary/pdfmagazine/

## About the Author and Illustrator

**Trina Bates Boice** grew up in sunny California and later braved the cold and snow at Brigham Young University where she earned two Bachelor's degrees. While there she competed on the BYU Speech & Debate team, and BYU Ballroom Dance Team. She was President of the National Honor Society Phi Eta Sigma and ASBYU Secretary of Student Community Services.

Trina also studied at the University of Salamanca in Spain and later returned to serve a full-time mission to Madrid, Spain for the Church of Jesus Christ of Latter-day Saints. She earned a Master's degree from California College for Health Sciences. She worked as a Legislative Assistant for a Congressman in Washington D.C. and wrote a column called "The Boice Box" for a local newspaper in Georgia where she lived for 15 years. She has a real estate license, travel agent license, a Black Belt in Tae Kwon Do, and helps her husband, Tom, with their real estate appraisal and investment companies. If she told you what she really did all day, she would have to kill you.

Trina was honored in November 2004 as George Bush's "Points of Light Volunteer" and also received the President's Lifetime Volunteer Service award. She was the "2004 Honor Young Mother of the Year" for the state of California and lives in beautiful Carlsbad with her four wonderful sons. They keep busy with Scouting, all kinds of sports, and are surfer wannabes now that they live closer to the beach. They now brave the cold and snow of Utah together to go skiing and visit family!

Trina has served as her ward's Young Women president and in her stake's Young Women presidency. She currently teaches Seminary and works in the beautiful San Diego Temple. Check out her website at www.boicebox.com.

Because Trina only has sons, she selected her Mia Maid niece, Brittany, to do the illustrations at the start of each chapter for this Young Women's book!

**Brittany Long** entered the world during the October 1990 General Conference as the Mormon Tabernacle Choir sang "Hallelujah!"

A born book and art enthusiast, she has marched through her teenage years with a book under each arm and a pencil behind her ear. In addition to getting straight A's and being top of the class, Brittany participates in her high school's theatre department as an actress and director and enjoys it very much. She has played the piano for nine years, is president of her Mia Maid class, and in any spare time she finds loves drawing as well as reading, writing, acting, speaking French, cooking Pasta Roni, being vegetarian, and procrastinating.

Brittany's ambition is to become an author and one day illustrate her own books. Until then, she writes for her English teacher and posts her doodles on her personal website at www. brytning.hatesmonday.com. She lives in Las Vegas, Nevada with her family and her beagle, Joy.